SOLACED

101 TRUE STORIES ABOUT CORSETS, WELL-BEING, AND HOPE

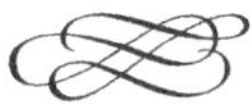

LUCY WILLIAMS

Published by Middlow Publishing

Cover photography by Rosalind Guder
Compiling, editing and formatting by Lucy Williams
Copyediting by Roger K
Photographs credited in captions

Ebook ISBN: 978-0-9951917-0-9
Paperback ISBN: 978-0-9951917-1-6

DISCLAIMER

Efforts have been made to recreate events, locales and conversations from the memories of the contributors, and to ensure that the stories in this book are true, and that any statements made in them based on information and belief were believed to be true at publication time. Some names, places, and identifying characteristics and details may have been changed for anonymity or to protect the privacy of individuals. All of this said, the authors, editor and publisher do not assume and hereby disclaim any liability to any party for any loss, damage, or disruption caused by errors or omissions, whether such errors or omissions result from negligence, accident, or any other cause.

The contents of this book are provided for information and entertainment purposes, and not as medical information or advice, nor as a substitute for or supplement to the medical advice of physicians. The information herein is not intended to help in the prevention, diagnosis, treatment, or cure of any ailment. The use of a corset for any reason poses some inherent risk. The authors, editor and publisher do not assume and hereby disclaim any liability or responsibility in this respect, and advise readers to take full responsibility for their own safety. You should consult a healthcare professional for any of the foregoing matters, before using or continuing to use a corset for any reason, and to regularly monitor your health and well-being, particularly with respect to any symptoms that may require diagnosis or medical attention.

CONTENTS

INTRODUCTION: LUCY'S STORY

SoLaced: Lucy's Story

solace (n.)

"comfort in grief, consolation," late 13c., from Old French *solaz* "pleasure, entertainment, enjoyment; solace, comfort," from Latin *solacium* "a soothing, assuaging; comfort, consolation," from *solatus,* past participle of *solari* "to console, soothe."

Related to Latin *solaris,* meaning sun or of sunny disposition.

— (ONLINE ETYMOLOGY DICTIONARY)

I was first introduced to corsetry when I was six years old. My parents had rented the movie *Gone with the Wind,* which was set during the American Civil War (in the early 1860s). The plot of the movie was terribly boring to me at the time, but I couldn't stop staring at the costumes: the ladies all looked like dolls come to life.

Although I was painfully shy and never dressed fashionably

throughout my childhood (I always got the hand-me-downs from my siblings and cousins), my love for the "big skirt, small waist" aesthetic stuck with me through my teens. After years of hand-sewing outfits, I finally overcame my fear of sewing machines at the age of 14, and from there my passion took off. In my freshman year of high school, my mother and I worked on and off for nearly a month on my most ambitious Halloween costume yet: a heavy, black velvet Victorian mourning gown. For a more authentic silhouette, we took the time to also search for old petticoats at a second-hand store, and we fashioned a "pseudo-corset" from a vintage longline bra—after its alteration, it brought my waist in by barely two inches. Although it was far from period-accurate, I was proud of the heavy velvet gown and its underpinnings; it was the largest and most difficult project my mother and I had so far attempted.

My first Halloween in high school was not a day I look back on fondly. I distinctly recall having a handful of fine glitter tossed on me by a "fairy" (a minor annoyance as it's difficult to brush out of velvet), having water spilled on me (which permanently water-stained my gown), and, during the costume contest during lunch hour, being booed off the stage—first by a small group of senior boys, which then quickly grew to a crowd of several hundred jeering students.

While my first instinct was to make myself as small as possible (or possibly to run to the restroom, which would have made even more of a spectacle), my "corset" didn't allow me to hunch over. My face was hot and my hands shook as I carefully lifted my skirts to step off stage and weave through the still-sneering audience. I found a vacant seat in the crowd and planted myself there, staring straight forward at the stage and avoiding eye contact with anyone around me. I was determined to watch the remainder of the Halloween contest with my shoulders squared and my posture tall.

Although I felt a panic attack threaten to bubble to the surface, it never came. As I sat in class during the following period, I remember feeling oddly, remarkably zen-like about what had just happened. Knowing my own nature as a sensitive young teen, the scenario over lunch period would normally have been devastatingly embarrassing and *should* have induced bouts of anxiety and crying for days. But the tears and the waves of panic never came. This was my first experience with the armor-like charm of corsetry.

(For the record, I think some guy in junior year with a commercially made tampon costume won the contest.)

My interest in cosplay and historical dress grew over the years and drove my fascination with corsets even further: corsets, although compact, were in some ways more difficult to sew than voluminous, poofy skirts, and I viewed it a personal challenge to master their construction.

I created my first genuine corset from a Simplicity 9769 pattern at the age of 18 and wore it occasionally for fun, but it wasn't until I went to university that I started wearing corsets on a regular basis, due to back pain from my field of work.

For a few years I had worked as a student painter in the summers, which involved regularly hauling four gallon-sized cans of paint at the same time, carrying 30-foot ladders by myself, etc. As an overachiever, I prided myself on being one of the most professional painters on the crew—and to me, "professional" meant not only working quickly and meticulously, but also not asking for help while doing heavy lifting.

Although I adored moving my body and working outdoors in the warm, sunny weather, these tasks took a toll on my back, and I begged for back massages from anyone who would listen. I consider myself very fortunate that the pain was only muscular and I didn't suffer any long-term injury to my spine.

My backaches continued when I went back to university in the fall: I was required to carry my heavy backpack all over campus, and to stand at the bench or in front of a microscope for long hours in my laboratory studies. I dug out my old Simplicity corset and wore it when I returned home most evenings. I appreciated the back support and posture control it gave me, even when laced loosely (at most an inch or two of waist reduction). By the time I had made dinner and removed the corset, my muscles felt relaxed and refreshed.

I continued this routine for several months, until the bed-sheeting I had used for the corset's fabric tore beyond repair. By that point, I already knew I wanted to make another corset (not only for support but also for cosplay purposes) and, although I hadn't experienced any negative symptoms, I did admit to being concerned about its possible consequences on my health.

It was at this point that I began to research corsets more heavily, and I happened upon the Corsetmakers community on LiveJournal, which led me down a rabbit hole of information where I discovered, most notably, Romantasy Exquisite Corsetry and the Long Island Staylace Association (LISA). I also embarked on a personal research project, using my university's scientific journal subscriptions, to read any peer-reviewed publication I could possibly find on the physiological effects of corseting.

I decided that in order to draft and sew a perfect corset for myself, I had to first know what a real corset (not made from a bedsheet!) was like, and theoretical online research wasn't cutting it—I had to study a real corset in my hands. There were no local shops that carried genuine corsets, nor were there any nearby museums where I could study extant corsets, so I went to eBay to purchase an off-the-rack (OTR) corset.

I must have spent a few hours every evening for weeks, thoroughly comparing the details and stats and prices, and agonizing over which brand and style to choose. There was very little information provided in product listings, and very few corset reviews at the time. This would be my most expensive purchase to date (apart from rent and tuition) and my finger hovered over the mouse in trepidation before I finally clicked the "Buy Now" button. The corset I chose was an emerald brocade underbust from Timeless Trends.

When I finally received it, I was blown away by the quality—although I had made "corsets" before, they were nothing like this! The weight of it, the smoothness of it, the fineness of the stitching, the support it provided ... as much as I had read corset-making books, commercial patterns, and tutorials from corsetières online, and as much as I had tried to guess at correct construction on my own, there was nothing quite like holding a real corset in my hands. I suddenly had a new appreciation for hands-on learning; everything I had previously read about corsets suddenly clicked in a new way.

Putting on this corset—and seeing it create curves that hadn't existed before—was also a revelation. From the ages of 13–20, my weight hadn't budged no matter what I ate or how active I was (or wasn't). I was a late bloomer, still growing in height in my early 20s. Then a "second puberty" seemed to suddenly hit at 21—and with a combination of stress, hormones, and a sometimes-unsteady income that directly affected the quality of my groceries, my weight fluctuated by as much as 30 pounds (14 kg) over several years, and I was forced to redefine what I knew and believed about my body.

I didn't necessarily dislike my figure at any particular weight, but no matter how much I had gained or lost, my waist and hips were never clearly defined. I was interested in obtaining an hourglass figure—or in the very least, interested in getting a glimpse of what I might have looked like with one. As I pulled my vivid green corset around me and a gentle ski slope appeared from my waist to my hips for the first time, I also thought about its potential in cosplay and costuming, and I may have jumped with glee.

I was still interested in the corset as back support, so after clearing my corset-wearing with my supervisor, I started wearing it under my lab coat to work. I noticed that my shoulders didn't round forward when I worked, and that my weight was evenly distributed between my feet. Even when I had a particularly long day in the lab, my back and feet didn't hurt when I left for home. And if I kept the corset on in the evening, I was better able to listen to my body's natural cues and was less tempted to give in to emotional eating.

I also began to experience a rise in self-assurance. The straight posture encouraged by my corset created an air of confidence, and others started to take notice that my body language had changed—even when my corseted silhouette was concealed under loose clothing. Its gentle compression gave me constant biofeedback with every breath, and its armor helped me take setbacks in stride. With this portable, discreet, deep-pressure-therapy device, my anxiety lessened and I found myself better able to accept constructive criticism at work and school without feeling personally slighted. With my family and boyfriend living many hours away, I didn't get enough hugs in my day, but my corset provided quiet solace, allowing me to remain productive during periods of stress and isolation.

In time, my posture improved and my body language became more powerful. Where my voice used to have a raspy, trembly quality, I learned to lift my rib cage and push my lungs against the rigidity of the corset to project my voice. Public speaking became easier for me, and unexpectedly, this allowed me to excel in my side job as a teaching assistant—in fact, I started *looking forward* to presentations instead of dreading them. The undergrad students began to look up to me, and my perception of myself began to improve as well. The year that I started wearing my corset to work under my lab coat, many of my "kids" wrote on their teacher evaluation forms:

"Lucy is the BEST T.A.!"

"Lucy's lessons were the easiest to understand."

"Lucy was always patient and helpful."

Something inside me started to glow. I loved teaching—more than any other job I had had up till then—and I felt that teaching in one form or another was going to be an important part of my life.

Over several months, my waist shrank and my first corset closed. I needed a new corset, and I decided that I would go back to making my own corsets, as it would be cheaper and would give me another creative outlet.

At the time, I believed that there had to be one single, perfect, correct way to make a corset. How could there possibly be so many different construction techniques, so many different ways to stitch a seam, so many different silhouettes and patterns in existence? In the interest of learning "which corset is the *best* corset," and avoid reinventing the wheel with my own creations, I started purchasing more off-the-rack and custom corsets online.

And over the months and years, that collection grew.

I pondered over how to document my research, so I could refer back to it when needed, and could easily share it with others. Written-out descriptions were all right, photos were better, but I wanted my documentation to be exceedingly detailed, as though the corset were right in front of the viewer and they could study the corset in person with me ... what about video?

At the time, there were very few people making YouTube videos about corsets, Phoenix (mmsnafaioopoofeeker) being the most notable due to her willingness to show her face on camera and talk frankly about the reality of daily corset wear. She had much charisma and spoke with much candor. I uploaded a short video of my own in 2010, thanking her for convincing me that perhaps my fascination with corsetry was not so weird and taboo after all.

That video went semi-viral within days.

Suddenly I found myself with a platform to talk about something I loved, to enlighten others, and to share what I learned each step of the way. Although my channel later took on more of an educational tone (as opposed to being the originally intended personal video diary), it is still very much an implicit chronicle of my own growth. Looking back through my video archives over the past decade, I can see how my shyness fell away and a new assertiveness eventually shone through, and I see how my studies and the international corset community have "shaped" me in more ways than one. I hope to continue to share my acquisition of knowledge and the refinement of my philosophies surrounding corsetry with this wonderful community for many years to come.

THE INSPIRATION FOR SOLACED

Although I have personally experienced a multitude of benefits from wearing corsets, for many years I was apprehensive about sharing my positive experiences (even within the corset community), lest I be seen as a delusional nutbar. So, instead of focusing solely on the benefits of corsets, I took a more even-handed, scientific approach and—with the help of my university-based access to scientific publications on abdominal support and pressure—set forth merely to justify that a well-fitting, responsibly used corset *could be* neutral or benign.

But part of me still felt somewhat ashamed about my preoccupation with these pretty garments that came bundled with a controversial, bias-laden history. The mere topic of corsets seems to be inflammatory and polarizing. Were the benefits I experienced nothing more than a lame attempt to resolve my cognitive dissonance and rationalize wearing a rigid garment that is widely considered frivolous at best—and oppressive or potentially injurious at worst?

As a biochemistry graduate as well as a nutritionist with numerous anatomy and physiology courses under my belt (or corset, as it were), the mechanical consequences of corseting—positive or negative—have never been far from my mind. This was the inspiration behind the *Physical Effects of Corseting* series on my YouTube channel. Of course, I've always known that this was merely reporting on past research, and that it would be more credible to design a longitudinal quantitative study on the effects of corseting on a large group of consenting corset wearers around the world—but this would require significant time, funding, and reasonable assurance of compliance by the subjects. While I would love to lead this study (and I now know that such a study would also contribute significant research to the development of more comfortable and more effective orthoses in the medical industry), the first challenge is to go about convincing the reader that such a study would be of any value—and more to the point, that corsetry itself still has a place in the modern world.

It wasn't until after meeting Jody Hewitt (phoenixjodirae on YouTube) that the potential benefits of corsetry—as opposed to merely their neutrality—began to precipitate. Jody battled cancer, a spinal injury from a car collision, hearing impairment, a chronic staphylococcus infection from a failed cochlear implant, and some other, more unspeakable stresses in her life. When I learned that her insurance company refused to cover a medical back brace, I sent her my then-retired first off-the-rack (OTR) corset—my emerald brocade underbust—as a gift in hopes that it would help to somewhat relieve her constant pain. The gratitude she showed from owning such a simple device, and seeing what it did to improve her quality of life, was the catalyst for my *Corset Benefits List*.

Since Jody's passing in 2012, I've honored her memory by conducting regular corset giveaways and by requesting true stories from other corset wearers—asking them to describe how corsets have helped them, whether by reducing their chronic pain, consoling them with an embrace, encouraging self-acceptance, or otherwise changing their lives for the better.

In the four years between her passing and the first edition of this book, I received close to 2000 such responses regarding the positive transformative benefits of corsetry, and thousands more since then. Not only did I realize that I wasn't alone, but that I was actually part of a global crowd, thousands strong, that had issued a figurative roar.

THE TRIALS AND THE MISSION OF THE SOLACED PROJECT

AND HOW TO READ THIS BOOK

The 101 true testimonies in this book are just a small selection of how corsets have improved many individuals' physiological, emotional, mental, and even spiritual well-being. The stories have been categorized as best as I could by the type of condition that the corset was used to alleviate or stabilize (e.g., scoliosis, hypermobility, fibromyalgia) or by theme (e.g., corsets as armor or for gender expression).

Writers were chosen based on several factors, starting with their willingness to share their stories with the world and to attest that their experiences were truthful. Stories were also chosen based on the strength of their message and on whether these stories provided a unique perspective—e.g., through using their corset for a condition or syndrome not previously covered by another writer, or through expressing a viewpoint that had not been yet explored.

Every chapter is stand-alone, as is every story within each chapter, so readers are encouraged to start by reading the parts of the book that interest them most, skipping the chapters that don't resonate with them.

Some stories contain varying and sometimes contradictory personal views, as is likely to occur in large groups of people. Of course, the writers vary in gender, ethnicity, country, belief systems, etc. These views are provided for a broader perspective and reflect the heterogeneity of the global corset community. Some writers don't believe in tightlacing, while others do practice it. Some writers are wary of mainstream medicine, while other writers have a trusting relationship with their practitioners and openly discuss their corseting practice, and still other contributors are healthcare workers themselves within the medical industry.

It is also worth noting that the beliefs of the writers do not necessarily represent the opinions of the compilers and editors, or the other contributors—for instance, I personally do not condone the use of corsets by people with certain pre-existing medical conditions, including (but not limited to) hypertension, acid reflux, pelvic prolapse, or hiatal and inguinal hernias. While two writers in this book disclosed that their scoliosis seemed to resolve over time from corset use, these results are not typical—the vast majority of corset wearers with scoliosis will not "cure" themselves of spinal curvature, although the corset might help to alleviate some of the pain and muscle tension associated with scoliosis. I would also not recommend using a corset before the age of 18, nor during pregnancy unless it were a specialized garment made for the purpose of prenatal support and approved by a doctor. I hope it also goes without saying that a corset should not be used as a bulletproof vest!

Conversely, some readers may find that certain stories seem repetitive. This is not an oversight. Some writers, like Claudia and Dawn, who both have EDS, may seem at first glance to have similar issues, but in reality Claudia's pelvis did not tilt forward enough (posterior pelvic tilt), and Dawn's pelvis tilted too far forward (anterior pelvic tilt). Both writers claimed that their corsets corrected their respective pelvic tilts into a more neutral position to alleviate their pain.

Additionally, you may find many parallels among the writers with fibromyalgia—logically, people with similar conditions often find that corsets are useful in similar ways. More importantly, it was once believed that fibro sufferers *cannot* wear corsets due to their trigger points, and as such many people with fibro dismiss the corset without ever trying one. The more people with fibromyalgia who come forward with confirmation that gentle corset wear is potentially helpful for their condition, the more likely therapeutic corsetry will be considered a viable treatment in the future.

You will also find that many stories don't fit cleanly into one category. Take for instance Tara D's experience, where she used the corset to stabilize her sacroiliac joint, provide breast support, and relieve her fibromyalgia pain—but I felt that her story focused most around her SI injury.

While working on this book, I found myself repeatedly in *sonder* (which John Koenig defines as "the realization that each random passerby is living a life as vivid and complex as your own") and in awe of the writers and how each has used a simple garment in many different ways to overcome their trials or cope with their chronic conditions. People are wonderfully multifaceted and complex, and these writers are no different—so their use of corsetry is not always limited to one purpose either. While I've done what I could to categorize the stories, you may find some overlap with other themes, and that is okay. Stories that didn't quite fit into any of the categories were placed in the Potpourri chapter, which is arguably one of the most interesting chapters due to the broad spectrum of experiences and perspectives therein.

One of the most difficult tasks in compiling this book was editing down or cutting some of the stories, since I consider each person to be as important as the next, and I felt that all stories deserved to be included and unabridged.

There were other stories I wished to include but could not due to time constraints, such as the stories of:

1. **Sasha**, "Brisbane's Million Dollar Woman" whose abdominal muscles were so damaged in a motorcycle accident that she wears a medical corset from Delicate Facade Corsetry to keep her organs in place.
2. **Kat**, who was punched in the gut by a violent aggressor, but

whose corset busk protected her from harm and broke the assailant's hand.
3. **Megan**, whose use of a corset assisted her recovery from anorexia. Too weak to walk or hold herself upright, she used a corset to support her torso during physiotherapy sessions until she gained enough strength in her legs to learn to walk again; then, gradually, she loosened the corset over time, allowing her core strength to build.
4. **Kitty**, whose corset by Lace Embrace Atelier was specially built to accommodate her ileostomy, support her scoliosis, and help keep her liver from floating (hepaptosis) due to her congenital ligament disorder.

Nevertheless, I believe that readers will still be pleasantly surprised by some of the unconventional and creative uses for corsets included in this book. Some you will find more familiar like Jessica's alleviation of her sciatica, Raquel's reduction of her lordosis and turned foot, Lelanie's abdominal support, and Kim's breast support. Other stories will have you consider corsets in a different way, such as Molly's remedy for her sensory processing disorder, Heidi's management of chronic complications due to mega-colon, and Grace's practice for making her intracranial hypertension more manageable. Some writers just got lucky by wearing their corset that day, like D'arcy's corset saving her life in a car accident, Birgit's encounter with a mugger, and the numerous Victorian women whose corsets deflected bullets or knives. And many stories discuss the relationship between corsets, body positivity, autonomy, and relationship with oneself, notably the stories by Tara Moss and Rose Guildenstern.

THE MISSION OF THE ONGOING SOLACED PROJECT

I should note that it is not my mission to put every "body" into a corset. Not everyone wants, needs, or cares for corsets, and that's all right. My mission is to ensure that anyone who *does* become interested in corsetry will be able to easily access reliable information as to what a corset can and can't do (a corset is not a miracle worker), and can thereby make an informed choice as to whether a corset might be right for their needs. It is important to enable prospective corset wearers to make educated decisions on how to find a reputable maker, ascertain good quality and fit, and use corsets responsibly under the supervision of their trusted health practitioner. Whether as a therapeutic device, as an aesthetic accessory, or as a tool for body modification, there is no reason that anyone should feel isolated, confused, or uninformed.

Nor is it my motive to have anyone come to permanently depend on a corset. Corsetry should not bind a person to their illness, but rather should be considered an aid—a leverage tool to help the wearer reach a place of better function and quality of life, *if it happens to work for them*. While many of the stories you'll read in this book are from people with life-long conditions who may very well rely on back support indefinitely, equally important are the stories where corsets have been used temporarily to help the wearer regroup, rebuild, and rehabilitate—at which point the corset can be retired to the status of a "pretty garment" to be worn occasionally for enjoyment.

My goal for this book is to start a conversation and encourage more open communication among corset makers, corset wearers, and doctors, so that more patients can be assessed for eligibility for a medical corset in an environment free of negative bias.

Modern back braces, post-operative or postpartum compression bands, weight-lifting belts, kidney belts for riders (of horses or motorcycles), etc., all have their roots in corsetry. The line between a customized textile therapeutic brace and a high-quality bespoke corset is now fairly thin. Corsetières are forever experimenting with modern materials (even carbon fiber reinforcement and space-age textiles), and discovering innovative ways to make corsets thinner, lighter in weight, more breathable, better tailored to the individual, more comfortable, and more durable, requiring less repair or replacement over time.

One wonderful thing about corsets is that they don't "look" like the purely utilitarian, traditional medical contraptions. Bulky back braces tend to draw pity and awkward stares from strangers (potentially leading to self-consciousness of the wearer, or soliciting emotional labor from them to be a "teachable moment" to intrusive onlookers). Conversely, even therapeutic corsets tend to attract admiration for their lush fabrics and intricate details—or they can be discreet enough to remain completely hidden under clothing to prevent unwanted attention. To alleviate one's pain, and at the same time have a say in how one presents themselves to the world on a given day, can be powerful for one's confidence and personal autonomy.

Naturally, corsets can remind the wearer that they are beautiful, exceptional, cherished, and worthy. But even more broadly: when combined with proper therapeutic support and bracing, these factors —a corset's aesthetic customizability, comfort, luxuriousness, and elegant appeal—may improve patient compliance and encourage faster rehabilitation overall.

The incredible work of independent corsetières is starting to be recognized by medical insurance companies. Physicians are now recruiting some corsetières to help their patients with long-term structural support for congenital conditions, or for short-term stabilization after injury. As you will read in the stories ahead, corsets are not only being prescribed by physicians for physiological support, but also for deep pressure therapy to reduce anxiety and depression.

While at present it seems a pipe dream, I hope to ultimately see reputable corsetières all over the world receive (deserved) recognition for their expertise in orthopedic technology and medical prosthetics. One day, I even hope to be able to financially support promising corsetières via a bursary to receive the necessary training at accredited institutions. By setting a global standard of quality for therapeutic corsetry, this may open up more opportunities for corsetières to collaborate with open-minded healthcare professionals and insurance companies—thereby improving quality of care for those in need.

—Lucy Williams
Lucy's Corsetry

PART I

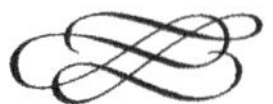

BACK INJURIES

MY EXOSKELETON

DEANNA C.

In the late 80s, I was riding my motorcycle as per usual, going around a curve I'd gone around a half-million times. I was daydreaming and hit the curve way too fast. It should have still been okay, if not for the wet sand on the edge of the pavement from the afternoon rains. In the summer in Florida, it rains every single day. After the rain, the sun comes out and just beams. It dries the top layer of sand, but the layer just underneath is still wet.

That's what had happened that day. The sand on top had dried and my back tire hit it at such a speed and severe angle that the back wheel slipped on the sand, out from under the bike.

That much I remember ... well, I do remember (and still get mercilessly teased about) pulling myself along the ground over to the bike and reattaching the linkage to the gear shift, just before everything went black.

I awoke in a hospital with half a front tooth, several broken bones, and a fractured spine.

Fast-forward to 1992: Hurricane Andrew slammed into Homestead Florida, where I lived at the time, and destroyed everything in its path. I spent somewhere between 6–8 hours in a bathtub with a bulldog named Badger under a soaked twin mattress, as the sustained winds ripped the house apart.

Although I wasn't badly hurt by the storm itself, what really wore me out was the strain of a hundred-pound dog who was scared out of his wits and a g'jillion-pound rain-soaked mattress, which were both on top of me for hours, and then having to dig us both out of what I'm assuming was the neighbor's roof and some of mine.

We all lived in FEMA tents for a while until we were able to be identified. There was almost nothing left. I got out with my dog and my baptism certificate. Thank goodness, my sister had taken my car to Clearwater the day before.

Fast-forward again to 2005: I was driving through an intersection, and a kid I couldn't believe was old enough to drive ran the red light and T-boned my car, hitting me squarely in the driver's side seat, pushing my seat into the console ... and that was it.

My body said enough. That was when my life almost stopped, other than work, church, and rest.

The doctors decided that I was too young for drastic surgery and started me on what became the all-too-familiar pain meds.

First, they started me on Tylox and found that I'm allergic to codeine. Enter Vicodin. At first, it was 5mg twice a day. After a year, it was four pills a day; and a couple of years later, it was the same routine with 10mg.

Then came Percodan, then Oxycontin, then Dilaudid.

Once they put me on Dilaudid, I got angry. I would get so upset that I'd lie in bed and cry ... not because of the pain, but because I knew I'd have to take more of that nasty stuff to do my job.

I have a small farmlette, and I raise my own hens for eggs and cockerels for meat. I bale hay, and I pressure-clean fences, roofs, and sidewalks. I have a fully functioning garden. I can and freeze what I grow, which means lifting heavy canning pots all day long.

On top of that, I have a full-time business as a master pet groomer. I work on a concrete floor anywhere from 10 to 16 hours a day, five days a week. I routinely lift 100-pound (45 kg) dogs. I've thought about restricting the size of the dogs I groom, but the bigger dogs have more intricate cuts and therefore bring more income.

For years I wore a bulky eight-pound (3.6 kg) back brace, which I called "The Hulk." This brace didn't really give any lumbar support, and it rubbed against my hipbones, but it was what I had and I made do. I'd gone as far as wearing two braces at once—pulling on a smaller, elastic brace first, then taking some of the foam out of a pillow and making a lumbar pad, and then putting on The Hulk so the pillow was sandwiched between the two braces.

In mid-2014, when I went for my umpteenth MRI, the orthopedic doctor told me that he thought it was time to fuse my vertebrae. He wanted to pulverize three discs, fuse the four vertebrae, and install a titanium cage, making a false spine.

That's when I went on a search. I realized that my lifestyle is not much different than the life of a woman 150 years ago. What did they do for relief? How did they keep going? CORSETING is how!

Before there were orthopedic surgeons, there were corsets. Before the pelvic sling and hysterectomies, there were corsets ... hundreds of years' worth of women had to be on to something more than just wanting a tiny waist.

Even the poorest of kitchen maids wore them ... now I know why!

It was through endless hours of reading everything I could find, starting with lucycorsetry.com and reading all the way through history (and everything on corsetiere.net), that I decided to find a cheap but reliable "starter" corset.

After considerable research I decided upon two corsets from Orchard Corset.

Since wearing my first corset, which actually fit quite poorly at the time, I realized that I was awakening with little to no back pain. The first morning that I awakened with zero back pain, I was actually scared to move. I thought I'd finally twisted in my sleep and paralyzed myself. That's how long I'd been in serious pain.

The last time I had had no back pain whatsoever was five months prior, when I took a step up into the dining room and all of a sudden, there was no pain. I mean NO pain. I felt a "shift" in my lower back, the pain stopped ... and then my legs gave way and I dropped like a rock.

So, that morning waking up after sleeping in my corset and being pain-free, I was literally scared to move ... but dawn was coming and I HAD to let the flock out. Once the rooster starts crowing, the hens will fight one another to get out to the feeders. I don't think I've ever moved so slowly in my life.

Once I started wearing that corset, in early August, the (extremely dangerous and high powered) pain medications I'd been on for almost nine years were gone. I got rid of every single one. Of course, the doctors have given me something to take the edge off the dependency that I'd developed over past nine years of taking ever increasing levels of opioids, but even that was given at only 8mg ... and within a week, I was back at the doctor's, having them reduce the dosage to 2mg.

I wish I'd realized sooner that corsetry didn't start out as a fashion statement, but rather, a means to an end. It took almost a decade and fighting The Hulk, being sick for several hours a day from the medications, and facing the prospect of major surgery to get fully fed up and try to find an alternative solution.

If I'd not started corseting, I very possibly could have been in a whole different and very bad situation. If I had agreed to the surgery that the orthopedic surgeon was pushing on me, I'd have lost my business and possibly my home. I would never have been able to ride my motorcycle again, my only mode of transportation.

My corset is my new spine. The only difference is that my corset is an exoskeleton instead of an internal titanium spine, and it's a lot prettier than a surgical scar—plus even more pain meds. Now I can get through an entire day of HARD physical labor with so little pain that I don't even need to take Aleve or Advil!

I've become a serious advocate of people trying a corset before they allow doctors to start prescribing addictive drugs and surgeries.

When I realized the limitations and the fitting issues of my starter corsets, I commissioned two asymmetric, bespoke corsets from Mina at L'Atelier de LaFleur. While she was vacationing in Florida in late 2014, she was coincidentally within 18 miles (29 km) of my house, so she took time out of her own trip to ask me to come to the hotel so she could fit the mockups in person, instead of me going to a local bridal dressmaker to have her fit it. Her service has been nothing short of spectacular.

I've even convinced two of my male clients, who have degenerative disc disease and sit at a desk all day, to be fitted with a bespoke corset; and, if they had insurance to cover it, I direct them to Fran of Contour Corsets, who makes heavy-duty back braces and will work with insurance companies.

I wish I'd known about this years ago. I can now ride my scooter with my shorter underbust and I can lift several hundred pounds over the course of a day with my longline underbust.

I never intended for a corset to be anything other than a way to stay upright and out of pain, but I will admit that having a visible waist for the first time in 20 years is not unpleasant!

If it hadn't been for the in-depth online corset tutorials, the attention to anatomy and the physical aspects of corsetry, I might very well be on my way, at 48 years old, to a nursing home.

My husband is 14 years older and much more physically damaged than I am, and I couldn't let him try to do this all by himself. My poor mom is in her mid-70s and although she retains her nursing license, would have had a very, very hard time dealing with me and my inability to do much of anything for the recovery period after the surgery, and then ... what?

How then would I make a living? I had to become the best groomer in the area to be in high demand without advertising. That took almost 20 years of honing skills.

I'm not going out on a very long limb to say that corsetry saved my life. I'm also finding that the extra $200 a month that used to be spent on pain medications is much better spent elsewhere. (Like on new corsets! I told Mina I expected to wear out at least two a year.)

As of this writing, it's been a year and a half since wearing that first corset, and I'm in the process of having my fifth custom, asymmetric corset made by Mina. In this time two more benefits of corsetry have become apparent:

1. My corset kept a post-surgical hernia in place ... one I didn't know I had, until it was discovered during a doctor's appointment. My corset had prevented it from pushing through.
2. And I had another, minor motorcycle accident recently—in 2015—and, although my knees and ankles received some damage, my severely damaged spine received nothing but solid support from my corset, which braced my torso against further damage!

Thank you for letting me tell what corsetry has done for me medically. I think it's much, much more important to have a supported, stacked spine than a tiny waist, and I think that more people, women and men, should know about the therapeutic benefits of this simple device.

ARE CORSETS GOOD BACK SUPPORT?

AUTUMN ADAMME, CORSETIÈRE AND FOUNDER ~ DARK GARDEN UNIQUE CORSETRY, INC.

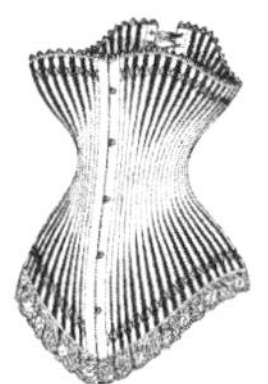

Corsets are an incredibly important part of my life for a variety of reasons. At the top of the list is my awareness that they completely affect the way the wearer feels. This is emotional as well as physical. At their most basic, corsets are excellent core support —and in today's world, where posture is quite neglected, we need all the help we can get.

I don't often speak about myself, my body image issues, or my background outside of corsetry, but a lot of things have brought me to be very interested in the human body and its abilities. I grew up not only being very interested in costume history, but dance as well. I've been a devout yoga practitioner, I love Pilates and swimming, and I have trained in circus arts for several years, constantly testing my own limits physically and mentally. All of this training has made me very aware of how everything in the body connects to everything else.

I look at corsetry as sculpting—both as a corset wearer, being able to affect the shape of my natural body, and as a corset maker, creating line and form from simple pieces of fabric and steel.

I studied ballet very passionately until I was 12, when a run-in with a school bus while on my bicycle cracked my pelvis and made dance nearly impossible for several years. It may have been that injury, or some other predisposition to hyper-mobility, that means I often have severe pain in my hips. Lately it's been shocking to me how much pain I experience on a daily basis.

I suggest to clients and friends frequently that they try a corset for relief from back and pelvic pain, but it took me over a week to listen to my own advice. Because of my dance background I focused first on stretching, strengthening, chiropractic, acupuncture ... but as far as *instant* pain relief goes—the corset wins. Don't think I won't pursue these other things—I'm not remotely interested in chronic pain, nor do I ever want to feel like I *have* to wear a corset, but it is a wonderful thing that I can feel instantly held and supported, and feel the screaming pain melt away, simply by wearing my corset.

The other bonus is feeling more elegant: I like the line of my body better, and I like sitting up straight at my computer or drafting table. The mind-body connection may never cease to amaze me. Better posture genuinely leads to feeling more confident—a positive feedback loop if ever there was one.

Some people worry that corsets make your core weak, that you can be lazy, but as I've been sitting typing this, I've felt myself try to slump back into my bad posture several times, only to have the corset remind me to sit up straight. The corset isn't doing the work for me, it's keeping me present to the work that I need to be doing. It's also stabilizing my sacrum, which doesn't come easily.

I've worked with two women so far who have needed expandable bespoke maternity corsets; the most recent one needed bust support as much as back support. She has since delivered a healthy baby and will be getting a new postpartum "belly section" to her two-part corset, to help her body return to its pre-pregnancy shape. My first maternity corset client was a repeat client who wore corsets daily to help her walk, as she suffers from extreme hyper-mobility in her pelvis. When she started considering having a second child, she came to me to make sure I would make a maternity corset for her, because she was certain she wouldn't be able to handle the pain involved with pregnancy without a corset to help her through it.

I work regularly with clients of all ages who have been referred by doctors, chiropractors, and physical therapists for lower back support, upper back support, scoliosis support, bust support as back pain relief, hernia support, full torso support … the list goes on. Some of them walk in, others roll in in wheelchairs—it's always a delight to see people move from pain into comfort, and to see the emotional transformation take place at the same time.

GETTING BACK ON THE HORSE

NORELL

Having always been a fan of historic costume and fashion, especially of the early-to-middle twentieth century, I have been drawn to the beauty and craftsmanship of the corset and the lines it produces. Throughout my life I have owned several corsets, all overbust, which I only wore for special occasions. I had not until recently done anything that resembled waist training. But now, I can't wait to expand my collection of these wonderful garments, as I'll explain.

I ride horses. Contrary to common belief, this is an activity that takes toughness, courage, and dedication. It also takes balance and good muscle coordination, something I lost temporarily when my horse fell and rolled over me last spring, breaking my pelvis. I felt like I broke myself. I couldn't walk, drive, or see over most kitchen counters and desks with my new friend, Mr. Wheelchair.

Horses are a huge piece of my life—and taking care of mine, as well as those of others, is part of my income. I couldn't get out to see my horse very often and that bummed me out the most. I couldn't do my job, a job I love. I was used to being a rather physically active person. That came to a halt for a while.

After a few months in a wheelchair and then learning to walk again, many things have changed about me physically. At 34, I am not as young as I used to be, but I am in one of the primes of my life. Luckily, after so much involuntary downtime, I was fully motivated to get out there and do all of the things I love, all of which require being very physical.

Everything was harder than it ever was before. I quickly discovered that my body just couldn't do what I thought it could; those activities I had always done easily before were now a challenge. The uphill battle left me in a lot of pain, especially in my back and legs. I could get only so far or do so much before my body said, "You're done for the day."

One of the hardest parts about coming back from an injury like this is building back your body strength and function. It's so tough to train yourself to not favor your more injured side, not lean on one hip, etc. Nobody breaks their body proportionately, and it can be difficult to redevelop the muscles and joints evenly. My hips and pelvis now have a slightly different slope and angle than they used to, so my silhouette has changed—and walking and pretty much everything else has changed too. I have always had slight scoliosis; my spine has an S-shape from the back, so I am especially susceptible to the uneven stance that would make my muscles not redevelop evenly and cause future chronic pain.

I decided I wouldn't just get back to where I had been —I had to come back stronger than I was before, and I had to make changes in my life. I figured this was as good a time as any. I bought my first underbust corset to help me mentally and physically develop a stronger posture, as well as to offer some support.

I started lacing the corset on every other day, each time for a little longer. As time went on I pushed myself to do more and go outside with my corset on. In the weeks that followed, I fully closed the corset for the first time, and I felt so empowered.

Eventually I noticed that even without the corset I was finally holding myself up much better, and my back wasn't fatiguing as easily —I was keeping my back straighter. The corset itself doesn't hold my back up, really, but it makes me feel taller and reminds me to sit up straight and put my shoulders back. I don't get as much strain in my lower back. I feel confident and I love the way it hugs me.

I have achieved a slightly curvier silhouette as well, which I appreciated given my boyish athletic figure. I feel so damn pretty in my corsets, so that's a reason by itself right there. I feel more confident when I ride, because my position over my horse is so much better—horses are very sensitive to our position on their backs.

Corsets have helped my body to rebuild correctly. They have instilled hope that I'm on a journey to a long-term healthy body. I am able to do the physical labor necessary to achieve my goals. I still have a long road ahead, but I'm getting there, improving every day.

Corsets have helped me in many ways, but most of all they helped me (quite literally) get back on my horse, and thereby gave me my life back.

SEVENTY-FIVE RABBITS & SCHEUERMANN'S DISEASE

STEPHANIE H.

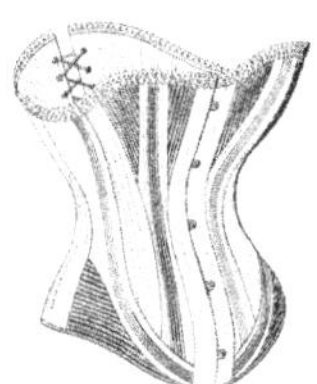

It was the late 1990s and I was a freshman in high school. I was invited to be part of a gifted program, taking college courses and high school courses at the same time. I lived far from the college, and had to lug a 50-pound (23 kg) backpack full of college textbooks around for five hours a day, every day.

At that same time I was raising and showing rabbits, and I was a member of the Future Farmers of America (FFA) council at my school. I owned and took care of 75 rabbits, which involved regularly hauling 50–75 pound (23–32 kg) loads around on my back. It was quite a lot of backbreaking work for a 15-year-old to do!

I started to have back problems in sophomore year. My mother, wanting to help me, took me to a chiropractor. I got some relief, mainly from massages that helped to loosen up my shoulder and neck muscles, but my back never was the same.

Cut to senior year: I was working three jobs and taking care of my ill mother and grandmother. One of my jobs was training horses to stop their bad habits, like biting, bucking, etc. Needless to say, I was bucked off these horses a LOT, constantly landing on my tailbone and back, which set the stage for massively herniated discs later on.

I got married at 19, and had my first child shortly after my 20th birthday. Maybe it was the bone loss from pregnancy, or the pregnancy weight I carried, but my thoracic spine started to hurt badly every day.

I was referred to a spine specialist, who diagnosed me with Scheuermann's Disease of the Thoracic and Lumbar Spine.

This disease causes irregularly shaped vertebrae and changes to the vertebral discs in young people, and it quickly leads to the development of a hunchback.

My doctor decided to put me on pain medication and put me into a kyphosis cast, which is essentially a full-body corset made out of plaster. It forced my spine mechanically into proper posture, and when your bones want to go in one direction but the plaster is pushing in the other ... damn that hurts!

After escaping the plaster cast, my doctor put me into a full-body orthotic corset, with a bajillion belts, laces, etc., which extended from my hips all the way up to my neck!

I was required to wear that brace for a year, but it worked—and from 2006–2011 I was doing wonderfully! Then one day, a seemingly innocent rule change at work essentially destroyed my life. In the summer of 2011, I was working as a night manager at a gas station. One of my job responsibilities was to mop the store at night before I locked up. This particular night, I was supposed to have a helper with me, but the storeowner had been dragging his feet about hiring new help.

The district manager saw that I was dumping the mop water outside, and said to me, "That's an eyesore for the patrons; dump it in the mop sink in the back room."

The "mop sink" was four and a half feet (1.37m) off the floor, and the industrial mop bucket weighed close to 65 pounds (25 kg) when full of water ... but working alone that shift was no excuse for not getting the job done, so I complied.

I finished up mopping, and headed into the back room to empty the bucket in the sink. As soon as I hoisted the bucket over the sink edge, I heard the door chime—a customer had just entered. The register was unattended (big no-no), so I quickly tipped the bucket, and it slipped from my hands. Instinctively I reached to catch it, twisting my body as I went … and the second my grasp connected with the bucket, I felt a gunshot-like "pop" in my lumbar spine. In agony, I called the district manager explaining what happened, but she forced me to finish my shift.

The damage was four herniated discs. They had been weakened from years of abuse, and they finally went out with a bang. My spinal cord was so squished from the disc matter, it looked like a pinprick on the MRI results. I lost the use of my left leg and became practically bedridden.

On July 2, 2014, I was scheduled for surgery. My neurosurgeon cut a 13-inch-long gash in my belly and moved my organs aside to access my spine, where he performed a hybrid fusion on the damaged discs. The second I woke from surgery, the staff wrapped me up in an Aspen Horizon 456 TLSO back brace—it's like a cincher, but the back extends up to shoulder-height with padded steel rods that hug to your back, with straps fitted around the shoulders like a backpack. The cincher part had strap-pulls that allowed me to lace it tighter for more support.

I lived in that brace from July until November of 2014, during which time I wasn't allowed any kind of physical work—I was forbidden to even lift a gallon of milk or dust the house!

Everything was going well, until scar tissue started to grow around the sciatic nerve going to my left leg … it made me bedridden yet again. Searching for relief, I found an inexpensive longline overbust corset on Amazon. I ran the idea by my doctor, who said,

"Anything is worth a shot—just don't try to bend at the waist in it, you'll aggravate the lumbar by pulling your muscles."

That overbust corset was my life-saver! It held my torso stable from my breasts down to my bottom. It distributed the weight away from the injured and damaged areas, and made my spine feel as if it was suspended in an anti-gravity chamber. It drastically reduced my pain, allowing me to do chores that I wasn't able to accomplish before, and it even allowed me to sleep peacefully, since it discouraged my waist from twisting and causing pain.

I more recently purchased an Orchard Corset Longline CS-426 with hip ties, and I love it! The CS-426 fits my body like a dream and has become my daily corset—although it's only an underbust corset, it gives awesome support. It's so comfortable I can even sleep in it.

Without a corset, I cannot stand longer than 15 minutes before my lumbar spine begins to burn and my legs start going numb. When I wear my corset, it takes 90% of the weight off my back, and gives me at least five hours of standing time. I informed my doctor, and he said that he saw no difference between the corset I wear and a medical brace ... and if it allows me to stand, to keep it up.

I can manage my pain and live a full, productive life again, as long as I am tightly encased in a well-fitting, quality corset ... so I can honestly say that a corset saved my life.

CORSETS SAVED MY CAREER

VEDA D.

I started working as a Certified Nursing Assistant back in 2002. Part of the job requires lifting patients throughout the day. I had no problems with my body; everything was fine—or so I thought. A few years down the road I started having pain in my lower back. I never went to the doctor for it during this time. I would just pop the joints in my back and go on with my work.

In the years that followed the back pain worsened, but not badly enough that I couldn't function. It wasn't until after the birth of my daughter that I started bringing it up to my primary care physician. Eventually he had an X-ray done and it was determined that I was missing some cartilage between my lower vertebrae.

I continued in my line of work and the pain kept getting worse. A few years down the line, well after I had my son, my nurse practitioner had an MRI done on my spine, which showed that I had a bulging disc in my lower back. The problem was so bad that if I turned my body the wrong way, for example just to move a small trash can, my back would lock up.

As many people know, pain can lead to depression. This added another problem to my already stressful life. I couldn't face being disabled and not being able to care for my family. It was already hard enough with my husband having lost his hand nine years ago from a work-related incident. I had to figure something out. I wasn't eager to drive 45 minutes routinely to get injections for my spine, so I started looking for something to support my back.

I was on YouTube one day when I came across a video of someone putting on a corset. I asked my mother whether she thought that a corset could help me with my back problem. She told me what she knew, and I set out to doing more research on corsets, surfing the web to find as much information as I could.

I wanted to find someone who had authentic corsets locally, but that was a no-go. While watching some of Lucy's reviews on different corsets, I would go back and forth to Amazon, Orchard Corset, True Corset, and other sites, comparing their corsets with my measurements.

Eventually I ordered my first corset through Amazon. I loved it and wore it the majority of the time, whether I had to work or not. It laced closed within a month. I put in some work on that corset, and when it started to fall apart, I got another one in a smaller size and different color—and so my collection started.

None of my corsets (all off-the-rack) fit the way I need them to, but I made do. I ended up getting a vintage sewing machine to do some repairs on my old corsets and eventually made one that is customized to my measurements.

Just having them on makes moving a lot better; I can't work without wearing one. Had I not discovered corsets, I probably would have given up. Corsets have saved my life and my career.

A VET'S EMBRACE

ALESIA R.

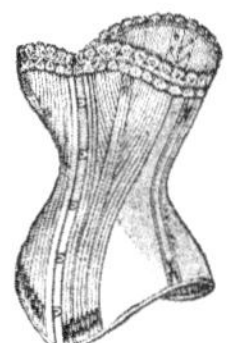

I am a 50-year-old kid who has decided that back pain has no place in my life.

In my youth I was fascinated with retro fashion and all things pinup. Enter my initial love of corsets, which, until recently, I had never thought that I could own.

I have a herniated disc at the L5–S1 level from a work detail while serving in the United States Air Force. For many years I suffered from low back pain, and suspected that I was walking around with a disc herniation. After 21 years of pain, an MRI was finally taken to reveal the source of my pain, and I was sent to physical therapy and given a back brace.

Because my brace came from the VVA Hospital, it was tailored to a man's shape and didn't fit as well as it should have. The prosthetic tech looked through a few medical supply catalogues until we found a somewhat attractive brace that was built for a woman's body—but it still did not fit very well due to my hip-to-waist ratio.

My thoughts soon turned to corsets. Since I had to use a brace, I decided it might as well be beautiful and fun. I took a class on corset making and made a rather whimsical natural denim corset trimmed with leopard-print external boning channels and lining, which in the end was ill fitting. But even the poorly-fitting corset and medical back braces offered relief from pain and showed me what was possible.

While at a renaissance festival I was gifted with a beautiful, ready-to-wear steel-boned corset, which felt like heaven until about an hour passed and it started digging into my hip. But I would accept the hip-digging in exchange for the back support and pain relief.

I started taking dance lessons in American smooth and rhythm ballroom dancing. The counter-body positions, dips, and lunges proved challenging to my back, and after an hour I needed traction, followed by wearing a corset. I started wearing a corset to class, which greatly reduced my back pain.

If 25 years of suffering weren't enough, nine months after I found my passion in the ballroom, I was rear-ended by a drunk driver, which exacerbated that injury and added C3-C6 herniation (in my neck) and T9-T11 bulge (in my upper back). All dancing stopped. Four rounds of physical therapy later, I'm still suffering and have found exercise to be the key. I pulled out my trusty yet ill-fitting braces and corsets, which had never failed to relieve some of the pain.

There are days when my 5′8″ (173 cm) frame feels like it is 5′4″ (162 cm) and my spine feels as compressed as if I had been hit on top of the head by a giant Acme mallet wielded by Wile E. Coyote. When I lace into a corset I can feel the compression start to relax as I regain those four inches in my spine.

I have yet to order a custom-fit corset, or to finish the custom one that I started sewing—but I love the way a corset feels, as though I'm in a tender embrace. It's what Temple Grandin discovered with her "squeeze machine": the power of a hug to fight depression. I have found in corsetry something to fight pain, the ability to help with posture, and to relieve disc compression. Plus, they're just so darned pretty.

I did eventually return to dancing and sports, recently winning multiple first place awards in a local competition. I still wear my ready-made corsets during practice, when needed.

FROM THE HEART

DEBI M.

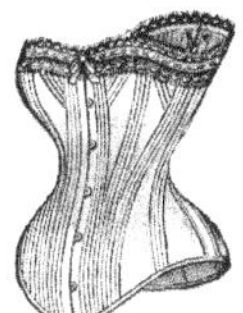

On September 10th, 2015, my nephew in Atlanta posted on his Facebook page an image of, and an article by, Sarah A. Chrisman. Curious about this picture of the pretty lady with the teeny waist, I read the article about Sarah and her husband, Gabriel, and how they have chosen to live a different life—a life of the Victorian period. Then I saw Sarah's book, *Victorian Secrets: What a Corset Taught Me about the Past, the Present, and Myself.*

"What?" I asked myself. "Teeny waists can be achieved in this day and age?" This question soon turned to, "Where on earth would someone like myself even find a place that sold corsets, in today's world?"

Natural inquirer and lifelong learner that I am, somehow I found Orchard Corset's online site, and I read and devoured all their information, including their corseting videos and their helpful blog articles. I studied corsetry the rest of the month of September ... and on into October ... day and night I read and studied.

Then, Orchard Corset posted a video interview of Lucy, of Lucy's Corsetry. What is this? In the School of Lucy's Corsetry, I studied online lessons, instructions, and reviews. I was in heaven, learning about the world-wide Corset Community! So much to learn! But I was now a stay-at-home newlywed and had time to study.

In the 1990s I had been a Champion International Ballroom Dancer, competing internationally for Denmark. I trained and lived in beautiful Copenhagen for several years, in a Hans Christian Anderson Fairytale! Then I moved back to Los Angeles, teaching American and International-style ballroom dance, and also performing shows and competing in Los Angeles with my brother David Woodbury, owner of the Arthur Murray studio in Santa Monica. Then I moved to Nashville, Tennessee to help my aging parents, who have since passed on.

For the years since 9/11, I have been teaching children near Vanderbilt University in Nashville. Then two surgeries within three days in September of 2014 took that teaching career from me. I had thyroid surgery and knee surgery in the same week. My body did not recover enough for me to go back to the classroom. It was a rough era, with ongoing negative side-effects. Healing was very painful, slow, and sporadic at best.

I had met my Charlie, who is a military war hero and a disabled USAF Combat Control Veteran, of whom I am very proud. Charlie took (and still takes) care of me like no other, honorably and with all of the love in his heart—I am hopelessly devoted to my sweetheart ~ we married in the spring of 2015. We then left Nashville and moved to a tiny country town of 400 people. Our 1930s farmhouse is surrounded by nature, mountains, water, and sunsets.

Charlie and I have both had lower back surgeries (laminectomies). Charlie's injuries were mostly from tough parachute landings. In addition, once his plane crashed and landed upside down high up in a tree surrounded by enemies; another time he was blown up. As for me, I had back issues from my many athletic injuries. Charlie and I both understood and empathized with each other's reoccurring back pains (even after having those laminectomy surgeries that were supposed to eliminate further pain). Today we stay grateful to be walking at all, and we count our blessings from the Good Lord.

Fast-forward to September 2015: I was reading all I could about corsetry, and I learned that there were many potential benefits of corseting … so I thought that maybe corseting could help me, too. I was hopeful.

I ordered my first-ever corset via Lucy. The second day I went to gently lace it up, I felt a weird, new sensation in my back … my back and body and muscles RELAXED—relaxed into the corset itself. I wept with relief and happiness—with gratitude to Sarah Chrisman and her memoir of her own successful corseting experience; to Orchard Corset for their educational corset blogs and videos; and to Lucy's Corsetry, for her extreme knowledge and scientific approach to corsetry, and for her unrelenting, persistent patience, answering her followers' question after question.

Corseting has relaxed my back so much that I'm not taking back pain medication now. Corseting has straightened my posture, relaxed my shoulders, and lengthened my torso. Corseting makes me feel proud, sassy, feminine, and in charge of my body.

The first time I put on a corset, I told my Charlie to take a "before" picture of me in our living room. He agreed, but pointed out that I was wearing black. Charlie said that the corset is also black and he would not be able to tell when I put the corset on. We would see about that! In our bedroom I then put the corset on, laced it up by myself, and walked back in to him in the living room.

Charlie saw me walk in … then his mouth fell open and he said in surprise, "Baybee … Baybee!!"

Corseting has brought back such feminine joy to me … and wearing it reminds me of when I was in my ballgowns, dancing like the wind in my high heels! I feel beautifully magical with my corset on. Truly I love the secure hug it gives, and my posture is again erect and proud. I am most grateful for the relaxation of my muscles and the absence of back pain (and now less pain from knee surgery) since I am now wearing my corsets daily. I now have three corsets, and I know that this is only going to be the start of a new collection! My study of, my passion for, and appreciation of The Art of Corsetry has just begun.…

I look forward to many more positive personal outcomes from corsetry, and now I am hooked for life.

A NEW LEASE ON LIFE

TARA D.

I was named after the mansion in the movie *Gone with the Wind*. I loved watching the movie and reading the book. I grew up in the South.

I always had a fascination with Victorian dress and corsets, as I have a very large bosom, and have since 6th grade. My back would regularly spasm due to its weight. I would commonly be found hunched over, frozen in pain.

My journey with corsets really started 20 years ago, when I was 23 years old. I was putting myself through college, working full-time as a waitress and dishwasher at a restaurant. This particular restaurant was bad about following safety laws, and I took a bad fall in the dish-room, where the drain had backed up. I put my foot down on the wet floor and one leg slipped forward, and the twisting action ended up pulling my sacroiliac joint out of place. I went through the entire school year in pain, still working and going to class, but not knowing what was wrong with me. It was finally diagnosed as an SI injury at the end of the school year, and my insurance company approved me for a rehab plan at the end of June.

That summer I flew to Oxford, England, staying at St. Bennet's college for a Shakespeare program. How I wish the Oxford Conference of Corsetry existed back then!

My two friends and I went to Piccadilly Circus in London on our day off, and we found a booth where we could have one of those "Old Time" pictures taken. The workers decided to put me in their Saloon Girl costume. None of the costumes had backs since it was supposed to be just a quick picture. But since my costume was supposed to be tight-fitting, I had several workers behind the edges of the curtain behind me, pulling the back of my costume hard so the strapless overbust "corset" would be tight over my torso! It must have looked comical backstage!

My shoulders and back immediately sighed with relief. For the first time, there was something else supporting my chest apart from my own tired, spasming muscles. It was so freeing for those few moments, I was amazed.

But corsets have always had that bad reputation, and I didn't have a lot of money, so I didn't have a clue how to follow through on finding a corset. Therefore, at the end of my study, I went back to America, returned to work and school, and graduated from college in May of the following year (1996).

That June, I slipped on another wet spot at work. I tensed my body to try and prevent myself from falling again, but ended up straining one of the muscles that ran through my previous SI joint injury ... and then I fell once more in July. After that last fall, the immense pain from the sacroiliac joint was all consuming.

The SI joint connects two bones on each side of your pelvis and acts as a shock absorber that comes into play every time you walk, jump, or otherwise do anything apart from lying flat on your back. There is a muscle connection called the Superficial Back Line, in which muscles that keep your spine erect run down through the SI joint and turn into your hamstrings, and also run up to your neck into the sub-occipital muscles in your head. I learned this the hard way when I dislocated my SI joint and pulled the entire length of this muscle out of line.

Subluxation of the SI joint can happen easily—but it's designed to slide and go back into place, as it's a shock absorber. But for me, my bones would not stay in place. After repeated injuries, the sacrum and ilium bones of my pelvis were scraping together.

The team of doctors tried to stabilize my SI joint long enough that I could make some progress in physical therapy and develop the muscle to stabilize my pelvis, but it continually dislocated, causing excruciating pain.

I fought for years with my medical insurance company, but they barely recognized my type of injury and were unaccommodating—however, I felt that if I didn't get help, this might lead to my becoming crippled. My insurance gave me a wrap-around bandage to stabilize my pelvis, which I wore all the time except to shower—but as soon as I removed it, my joint would slide out of place again.

My doctors and therapists did everything they could until finally they said that the only option left was surgery. They inserted a bolt through my pelvis to hold the SI joint in place. But almost immediately after the surgery, we realized that not only had the first surgery failed (the bolt was still allowing too much movement), but I had waited so long to qualify for social security that now my left side was out of alignment from compensating for my right side. A year later, I went back for my second surgery to not only correct the alignment of my left side, but to also fuse the bones of my SI joint together on my right side.

The second surgery stopped the subluxation, but my shock absorber was now gone. I could feel every time I put my foot down, every bump in the road while in the car, anything that shook my body or caused the slightest impact. Additionally, they found a bulging disc after my surgery. I couldn't stand or sit for more than 20 minutes at a time, or lift a 5-pound object more than a few times. My back spasmed more than ever. I was put on semi-permanent disability; I was terrified of losing my ability to walk.

I appealed the denial of my insurance claim, and in 1999 the agency sent a doctor to speak with me. He suggested that I should wear a girdle or brace for the rest of my life, and then I should be able to go back to work. I didn't understand his suggestion and immediately rejected the idea; the thought of it seemed ridiculous.

Life went on, and I slowly worked to regain my strength. If I wore a knee brace, I was able to walk. My best friend and I would go on daily walks together—and it was around this time that I noticed strange things starting to happen in my body. My wrists started hurting, and I figured that it was probably carpal tunnel syndrome from all those years of waitressing in my early 20s, carrying around heavy platters in awkward positions. I didn't think too much of it, and began wearing wrist braces. Little by little, my body started doing more strange things.

I moved in with another friend who was a nurse, and she suggested I see a pain specialist. When I first went in to see this pain doctor, he didn't initially tell me the reason for the specific tests he ran on me—I thought he was just checking my range of motion. As it turned out, he was checking me for fibromyalgia. It had been building over several years, like small cracks in a dam, but shortly after my official diagnosis, it was like the dam completely broke and the symptoms hit me all at once.

I started doing what I call "the fibro dance." My best friend has had fibro since her teens, so she educated me on how to keep active and manage my symptoms as best as possible, while the doctors were trying to figure out the right cocktail of meds for me.

Following this, I had a string of bad events for a few years, and my mother took me in again as I had nowhere else to go. At this point I couldn't walk and I gained a significant amount of weight. Possibly from the combination of stress and my medications, I developed elephantiasis of the breasts. They grew to the point where I was not able to even stand up because they were so heavy. I had a breast reduction and got the weight off—and for a little while, I was so happy to finally have a smaller chest … and then the elephantiasis returned and my breasts grew back (something that no one understood). My extremely heavy bust would aggravate my injury, and I didn't know at the time about proper bra sizing for bust support.

If I tried to get up and do dishes, after 3–4 minutes my entire lumbar area flared and swelled into squishy cushion filled with pain, and my legs went numb.

The doctors were yelling at me saying I wasn't trying. I was told to walk for exercise and to go to physiotherapy (which I couldn't afford), and they didn't understand that my muscles had atrophied and I was unable to do my required exercises. With everything going on in my life, I spent most of my time asleep.

My mother started leading a creative writing class for adults at a school in Dallas, and one day she asked me to come with her to class. I agreed. I sat down in the classroom and within a few minutes, a guy walked in and drew me in like a magnet. We started talking to each other, and it was as if no one else in the class existed. After the class, I turned to my mom and said, "I think I met my future husband." What I didn't know at the time was that he felt that way as well. We went on our first date at the end of May.

Our dates consisted of him taking me out for rides in the car to help me get out of the house and get stronger. Our dates would often be cut short when I started to feel pain or become worn out. He took interest in how my illness worked and showed empathy for my pain.

By December we were engaged, and we planned a wedding for exactly one year to the day. When it came time for me to find a wedding dress, I tried on my first longline strapless bra with steel boning (not a true corset, but proper bust support nonetheless). It was revolutionary!

I found my perfect dress: a heavy strapless gown, plus all the bells and whistles for undergarments (including that longline bra). I was able to go through my entire wedding, including the reception dance and after-party, and feel great. In retrospect, I shouldn't have felt that good, because my back would have normally flared up even in the time it took to get dressed and ready that morning.

I didn't think too much of it at the time, and after the wedding, my dress and undergarments were stored in my closet until sometime later, when we were invited to a family celebration, which was an hour's drive away. I wanted to wear a strapless dress to the event, so I pulled out the longline bra from my wedding and put it on again.

I had no clue how I was going to get through the day. Normally within a couple of hours of sitting I would be shifting in my seat, pulling out the painkillers, etc., and by the time the event was done my body would shut down. But that day ... I was fine. I felt alert and unusually good the whole time.

When we got home, I took off the longline bra, and then the pain hit me like a wall—to bed I returned. I was tired of being bedridden. I wanted to get in shape, I wanted to be active. This got me thinking, and I started doing some research. First I found Georgina of *Fuller Figure Fuller Bust* and she taught me the importance of getting properly sized for my bras.

I talked to my husband, saying that I thought I needed to get sized properly for a bra, and that I needed to learn more about supportive corsets. This was in 2011; more than a decade since the insurance doctor had recommended a girdle for me—the irony was not lost on me. But a soft girdle and a supportive, full-torso corset are vastly different, and I also think the surgery to fuse my SI joint was necessary before bracing, as my pelvis constantly slipped out of place prior to the procedure.

I bought an underbust corset from Orchard Corset, and at home I was able to do some light housework without my back spasming. It was wonderful! I could take my dog for a walk, I could go pick up groceries—I felt like I could do anything. I finally started to believe that the old, active Tara was coming back! I was full of hope.

To this day I can hardly believe that a simple corset could change everything. Over the last few years, I built up a small collection of corsets and wore them whenever I could—to family events, birthdays, Christmas, going out to dinner—over my clothing or under, it didn't matter as long as I had my corset.

I always had to deal with the fact that when the corset came off, the pain would be there. I'd prepare myself for it, using Lidocaine patches or ointment to help with the muscle spasming. But apart from that, I finally felt normal—having normal interactions, being able to visit family, going on dates with my husband, etc.

With my corset, my husband and I were dating more than before we were married! My corsets also helped me with my heavy breasts, even my underbust corsets. The top edge of the corset contoured under the bustline, improving the support of even my ill-fitting bras and taking some of the weight off my upper back and shoulders.

I also gained 3/4 inch in height in the last few years—I had scoliosis in my upper back, and I had an extremely short torso. I wear mostly high-back corsets to support as much of my back and ribcage as possible, and my height actually increased!

A corset not only gives me pain relief and allows me to get out and do things and be independent, but it also makes me feel feminine and strong. With a corset, I can hold myself up and not have to suffer.

PART II

SPINAL CURVE

A HAND IN POSITIVE CHANGE

KATRINA MIOR, CORSETIÈRE ~ BONE & BUSK COUTURE

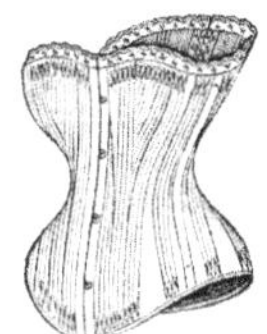

In 2014, I began working with a client whom I'll call Dominique. She had messaged me through my website, expressing that her expensive back brace was not easing the pain from her moderately severe scoliosis.

The severity of a scoliosis curvature is defined by Cobb degrees, or degrees of curve in the spine. 10–15 degrees is relatively unobtrusive, and people in that range can usually wear standard sized corsets. Between 20–40 degrees is specialty brace territory, and the need to prevent further curvature becomes very important. Greater than 40–50 degrees is beyond the capabilities of a corsetiere.

Generally speaking, I won't touch a client who has greater than a mid- to late-30 Cobb-degree curve. I would have put my limit somewhere between 25–30 Cobb degrees.

Dominique lived in Montreal and was willing to come to my studio in Toronto to be measured, so we made an appointment to have a consultation later that month. Generally, if the curvature is too great, then I do not recommend a medical corset, so I had to see her in person to decide if an exception was possible. She was a very fit and active person, much like myself, and I empathized with how limited she felt from being unable to perform her exercises and how she was in constant back pain. Her curvature was definitely on the more severe side than I had previous experience with, but it wasn't so bad that I wasn't comfortable working with her.

Typically, there are a few constants in my scoliosis clients: a protruding ribcage in the front usually, a twist, and extreme pulling from the weak side to compensate for the rock-hard inflexible strong side. I drafted my corset pattern as I normally would to accommodate for these issues, and we then set the date for her mockup fitting. She was so excited.

When she arrived, Dominique brought her partner and her extraordinarily expensive brace to show me what she was working with: it was effectively a multi-webbed tensor bandage, which she had to pay to have adjusted every six months. It was an impractical garment that didn't appear to be doing much for her. She was nearly in tears telling me about how much money she spent on it and how little it was doing for her.

I've had clients cry on me before: happy brides, women (and men) with body dysmorphia who see their corseted figures and become overwhelmed—so many touching stories—but this one ... this one was different. This was a woman who has spent her entire life in pain, throwing money at a problem she couldn't fix, and who was just exhausted. The fact that she believed in my work so much meant that I couldn't let her down. I resolved to do better for her. I took it personally. Little did I know what I would be in for.

The first mockup didn't fit. The pulling from her strong side was too extreme and there was a slight twist in the busk. I wasn't surprised, and I didn't give up. Because she was staying overnight, I offered to make another mockup to fit her before she left. I would NOT let her go home with a mockup that did not fit. I stayed up at my studio into the night (I must have left around 3 A.M.) determined to produce a perfectly fitting mockup. No such luck: still twisting of the busk, extreme pulling. Different draft, same results. I was stumped, but was definitely not giving up.

I ended up taking a week to think about it and ponder what was wrong. I grew obsessed with making the perfect corset for her. I consulted colleagues, but being a specialist in something most other corset makers either rarely or never execute meant that I was left on my own. Eventually, I had my "Aha moment," realizing what I had been doing wrong, and knocked together a third mockup.

By this time, our order process started to bleed over into other orders and my work touring schedule (I am a circus artist by day and tour globally, performing my show across six continents), so I had to mail the mockup to her to ensure she would get it quicker than trying to arrange for an in-person fitting. I felt confident that even if it didn't fit, we would make as many mockups as necessary until it fit exactly. I sent off her mockup before a short tour. When I got her email and photos showing a perfect fit, I shouted out loud in my hotel room and high-fived my colleagues on tour. Unfortunately, I wouldn't be able to finish her final corset for another three weeks when I came home.

She asked to keep the mockup because it felt so comfortable, and of course I agreed, and we would time her shipping for the week I got back so I could hit the ground running. I would be lying if I said I wasn't thinking about finishing her final corset even during my shows while performing for thousands of people.

When I got home, I began working on her corset right away. I finished it in record time, anxious to get it shipped out. Finally, I saw a message from her pop up in my inbox. I felt nervous, as I always do with bespoke garments, because anything can happen in that final fitting ... to my relief (and joy) she expressed her sincerest gratitude for how comfortable it was, how well it fit, and how her pain had all but gone away.

We had our final Skype chat later that day so I could see the fit. Now, I'm not exactly what people would describe as an approachable person. I admit to being intense, I flagrantly use scurrilous vernacular, and am viciously outspoken. But after our conversation I felt supremely uplifted, like I just paid some kid's tuition for a year. The only other time I have ever felt that way has been after a rocking good show and sometimes—even then—it's not meaningful. It's just adrenaline. But for the first time in my life, I felt that I had been a part of positive change in someone's life. I may have gotten a touch eye-sweaty myself.

FROM DUCK BUTT TO PIN-UP

RAQUEL SKELLINGTON

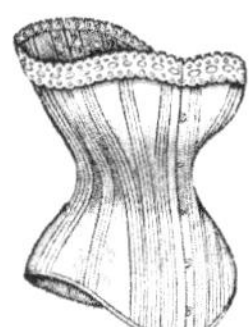

As I child I had severe swayback. My parents affectionately called me "duck butt" for the way my lower back was curved and how my butt used to stick out. In addition to this, I was born with one foot that had a tendency to turn inward. When I was 13, I started wearing soft shapers, not for waist reduction but to correct my swayback. My first shaper had shoulder straps to hold my posture, and I wore it every day. My friends at the time were all guys and they called this shaper my "armor." They would say, "Too bad I can't poke you anymore, you're wearing your armor today!"

I wore these shapers for two years until I was 15, when I got into a severe bicycle accident. I was at a camp in the Appalachians for the summer and had left my shapers at home. One afternoon during a bicycle ride, I was thrown from my bike and fractured my lower spine. I flew over the handlebars and, as I was airborne, I instinctively turned my body to the left and landed on my side so that I wouldn't take the impact face-first. As I turned, I skidded through the gravel. My face, arm and leg were skinned, my leg taking the worst of the drag. My left shoulder, hip and knee were all dislocated from the impact, and I had hairline fractures in my lumbar vertebrae.

The doctors also thought I had fractured my neck since they saw an anomaly in the X-rays, but it was later determined that I coincidentally had an unfused vertebra that was always there, which is why I'm not paralyzed today.

The only hospital nearby was a tiny, rinky-dink facility in the middle of nowhere, with limited resources. It looked like something out of a horror film, with the ceiling tiles falling out in places and flickering fluorescent lights.

They cleaned me up, stitched up my split lip, and bandaged my face, arms, and legs. They offered me a pillow for lumbar support as they said they couldn't do anything else for my spine, and gave me a single crutch to support me when I walked.

Returning to the camp later that evening was a moment I'll never forget. It was dinnertime, so everyone was in the hall. As I entered, hobbling on one crutch with half my face and body bandaged up, the entire place fell into complete silence. Naturally, the medical team didn't let me look at myself at the time, so I had no idea how bad the injuries were and how disturbing I looked until I saw the pictures weeks later.

That night, my back completely locked up in my sleep and when I woke up the next morning, I was unable to move. It was a very scary and painful experience; several people in the camp came over to help lift me up and slowly, agonizingly pull my upper body into a sitting position. This was my life every day for the next 3.5 weeks, until I returned home from camp.

At home, I started wearing my soft shapers again, but I was still in immense pain. At this point, I decided to invest in a steel-boned corset. Although I was only 15, I had a job and was able to save up to buy a Timeless Trends slim silhouette corset, which was not curvy but which relieved the pain and supported my back. It was easy to hide under my bulky school uniform, and I wore it every day and every night.

My parents weren't fans of my corset. My father hated it and my mother, a nurse and dermatologist, was concerned that it was doing more harm than good.

About three months after the accident, my mother took me to see a doctor in my hometown for a follow-up. I brought my corsets with me to show him exactly what I had been wearing and how I had been using them. He said that given the short length of time since the accident, it was impressive how much I had healed. He only saw improvements, and no side-effects from the corsets. He remarked that if I hadn't told him about my spinal fracture, he wouldn't have thought I had been injured so badly—and considering what I had been through, it was a surprise that I could even walk straight. He said I was lucky that I didn't need to walk with a cane.

Talking with my mother about my corsets, I showed her Lucy's online videos and articles on modern corset use, so she would understand that I had done tons of research into this. She knows that I'm not good with pain, so I would never do anything to deliberately hurt myself. Her opinion started to turn around once she saw the benefits that my corsets were having on my body: how well I was recovering from my accident, how my swayback was improving, how much straighter I was standing, and how my foot that had previously pointed inward my whole life was now facing straight. Especially after hearing the remarks from the follow-up doctor, she started to be more supportive of my use of corsets.

I wore that first corset day and night for the next year and a half, and I consider that year—the year I turned 16—as the year I really started to blossom. I became involved in LARP (live action role-play), I started modeling locally, and I landed a good job. I started going places and doing things ... I realized that these goals are tangible. Over the next few years, I started investing in other corsets: off-the-rack pieces from Orchard Corset, MystiC City Corsets, and Isabella Corsetry; and made-to-measure pieces from custom makers including SnowBlack Corsets.

Most of the other girls at those early LARP events and conventions wore cheaper corsets from eBay, so when I walked in with my real corset, some of them lost their minds. I quickly became the go-to girl at these events for corset training advice.

Now at the age of 20, my modeling has started taking off because I have grown into my corsets through my teens, instead of training down from a larger size as a mature adult. I know this practice is not commonly seen today or necessarily recommended, but it came about as a result of my circumstances. With a combination of inherited curves from my mother and my body developing in my corsets, my waist was formed into an hourglass. The other models within the agency previously only used cheap and badly made corsets, and I'm now teaching them what I know about proper, safe corseting.

Although I still have scars from my accident (especially on my legs) that have to be digitally edited out of my pictures for my modeling gigs, I still consider myself extremely lucky that I've healed as well as I did.

I'm afraid to even think what might have happened to me if I hadn't started wearing corsets after my accident. My spinal fracture would still have probably healed, but I might have been left in pain. It could have produced a lump or spurs on my spine, or my swayback might have become worse. I might not have been able to walk straight and would've needed a cane for the rest of my life.

I never thought about how much corsets have impacted me or how long corsets have been in my life until I joined The Tightlacing Society on Facebook. I've been able to meet amazing people in person through the online corset community and it's opened up new opportunities for my career, especially as corset makers are starting to become interested in having me model their work.

Corsetry has allowed me to express myself through modeling, art, and fashion. It's played a large part in making me who I am: my swayback is gone and my feet are essentially straight. Not only had corsets helped my recovery from my accident back then, but they now also play a part in self-branding through my work.

THE ACCIDENTAL CORSETIÈRE

JESSICA CRUTCHFIELD, CORSETIÈRE ~ TIES THAT BYNDE CORSETRY

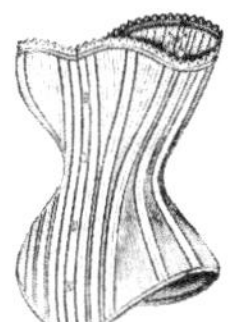

My introduction to corsetry was in a historical reenactment context. I started doing sixteenth century reenactment when I was 5 years old—I was in kindergarten when my aunt made me my first Elizabethan pair of stays (as part of her historic textiles thesis).

In high school I did an independent study on historical costuming, specifically the burial gown of Pfalzgräfin Dorothea Sabina von Neuburg from 1598, which is one of the earliest examples of what would be considered a modern-day corset. From there my interest snowballed—but it wasn't until after I hurt my back in a car accident that I became involved in Victorian corsetry.

In 2003 I was riding in a pickup truck with my aunt and uncle when we were T-boned by another car going 55 mph (88 km/h). Luckily my aunt (who was seven months pregnant at the time) and my uncle were both uninjured, but I was in the center seat of the cab, which didn't have a 3-point shoulder seatbelt.

My upper body traveled at 55 mph while my lower body was held still by the lap belt. The crash ended up twisting my hip and lower back, and my head hit either the steering wheel or dashboard (I wasn't clear as to which one, as I was concussed). I also had some soft tissue damage in the right side of my lower back.

It was 3–4 weeks before I could return to work. My doctors prescribed several different pain meds and got me into physiotherapy, and I also started seeing a chiropractor. After six months of physiotherapy, I still wasn't physically where I wanted to be, but the therapists kept saying, "Well, just keep up with the exercises to maintain your progress," and my doctors kept giving me different pain meds as I kept developing allergies to the previous medications.

After a year, I was still telling them that my back was in pain, that my leg was still numb and weak, and that I was not back up to normal, but the doctors decided that there was nothing they could do other than pain management. They started discussing options to burn the nerves away—not to solve the issue, but just to relieve the pain.

At this point I was nearly 24 years old and I knew that was not going to be the right option for me. They didn't know the long-term effects of those procedures yet and I didn't want to take the risk.

From the nearly two decades of prior reenacting, I knew that I had fewer back spasms while working long days if I was wearing my reenacting costumes, including my corsets.

At that point I had a single steel-boned Victorian corset from Fallen Angel and I figured, "What further damage could I possibly do? They're ready to burn nerves out so it's not like I'm going to do any more damage to my body than what was already done and what the doctors want to do to me." So I put on that corset and I noticed a definite decrease in my back spasms, and I was a little more functional throughout my day.

I was familiar with the Victorian myths that I'm doing horrible things to myself and all my organs are going to fall out of my body—but not much was available in terms of modern medical studies surrounding corsets.

At this point I started doing more research into modern corsets. I started my research online, at which time the Long Island Staylace Association (LISA) was one of the only major sites where I could read much about modern women who wore corsets on a daily basis.

Realizing the importance of a customized fit, I decided to make myself a corset and draft a custom pattern to my own body dimensions, as I already knew my proportions were a little unusual (my waist is very high-set and short).

Thanks to my long historical reenactment background, I was already comfortable with pattern drafting, so I started drafting my own corset patterns. My first few attempts failed epically (who knew that four layers of lightweight cotton shirting fabric doesn't make an adequate corset?), but soon I picked up a herringbone weave denim from JoAnn fabrics, made myself a two-layer longline corset that supported my back and hips, and started lacing daily.

I wore this corset every day for almost a year, from the moment I got up until an hour before bed. Each day I took the corset off and did my core and back exercises from my physiotherapist before bed.

Within three months I was having almost no back spasms. By the six-month mark, I no longer had numbness and deep pain in my leg from the car accident.

After about a year, the leg that had previously been numb started to become strong enough that I could stand on it again. I started to lighten up on how much I was lacing, so that I was wearing my corset for only ten hours a day, six days a week, and continued weaning off from there.

By the time 1.5–2 years had passed, my body had recovered enough to where I only laced up my corsets on days where I knew my job would have me on my feet all day and my back would be in strenuous positions.

Through those two years, I unexpectedly gained nearly an inch in height. I had mild scoliosis in my teens—which, after corseting, my doctors could no longer find any sign of. They guessed that it was due to the support from my corset, but they didn't understand why I used the corset, and didn't like that I used it. But they also couldn't complain, as I haven't lost any core or back strength, and I'm not in constant pain anymore. My chiropractor agreed with my use of a corset, especially after seeing how my corset was helping to hold his adjustments longer.

From there, my friends started asking me to make corsets for them, and within another two years this turned into a full-fledged business. Now, more than ten years later, it's taken over my life.

A few years into my business I started vending at conventions, and there was one romance reader / writer convention that I attended as a vendor. In the booth next to me was a tattoo artist who went by the name of Voodoo Monkey, and we got to chatting that weekend. He noticed how much better I was moving in my corsets vs. when I was not laced in, and next we started talking about men and corsetry, and what corsets do for the body. He threw a fit and didn't believe that men had ever worn corsets or that they could ever help his back (saying this while at the same time stretching his back every five minutes from crouching over his tattoo work).

Voodoo and I became good friends and continued to argue about corsets for another two years. One day we were in New Orleans for another convention and I was watching him work. His back was in agony, and he kept needing to stop and stretch. I told him to try one of my corsets because it might help him just a little bit. He was in so much pain that he agreed.

I laced him up into one of my men's style corsets: it was an underbust style that resembles a cummerbund, and it didn't give a high waist reduction—it gave him a "Superman V" shaped torso instead of an hourglass silhouette. Immediately he remarked, "Wow, my back already feels better." I explained that the corset was giving him proper support and correcting his posture. He said he would take the corset home, try it, and let me know how it went.

By the following year, when my tattoo appointment rolled around, he was able to literally double the work he did in the same length appointment. I have two tattoo pieces on my leg done by Voodoo, each of them took three hours—the first one is a small simple tattoo (4.5″ × 4.5″ or 11 cm × 11 cm), which he did before I gave him a corset. The tattoo above it is almost three times the size (4″ × 14″ or 10 cm × 36cm) and is a complex piece made to look like split-open skin showing a clockwork leg with multiple gears underneath. The second one he did corseted, and he completed it within the same amount of time as the first.

Currently, Voodoo wears a corset all the time in his shop in Rochester, NY. He tries to convince other tattoo artists to start wearing corsets as well, because he's found such a difference in how much he's able to do. He doesn't have to stop and stretch every five minutes, and when those breaks add up, the result is huge. When he's wearing a corset, he's able to sit down, get into position, and work through the entire session. He's more efficient, his clients like it because he's able to get more done in less time, and he's able to charge more for his tattoos because of this. It's improved his trade and income.

I'm very open with my clients about what corsetry has done for me, and at this point in my career, my clients are sharing their stories with me regularly as well. More recently, one of my repeat clients has just gotten her medical insurance to approve paying for her next corset from me, as my first corset had helped her so dramatically with her severe anxiety disorder.

I had taken my first commission from her in August last year. Within six weeks, she was able to go grocery shopping without needing her husband to accompany her out of the house (her husband also thanks me for this!). After three months of her wearing a corset, she started driving again—previously she hadn't driven in seven years. After five months, she was able to wean off the majority of her anxiety medication. She said that the corset was so comforting that it gave her that little bit of confidence she needed to push her out of her comfort zone.

When my clients write me and say that I've given them their lives back, I remind them that they should take the credit for the work and improvement they've seen in their own lives—I'm just happy to do my part to help.

THE GRACE OF A DANCER

KLAUDIA

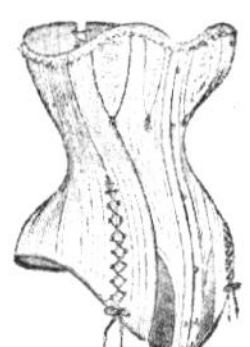

I started wearing corsets for purely aesthetic reasons. The sharply nipped-in waist and large hip shelves enticed me. I was unprepared for the unexpected benefits of having "a little secret."

Around two years after I started wearing corsets, it was required for me to visit a physiotherapist (for reasons unrelated to waist training).

During my first visit with my physiotherapist, I was asked to perform a few exercises in order for them to assess my movement. I noticed a perplexed look their face, and what they said next astonished me.

"So, are you a classically trained ballerina?"

I stopped what I was doing. "No! What would lead you to believe that?!"

"It's your posture—I worked in a ballet studio for a few years after graduation. You see the same stance again and again."

I couldn't believe what I was hearing. As a child and young teen I was constantly reprimanded for my poor posture. My general physician at the time informed my parents that I was developing a kyphotic curve, and advised that having me sleep on an extremely firm mattress would be the best course of action (to this day, I consider lying on softer hotel beds a luxury).

And yet here I was, standing in front of a wall covered in mirrors, with every angle displayed, being complimented on my posture by a medical professional.

Once I got home, I re-laced myself and stood in front of the mirror. It was in that moment that I lifted my head to its full potential and decided to embrace the newly realized posture.

Since this incident, I've been complimented by other people (including by a dance teacher and registered massage therapist) on my walk and my posture. Concurrently, my self-esteem has increased; I no longer see myself as that little girl who heard whispers from adults bemoaning my romantic future with a crooked back. Instead, I am a confident woman who is reminded every time I walk into a room to raise my head just a little higher.

It wasn't just my stride and self-confidence that changed.

I enrolled in nursing school during my waist training period. One of the things we had to do were lifts and transfers. While proper lifting technique dictates that one should use the knees and bend at the hip, many of my colleagues would bend at the waist and use their lower backs to lift. I quickly caught on to the correct method since my corset discouraged me from bending at the waist, and was there to remind me when I tried.

The routine lifts and transfers, combined with the constant bending over, proved downright debilitating to many of my classmates. Many of them would ask for breaks during lab sessions due to lower back pain. Many study sessions were lost thanks to one person mentioning their lower backaches, whereupon the choir joined in. Muscle strains were something that nearly everyone could relate to. I had absolutely no clue what they were talking about.

One day we had six ladies sitting on chairs while the rest of the class practiced lab skills, when our Professor lost her temper. "Why can't you all bend at the hip like she does?" She gestured in my direction. I was squatting on the floor.

"You're all concerned about developing varicose veins, yet you can't be bothered to learn proper technique to save yourself spinal surgery. You'll all throw your backs out by 40. What kind of nurses will you all be then? Disabled."

It may seem silly, but it never occurred to me until that moment why nurses would complain about back pain. Habits are hard to break, and I could see my classmates developing debilitating habits that might cost them their spinal health in a few years.

So, at the end of the day, it's not only my fingers that enjoyed trailing my hip shelf. My spine and my mind are just as pleased.

CORSETS AS MOBILE TRACTION

DIANNA DINOBLE, CORSETIÈRE ~ STARKERS CORSETRY

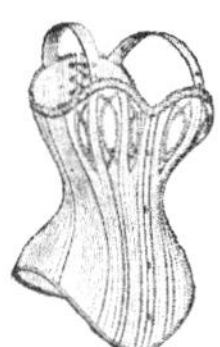

My daughter was born in 2004 and needed to be held constantly for the better part of her first year. I would shift between being hunched over, jutting one hip or another to bear her weight, leaning forward with her in a front carrier, or putting her in a back carrier to sit at a sewing machine. My back and abdominal muscles were constantly sore.

The first time I went out to an event where I could dress up after the birth of my daughter, I wore one of my handmade, custom-fit corsets. I felt instant relief and support when I laced up. It gently compressed my sore muscles and held my spine and ribs stable, almost massaging them as I walked and moved. At the end of the evening, when I removed my corset, the decompression was every bit as wonderful as the initial compression. My back muscles felt more relaxed than they had been in months. Wearing the corset soon improved all aspects of my daily life; it supported and reinforced proper posture when I was unable to do so on my own.

I actually felt a little ridiculous about how long it took me to think of wearing a corset for posture support, since I was (and am!) surrounded by corsets all day long. Soon enough I found that wearing a corset during the day also helped to reinforce my posture while carrying my daughter or bolts of fabric—or both at the same time. The slouching habit I had picked up while lifting an ever-increasing (and often squirming) weight that was leading to sore muscles had lessened, and my posture improved.

It wasn't just lifting that was causing me problems. When I was about 12 years old, I was diagnosed with mild scoliosis. It wasn't terribly noticeable and fortunately didn't produce the resulting muscle and joint pain that many others suffer from. However, it did cause some muscles to move incorrectly when I exercised (which I love to do), which led to a herniated lumbar disc at my L4 vertebra in 2012.

It began with a severe sharp pain in my low back with radiating sciatic pain shooting down my right leg. I saw several healthcare professionals, including a chiropractor who was only able to use acupuncture and traction to relieve the pain, since an adjustment could have injured my back further. We discussed the mechanism of traction, and how it was similar to a (properly custom-drafted and constructed) corset in the way that it held the ribs, spine, and hips relatively still, and prevented the vertebrae from compressing downward. He recommended that I might find it helpful to wear one of my corsets as a method of "walking traction." When I tried this method I certainly did feel relief from some of the pain. My corset discouraged me from making movements that would send sudden jolts of pain down my sciatic nerve, and the compression and mild traction provided relief from the vertebrae compressing my disc. It also served useful to hold ice and heat packs against my lower back when I loosened the corset a little.

As the weeks wore on, my doctor assured me that the disc would heal on its own—but it didn't. The pain increased and a series of MRIs showed that the disc herniation was getting worse. Eventually I was fully dependent on my corset being laced as tightly as it would go all day, keeping the torso immobile and compressed. I also needed it to sleep. Sleeping in a corset was tricky; even lightly tightened, it can limit full, deep breaths. While I wouldn't generally recommend sleeping in a corset, it was the only way for me to get an hour or two of sleep at night.

Finally, I was seen by a neurosurgeon, who determined that my scoliosis had prevented the disc from healing on its own. He wanted to operate immediately to prevent any impending nerve damage as a result of having my spinal nerves severely compressed by the offending disc. He also recommended that I put the corset back on immediately after his examination because it gave me some relief from the pain. I was allowed to keep the corset on for the X-ray prior to surgery, but not for the final, unbearable MRI.

After my surgery, I didn't want to see my corsets for quite some time, having worn them 24/7 for over three months. It's now been three years since my surgery. I've had lots of physiotherapy and coaching on how to correct my weight-lifting form to accommodate for my spinal curve. I'm much stronger now than I've ever been, and get to wear my corsets for dressing up instead of as a medical device. While I do love them, I cherish every night I sleep corset-free.

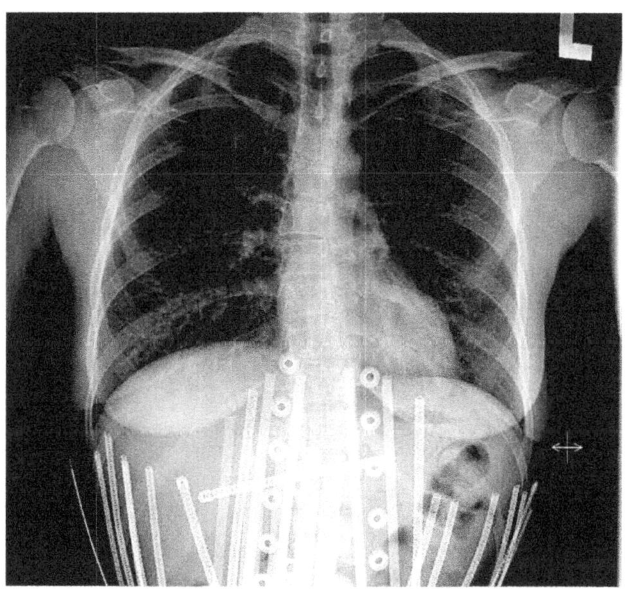

Dianna's X-ray showing steel bones, busk, and grommets from her Starkers Corset.

UPRIGHT

ALICE A.

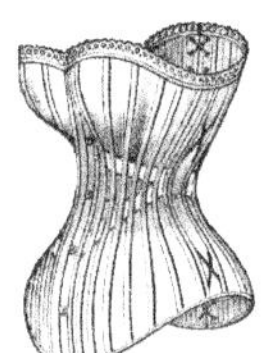

Although I don't recall my first introduction to corsets, I had always been fascinated by them, both for their beauty and the way they shape the body. The many hours of workmanship poured into a garment with relatively little fabric is something I admire.

My personal story starts when I found in fifth grade that my spine wasn't as straight as others'. It was determined that I had a case of minor double scoliosis, which I've always been grateful isn't bad enough to require treatment. However, I went to chiropractors on and off for adjustments whenever the back pain got to be a good ol' nuisance, to put it lightly. While not crippling, it was definitely distracting from life and school.

Sometimes I used a stretchy old back brace that my dad gave me to help ease pain and support my spine. It helped, but due to my body shape, the brace would slowly shift up, no longer supporting my lower back the way I wanted. So, I thought back to corsets and figured that since the shape is meant for a woman and they come in longer options, getting one might support more of my spine than just the eight inches the stretchy back brace covered.

The day I received my first corset, my mother brought it to me, happily announcing, "It's here!" She watched with curiosity as I dug into the package that contained my Timeless Trends underbust corset. When pulling the corset out of the box, it sure didn't feel as I expected—although I had no idea what to expect. The steel bones made it remarkably heavy and the layers of fabric made it stiff, yet flexible. Lacing up the first time took a little while despite the fact I'd watched many YouTube tutorials on how to do so properly. I knew what I was aiming to do, but seeing and doing are two different matters.

In my excitement I chose to wear it out the following day, which became a longer outing than planned. I wore the corset much longer than intended, and my ribs were sore. Lesson learned. I reduced the length of time I wore my corset until my body got used to it, and over time I learned how to listen to my body and gradually work up to wearing it longer. I often reached for that corset whenever my back was sore, seeking the relief that the gentle pressure provided. Whenever it started to feel uncomfortable I'd just take it off, feeling mostly relieved of my initial back pain.

After a year or so of this, I decided it was time to invest in a custom corset that was shorter and better suited for my body and needs.

So began the great online hunt! With even more information at my disposal from researching corsets for so long, I knew how to spot the right type of corset for me. I had a specific style and color in mind as I originally planned to pair it with a wedding dress design of mine. After careful deliberation, I chose to order a corset from La Belle Fairy in B.C., Canada. She was wonderful to work with and kindly answered my many questions, along with providing a fabric swatch so I could be sure of the color. I also wanted to be sure it was shorter than my first so it would not push up my bra so much or put pressure against my ribs where I did not want it to. The day it arrived was even more exciting than my first one, knowing it was made-to-measure! It looked so beautiful and the laces were softer than I anticipated.

With my new corset, I found even greater comfort and back support than ever before. Better yet, I began holding my shoulders more upright to complete the neutral, balanced position my spine feels best in. As time passed, I began holding myself like this even when not wearing the corset. I found that not only was it helpful in relieving back pain but also in helping me prevent the pain from happening to begin with. In turn this caused me to work at finding the best ways to stand to nearly eliminate knee, foot, and back pain due to uneven distribution of my weight. This made a world of difference at my job.

My corsets act as a confidence booster, a fun way to shape my silhouette for some fashions I enjoy, and a well formed back support to promote and teach proper posture, although neither of my corsets were made specifically for medical purposes.

PART III

BREAST SUPPORT

RELIEF FROM NEUROGENIC THORACIC OUTLET SYNDROME

BELLA BOMBSHELLA

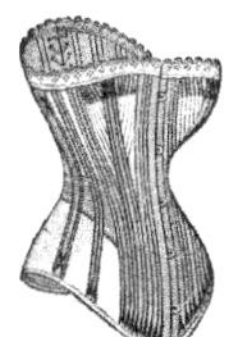

In 2012, I drove for five hours with my right arm at a 90-degree angle with my elbow resting on the top of the passenger seat. I did not have a pet gate, so I put my arm up to keep my chocolate lab from climbing into the front seat. This ended up causing a strain in my brachial nerve cluster around my shoulder and a strain in my ulnar nerve. I went to physical therapy and a chiropractor to address the pain and discomfort. Acupuncture addressed the neuropathy in my right arm for a time.

I had the pain managed until I took a new job that involved a lot of driving, which re-injured the brachial and ulnar nerves. I went to physiotherapy, orthopedics, and saw a physiologist. I tried gabapentin, an anticonvulsant and nerve pain medication, which helped minimally—but I could not take that and work at the same time, so that was not a long-term option. I did continue with physical therapy, which, coupled with yoga therapy, helped to minimize flares to occasional occurrences, rather than living through the pain daily. During my treatment with my physiotherapist, she informed me that I had been diagnosed with neurogenic thoracic outlet syndrome. The other specialists had not previously informed me of my actual diagnosis.

My workplace gave me the opportunity to attend Pain Week in

Las Vegas. This is a week-long convention for pain specialists. At that convention there were two presentations on neurogenic thoracic outlet syndrome. I attended both presentations and spoke with the presenters afterward. At that time one recommended that I use a corset to help with the tension on my nerves. He spoke about the reluctance of people to consider corsetry, but, as I was large chested (which tends to aggravate thoracic outlet syndrome), he felt that a corset could provide serious relief.

After that recommendation, I returned to my physiotherapist, who at this point was the healthcare provider who was most upfront about my health problems. She was supportive, and she wanted me to have relief and use whatever helpful tools I might have. She did caution me regarding retaining back strength and abdominal strength, so that started my research into corsets.

I started looking through blogs, conducting my own medical research, looking at the construction of corsets and how they provide support. I emailed several corsetieres and searched through social media, and as a result of several recommendations I chose Jupiter Moon 3. We discussed my medical concerns and the "overbust versus underbust" issue. The doctor I spoke to at the convention stated that an overbust would be best, but the corsetieres said that underbust corsets can also provide some support. I ordered an off the rack, on-sale corset to see what it was like. I really liked the support and shape it gave me, and recognized that this could be a game changer for me.

Armed with my research, I decided to order a simple bespoke underbust corset from Jupiter Moon 3. The first time I put the corset on by myself, the RELIEF was incredible. Instantaneous RELIEF.

The pain in my arm and neck was gone. The ache, the throb, the numbness—gone. I used to tell my physiotherapist that I had the sensation of working out my right arm all day while my left arm did nothing. That was gone. I'm now on no medication. No ongoing physiotherapy appointments. No acupuncture. Gone. Gone. Gone.

Now when I have a flare up, I put my corset on. I wear it for a few hours a day until the pain is gone.

COMFORT AND COMEDY

KIM RICHARDS GILCHRIST

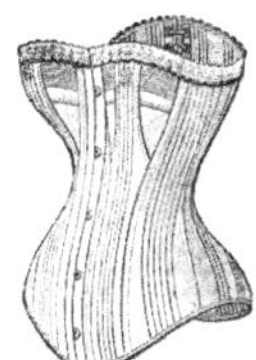

I've been wearing corsets seven days a week, including sleeping in one, for over five years now. They've helped me in many ways, both physically and psychologically. I started wearing them to relieve back pain. I have mild scoliosis, and I'm large enough up top that bra straps pulled on my shoulder muscles and stressed my back and neck. I had been experiencing a pain in my shoulder joint as well.

When I started wearing corsets, primarily overbusts, I found relief in a matter of days. The back pain, the neck strain, the shoulder injury—all of that disappeared with corseting. I also believe the corset is helping with my mild scoliosis. I will never go back to wearing a bra again.

Wearing a corset to bed has allowed me to sleep through the night without sleeping pills. At first I struggled with getting comfortable, and I warped the first corset I slept in regularly. One thing I did to help was make a waist roll. I got the idea from the bum rolls of ladies' historical clothing. I made a tube of cotton fabric and stuffed it. It took some trial and error to get the padding just the right thickness in each area of my waist. Then I sewed seams through the padding to prevent the stuffing from shifting over time. It looks a bit like a sausage with ties on the ends. I tie it around my waist and so, whether I sleep on either side or on my back, there is support to provide comfort and to prevent the corset from warping. So far it's working great. If pillows work for you, then use them. You have to find what works for your body, bed, and sleeping habits.

In a corset, I can sit comfortably on folding chairs, benches, and other standard community seating for long periods of time. Additionally, I work at the computer all day and the corset helps me to sit properly with my feet flat on the floor. It's helped me get through some long workdays. I do prefer to wear my corset than be without, feeling rather naked without it, even with clothing on. When not wearing a corset, I'm seeing permanent changes in my waist shape and I tend to sit erect as though I'm still wearing one.

Emotionally, it's helped me because I've always felt I wasn't girly enough. Wearing the corset makes me feel like a woman. The added benefit is the looks I get from my husband. He loves them on me and likes to lace me up, even though I can do it myself.

Recently I went to another state to stay with my mother through her late stages of cancer. She passed away in January of 2016. I have to admit that there were a few emotional times when my corset literally held me up under the weight of being a full-time caregiver and the subsequent grieving of her loss. When I wanted to collapse, it reminded me to stay strong.

Corseting has also provided some humor. The first time was when I was standing next to a young guy at the bus stop. I was wearing my corset stealth-like beneath a T-shirt. He turned and accidentally elbowed me right in the busk, and it made a fantastic "thock!" sound. I wasn't hurt but the expression on his face was priceless. I knew he wanted to ask about it but was too shy. I still grin when I think about it.

The second time was when I was wearing an open sweater with my corset visible from the front. A man in the convenience store wanted to know if I was "working." It took me a minute to realize he thought I was a prostitute. That's pretty funny when you consider that

I'm over fifty years old! It's like being carded when you're over twenty-one in that it's a sideways compliment.

The third incident involved my grandson, who was four at the time. My husband and I were visiting. I was sitting on the couch when little Sammy came up to tell me something. I leaned forward to give him my full attention but that wasn't good enough for him. He grabbed the top edge of my corset (which I wore overtop a light shirt) and used it to haul himself up into my lap. What a shock and surprise that was! The whole family got a good laugh over that one.

So, what's the downside to corseting? The most obvious one is going through airport security. I once took a corset through in my carry-on luggage but it caused the screeners concern. Since then, I don't wear one when I fly and instead pack it in my checked luggage. I admit it would be nice to wear while sitting in those awful plane seats, but the security staff is just not prepared for anything that's not a medical item.

I had to learn to pick up things off the floor differently. Now, instead of bending over, I squat down. It took a few weeks for my thighs to stop complaining at first, but it was just a reminder to exercise and strengthen my legs.

Bucket seats can get uncomfortable, as can restaurant booths—so now I ask for a table with chairs instead and I'm fine.

While not really a downside, I did change my wardrobe a bit. I took to wearing skirts more often. It didn't take long for me to learn to use a garter belt and thigh-high hosiery. Someone told me to wear my underwear on top of the garter belt for ease of use in the ladies' room, and it works great. I couldn't find thigh-high fleece lined hosiery, so I made my own by purchasing fleece-lined tights and cutting them at the hip. They work just as well with the garter belt.

I tried corset liners but discovered that a cut off T-shirt works fine and, when I plan to wear the corset in stealth, I just use a tank top beneath. They help soak up body oils and dirt, and keep the corset clean. I also use powder beneath my breasts to prevent rashes from perspiration or abrasion.

It's funny how these things like garters, powder, skirts, thigh-high stockings, and my corset all combine for a complete feminine experience. I guess that's something I was looking for most of my adult life.

Most of the time, when I'm going stealth, people don't necessarily notice the corset. I do get complimented on my appearance a lot. Part of that is the clothing but I believe a bigger part of it is my being more comfortable and more confident now.

The one recommendation I constantly make to others considering corseting is to learn all they can before they start: find out how to break in the corset, learn how to care for and clean it. Many online retailers, and some you find at conferences or conventions, won't tell you this stuff. They don't advise new corset wearers to start out on the corset path a couple of hours at a time. No wonder some women swear them off. Had I not found Lucy's videos, I might have, too, because I had no idea how to ease myself into corseting. I warped several of my first corsets and over-washed a couple more. Now I know better and am loving every moment of being corseted.

CORSETS IN ACTION: FASHIONABLE HEALING

IZABELA PITCHER, CORSETIÈRE ~ PRIOR ATTIRE

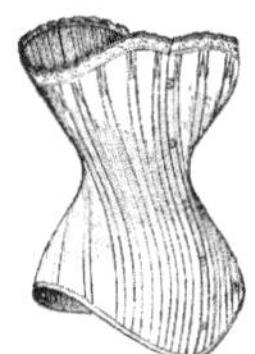

My corset adventure was inevitable. As a historical dressmaker, I knew that sooner or later I would embark on that particular journey... It was actually my engagement, and the decision to make my wedding a Victorian one, that spurred me to action. I decided to make my own Victorian gown as well as the bridesmaids', the matron of honor's, and my mother's gowns—so quite a lot in one go! Of course, for Victorian dress, if you are not wearing a suitable corset, you are simply not doing it right.

And so, my first corset was created to go under my wedding frock. But it was so much more than a corset for just that dress. I needed to wear it for dancing and for horseback riding, as we were planning a sidesaddle ride after the ceremony. It had to be a working item I could wear all day for all different activities, not just a fashion item to lace tight for a quick shoot and then take off an hour later.

So, we looked into original patterns—and the Symington collection. I still needed help with pattern drafting at that point, just in case, but the manufacture and all the slight alterations were up to me. The mock-up was made by Cathy Hay of Harman Hay and I took it from there. I tested it for riding, etc., adapted it as necessary and then created my first "proper" corset. It wasn't the best job, to be honest, and the techniques I used were not fantastic—but five years later I still have it and wear it quite often!

Needless to say, after that I got the "corset bug." I did more research and tried to learn from the best. Julia Bremble from Sew Curvy has been an amazing teacher and friend here, especially in the first few years when I was still very green on corset-making techniques.

In the last five years I have made over 100 corsets—Victorian ones, Edwardian ones, bridal ones, Steampunk ones, alternative ones—initially starting with a commercial pattern and gradually developing my own patterns, and hopefully, style. Our four bridal collections featured corsetry a lot, and I have made four different corsetry collections over the last three years (Steampunk Travellers, Steampunk Amazones, plus an Eastern-inspired and an Egyptian-inspired set), and the bug is not lessening one bit. Without any doubt, the best-sellers remain the historical pieces—Victorian, Edwardian, and riding corsets.

Apart from making corsets, I also wear them—and not just for photoshoots. I do not tight-lace or waist train, but I do wear corsets to work. As a historical interpreter and trader I often wear Victorian clothing (with a corset) for work. And work here means standing for long hours and entertaining visitors, giving talks, serving customers when trading, providing side-saddle or dancing demonstrations—all very active! And guess what—my corset has never been a hindrance; rather it has been a blessing. If I am on my feet for 12 hours, walking, sitting, standing, serving customers, etc., normally my lower back would be killing me. With a corset on—no problem! It provides just enough support when I need it. I have ridden, ice-skated, roller-skated, cycled, and danced in a corset—with no ill effects whatsoever. I actually started an online group, "Corsets in Action," where folks share accounts of their own active pursuits while corseted.

The secret to successful active corsetry is, of course, the proper fitting and style of your corset—not something to be found in the cheap mass-produced "corsets" on eBay—but a personally fitted, well-built-for-purpose corset that will last for a good few years.

Not only that—it has actually helped with some muscular issues. I recently pulled my pectoral muscle, and as if that weren't painful enough, costochondritis followed. My soft bras were not enough to support my 34F bust—and the weight of the breast pulled at the already painful muscle. Normal or sport bras were out of the question —they pressed on the ribs in exactly the place that hurt. I was at a loss —no bra and my pectoral hurts; wear a bra and my pectoral is better but my ribs are in agony.

Then we were out photographing some Victorian riding habits. I was modeling one—and realized that once I put the corset on, the pain was mostly gone. I rode around, posed, got back home, changed out of my habit—and the pain was back. I put the corset back on—eureka! I wore it laced very loosely, just enough to support the bust, but not to exert pressure on the upper ribs, and it worked! The corset is heavily boned, so it doesn't have to depend on tension too much to provide support (it is more like an exoskeleton!), and it rested gently on my ribs, holding my boobs up and allowing for the pectoral muscle to heal. I wore it for three days of my normal working life—bending down, sitting on the floor, cutting out fabric, all the usual tasks of a dressmaker—and it was bliss.

Three days were all my pectoral muscle needed to recover, and I was able to go back to soft bras (costochondritis takes several weeks to heal), but as soon as I was better I got back to riding—and that's where the corset proved useful once more.

So there you have it—an "instrument of torture" actually helping with a medical issue!

Izabela in her Victorian corset. Photo by Pitcheresque Imagery.

PART IV

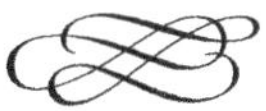

WEIGHT LOSS & LIFESTYLE

CORSETING AFTER BARIATRIC SURGERY

ROBIN J.

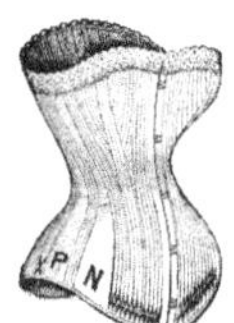

Weight loss for me has always been a struggle. Even in high school, I was always considered the fat one among all my friends. In reality, I was the average one at the time and everyone else was on the skinny side. It wasn't until I was in my 20s that the weight began to creep up on me. And, creep it did. For the next 20 years it was a constant battle with yo-yo dieting—losing 20 to 30 pounds (9–14 kg) at a time, but never keeping it off, and always gaining back more. As with all dieters, my frustrations were never-ending. It wasn't until I had bariatric surgery that I was finally able to gain control of my weight.

Although I have only been corseting for about two years, I have found the experience to be a very positive one. I love the way a corset makes me look, the self-confidence I feel, the improved posture, and I especially love the way my body has changed; not only because of the waist training but also because of the weight loss I have experienced.

I had heard about women losing weight with corseting, but I had never put much stock in it until recently. When I first began corseting, I wore my corset open in the back (i.e., with a gap in the laces) and I didn't feel any significant restriction. Once I began to lace tighter and my corseted waist was reduced by more than three inches, that's when I noticed it. After four months of being able to wear my corset closed, I noticed that the corset began to feel quite loose, even to the point of being able to put my hand down the front without discomfort and pull my tummy pooch up to help hide it. My muffin top above the corset in the back had also gotten smaller. My bra had gotten a little too big around as well. Even the rings I wear on both hands were much looser, too. I don't know how much weight I lost in the beginning because I hadn't stepped on a scale in several years—but these signs, along with the way I looked in the mirror, told me that I definitely had lost weight.

I know that not every woman experiences significant weight loss from corseting and that some will only lose a few pounds, if any. But, when combined with bariatric surgery (either lap band, sleeve, or bypass), the corset helped to keep me on track if my weight slowly began to creep back up, for whatever reason (especially since there are many ways to cheat and overeat). Given that roughly 53% of bariatric patients do not maintain significant weight loss over 10 years or more,[1] corseting can be a tool to help me remain part of the other 47%.

Because there is some compression of the stomach and intestines, the corset doesn't allow one to eat large meals, so the full feeling comes sooner—even for some who haven't had bariatric surgery. When this is combined with bariatric surgery, as in my case, the corset works in concert to keep those small meals in their doctor-recommended portions. Granted, there are still ways to cheat, such as drinking high-calorie drinks, and eating chips, desserts, and other high-fat meals (or taking the corset off). But, again, when combined with the corset, even though there is the ability to cheat that way, weight loss goals can be maintained easier because the volume of food is reduced.

My personal experience is with the lap band, which is an adjustable ring placed around the top part of the stomach to restrict the intake of food. I experience the full feeling relatively quickly since it is at the top of the stomach, and it is in this part of the stomach that signals for me to feel full sooner once I've eaten. This forces me to eat smaller quantities.

The food then slowly seeps down through the ring to the lower part of the stomach, much like sand through an hourglass. However, as I stated, there are ways to cheat, using calorie-dense, processed foods. These along with taking several hours to eat a large meal, or even taking sips of a beverage while eating, will all contribute to regaining weight initially lost during the first year after surgery. That is what had happened to me. I gained back almost 50 pounds (23 kg) of the weight I had originally lost after surgery.

All of that changed when I began corseting. I found that the corset made my lap band work for me again. Corseting makes me feel full when I'm supposed to. It doesn't even allow me to badly cheat with the "forbidden foods" because it doesn't let me eat as much of them. I have used it as a secondary tool to help me lose the weight I had regained, and now I'm going to continue to use it that way to help me maintain my weight loss.

When I began corseting I had a 39″ (99 cm) natural waist; through corseting and weight loss, it is now about 33″ (84 cm). I can close a 27″ (68.5 cm) corset and I'd like to close a 26″ (66 cm) corset eventually. I haven't thought about how small I want my waist to ultimately be yet; I think I'll just take it one corset at a time. In the meantime, I'm enjoying the benefits corseting has given me.

---

1. O'Brien, Paul E., Leah MacDonald, Margaret Anderson, Leah Brennan, and Wendy A. Brown. "Long-Term Outcomes after Bariatric Surgery." *Annals of Surgery* 257, no. 1 (2013): 87–94. https://doi.org/10.1097/sla.0b013e31827b6c02.

A HEALTHY KICKSTARTER

MAI MOLINAR ~ CORSETS AND DREAMS

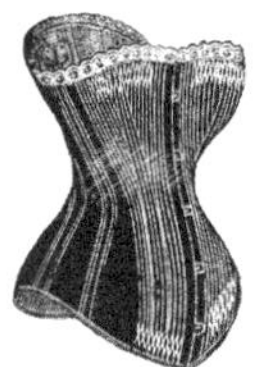

A couple of years ago, I bought my first corset—it wasn't a good one, but it still sparked my interest in corseting, so one could consider it one of the best purchases I've made.

I am a very curious person, and when corseting caught my attention it was impossible for me to let it go. I dove into research, reading for many hours a day and watching all the videos I could find about the topic.

I remembered seeing a girl who displayed corsets on YouTube. I first found her when I was trying to grow my hair longer ... by now you must realize I am talking about Lucy, but at that time I had to go through all of my old playlists to find her videos.

I spent months watching her videos over and over, and listening to her playlist at work, memorizing all I could about corsets.

And when I thought I was ready, I asked her for advice, and she helped me choose my second corset. This corset was of higher quality, and it changed my life.

Besides all of the usual health and beauty benefits (good posture, a smaller waistline, confidence), corseting gave me something more: a different lifestyle, lots of social interaction, and a very close friend.

It might sound weird, but wearing a corset really put me out there.

I am not so good at making friends, but I am very open and talkative when it comes corseting. My corset is a good conversation-starter: many times my co-workers have asked me how I got my waist to be so small, and I gladly share my knowledge with them.

That's how I became friends with Claudia, who is one of my closest friends today (she was even a bridesmaid at my wedding). One day we started talking about corsets and eventually became great friends.

Two other girls from our department started hanging with us because they loved to chat about corsets, too. I also became friends with my supervisor at my previous job, which was nice.

At my current job it happened again. This time one co-worker gave me a compliment about my waist, and asked me what type of exercise I do. I told her that I go to the gym and I am vegan, but I got my waist smaller by corseting.

She bought one of my old corsets and we became friends; I later learned that she's the finance manager; she gave me lots of advice and help when I had to travel for work a few months ago.

The corset helps people approach me, and they soon see that I am very passionate about corsets, and passion is something rare and interesting, and gives us something to bond about. So my corset helps me to "come out of my shell" and get to know new people.

On a more personal level: the second impact corseting has made on my life, which is also the most important change for me, concerns my eating habits.

I believe that a healthy lifestyle is like a snowball: once you see some results you become motivated to seek more changes and to create more and more benefits.

When I started corseting I had lost a few pounds by going to the gym and eating (kind of) healthy. I learned that doing core exercises is a must to keep your muscles strong while corseting. So I decided to go to the gym more often, and train my core muscles harder. After a few months my first corset was closed at 22″ (56 cm), but I still had some belly fat that I wanted to burn, and exercise and corseting weren't giving me any more progress on their own.

I needed to change my eating habits, so I started reading about dairy. The dairy we buy here is full of hormones and antibiotics, and it can cause inflammation and reactions in many people. After some research I completely cut it out of my diet, and I felt great. This is when the change started.

Over time I also gave up eggs, refined sugar, and finally meat. I was never a picky eater, and I liked meat as much as anyone else does, but while reading about the health effects it has, I came across something more important, and it really changed my perspective:

My eating meat caused animal suffering. It broke my heart and it still does. We are so used to buying beef, poultry, pork, etc., in the supermarket, nicely packaged, cut, and "clean," so that it is completely removed from the animal it used to be: cattle, chickens, and pigs. We give it a different name and completely forget that that product used to be a living being.

In this industrialized world and its factory farming, that living product does not have a name, it doesn't have much space to wander, and it doesn't have a good life.

Mass production reduces the life span of these animals to the minimum duration necessary for them to grow big enough to make their flesh and fluids profitable. Their health does not matter, nor does their pain.

Health brought me to this path, but compassion has kept me going. I started by wanting to see more benefits for myself, and I stand now for the benefit of others.

I hope my words can intrigue someone enough to research more about factory farming, and how its products affect our health, the economy, the animals, the environment, and the millions of people suffering because of world hunger.

My life has changed a lot since I bought that first corset. I love my body now, I am more socially available, I have a hobby and a passion, I feel so much more compassion and love for all life, and I am helping the world one meal at a time.

THE "SCARLETT O'HARA" DIET

JULIA S.

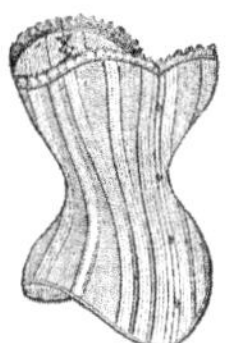

I never thought I would ever purchase or wear a corset. I was always extremely thin as a child, teenager, and young adult; so I never thought about corsets in relation to my body type.

I was a heavy reader of the classics. Most memorable to me were the scenes from *Gone with the Wind,* and the tightly corseted southern women of the 1800s. I had always believed the tales of corsets being instruments of oppression for women and that they were extremely unhealthy.

When I got married, I had a natural hourglass figure that remained until my first pregnancy. Then my thyroid began to fail and I was unable to lose the "baby weight" I'd gained. I started into a "gain, lose, gain" cycle with my weight.

Somehow, I stumbled across the idea of corsets in early 2013. I purchased my first corset in March and started wearing it on Easter week. That one corset started me on a journey.

While surfing YouTube, I came across several corsetry channels. The one that really hooked me was "Lucy's Corsetry." Lucy's well-reasoned and evidence-based defense of corsetry convinced me that not all corsets are instruments of torture, and that they may sometimes be used for good. I was intrigued to read from many women online that they have used corsets to successfully lose weight. As an added bonus, it's the only non-surgical method that provides instant gratification in the form of a visibly smaller waist the moment you put it on.

I have a basically non-functioning thyroid and take synthetic thyroid—which does not work anywhere near as effectively as normal human thyroid. After three children and the loss of my thyroid function, I had gone from my previous size 8, 115-pound (54 kg) self to 185 pounds (84 kg). After failing to keep weight off with other methods, being able to lose weight and get my figure back with corsets has been a miracle to me.

I am now on my fourth, ever-smaller, corset size and have lost 20 pounds (9 kg). I have even impressed my doctor with the improvement in my health since my corset training has started. Due to the compression on my stomach, I have to eat more frequent, smaller meals. And naturally I want to make that food as nutritious as possible.

I have recently been purchasing my corsets from Orchard Corset and just love their curvy longline CS-426 corsets. I now cannot imagine NOT wearing a corset. I wear a corset under my clothes about 10–12 hours a day, and it makes all of my clothes hang better on my body. Normally I wear a suit (I am an IT manager), and no-one realizes that I have a corset on. They just comment on what great posture I have.

The major benefits I experienced from wearing a corset include: losing weight, getting my hourglass shape back, excellent posture, high self-confidence, and the nice warm feeling of being always "hugged." The excellent posture and heightened self-confidence enabled me to do really well in job interviews, and I obtained my recent good position as an IT manager shortly after starting with corseting.

Sidenote: when my friends ask me how I have lost weight, I tell them that I am on the "Scarlett O'Hara" diet. *wink*

PART V

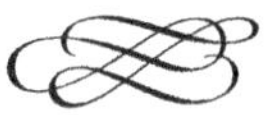

HYPERMOBILITY & EHLERS DANLOS SYNDROME (EDS)

ADAPTIVE DISABILITY LIFESTYLE

JO S. ~ JBOT | OCCUPATIONAL THERAPY, LIFE EXPERIENCE & CREATIVE THINKING

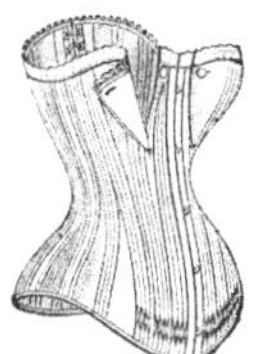

I have always been in pain: little twinges that catch me off guard, dull aches that never quite disappear, burning pain in my lower legs when I stand, sharp stabs like a knife in my back, muscle cramps that seem to go on forever. I distinctly remember leaning over for a pencil in drama class at age 15 and feeling the most horrible pain, as though I'd been stabbed. After an unproductive visit to the doctor's, I ended up seeing an osteopath; she spent hours working the knots out of my back and relaxing all of the spasmed muscles.

Until I was 19 I assumed that's how it was for everyone … all my injuries were just from an active lifestyle and a love of slightly risky after-school sports like gymnastics and rock climbing.

At age 19 I was diagnosed with Hypermobile Ehlers Danlos Syndrome (EDS) and suddenly my whole life made a lot more sense. Ehlers Danlos Syndromes are genetic conditions that cause faulty production of collagen proteins. Collagen is found throughout the body in skin, bone, blood vessels, internal organs, ligaments, tendons, cartilage, and even parts of teeth. With connective tissue disorders (like EDS), the faulty collagen leads to issues with one or more of these body parts.

There are several forms of EDS, the most common of which is the Hypermobility Type. Because of my EDS I have severe joint hypermobility, which leads to regular joint subluxations and dislocations. I also have soft and delicate skin that's allergic to everything and is always covered in scrapes and bruises, slow digestive transit with a very long list of food intolerances, an amazing ability to trip over thin air, and a strong gravitational attraction to door frames and work tops!

There is no cure for EDS or any of the other connective tissue disorders, but there are lots of ways to manage the symptoms. One of my management strategies is corseting.

Corsets help me in a number of ways; some are fairly simple and obvious, but others are a little more complex. First off, by supporting the joints in my spine, a good corset takes the strain off my postural muscles; this (in the short term) can help relieve spasms and provide pain relief. I also use it to crunch wonky joints back where they belong, although I wouldn't recommend anyone else trying that! This is a real relief, and it would be very tempting to stay corseted forever, but part of my condition is that I lose muscle tone very quickly—so I'm constantly having to balance the benefits of tightlacing for a few hours, and the fact that not using those painful muscles could actually do more harm than good in the long run.

In addition to my back, corsets have also helped me with my ribs. I have intermittent issues with my ribs partially dislocating away from my spine; this usually causes intense pain, and it can also, at times, affect my breathing. When this happens I wear high-backed corsets to help hold my ribs in place. This is especially helpful during allergy season—if you have ever tried sneezing with a rib injury, you'll know just how painful this can be!

When I first tried wheelchair basketball I was worried that getting crashed into at high speed would lead to serious back injuries—so I actually played in a corset for the entire first season! This (as you can probably imagine) led to a few laughs when I arrived for sporting tournaments kitted out in the team colors, running shoes, kinesiology tape, and a steel boned corset!

The second way I use corseting is a little more complicated. A few years after my EDS diagnosis I developed Postural Orthostatic Tachycardia Syndrome (POTS). This basically means my body can no longer adjust to quick postural changes; if I stand up too quickly I get very dizzy and can pass out. Part of this is because my blood pools in my stomach and legs—the blood that is supposed to be oxygenating my brain is instead lazing around in my lower body. But add in some abdominal compression and some (ever-so-stylish) compression stockings, and—hey presto!—I stop passing out. This has been a massive boost for me at university. Until I learned to manage my POTS with compression wear, I spent long periods of time lying on the floor in an effort to stay conscious. Not the best way to go about getting a degree since it made taking notes very difficult!

Another benefit of corseting is that it helps me with proprioception (which I seriously lack). I often trip over my own feet, and sometimes when I'm tired (which is most of the time) I genuinely can't tell if I'm standing up straight or not! Pop on a corset for a few hours and I regain some postural awareness. The benefits tend to persist a few hours after I take off my corset, so if I lace up for an hour before physiotherapy then I can do my exercises without having to worry too much about falling over!

Corseting for many people is about losing inches off their waist and creating a fab silhouette—but for me, it's so much more. I don't waist train as such, and I may even go months without lacing up. I use corsets for medical reasons; if I don't need my corset then it's usually a sign that I'm going through a good phase health-wise, and that all my physiotherapy is paying off.

That said, on the rare occasions that I head out for a night of dancing with the girls, I do usually lace up—not just for medical reasons but because I love the way corsets make me look and feel. I love the confidence I get from corsets and I love the interesting discussions I've had with total strangers as a result of my openly lacing up.

This brings me to the final benefit of corseting … I have met some truly amazing people. The corseting community is a massively diverse but very close-knit group of individuals that I'm very lucky to be a part of!

HOLDING THESE BANDS TOGETHER

LISA HARRIS ~ CLEVELAND CORSETERS

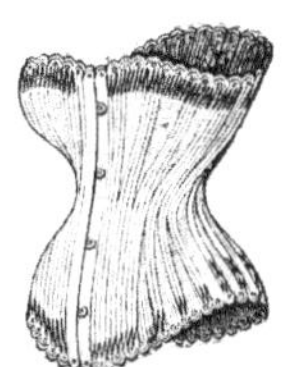

My name is Lisa Harris and I have been wearing a corset for medical reasons since January of 2014. My lifelong love of corsets (in history, fashion and costuming) had prepared me to take this path, which some may find odd, interesting and even controversial ... but yet "corseting" is not at all unique even in our so-called modern age!

I feel lucky that my exposure to corsets over my lifetime had always been a positive one. Through exploring history and art I came to realize that the general and "modern day" public are not privy to the "truth" or have an accurate historical perspective about the corset. I have made it a personal mission to help enlighten others about the beauties and benefits of corseting and expose the truth about this mysterious garment!

As I mentioned, I now wear corsets for medical purposes. It wasn't until 2011 that I finally found out why I've suffered with strange ailments since childhood and lived a life full of pain, fatigue, and easily induced injuries. I was finally diagnosed with an autoimmune condition known as Ehlers Danlos Syndrome (EDS), hypermobility type.

This disorder attacks all the various types of connective tissue in the body (skin, ligaments, tendons, bones, fascia, etc.). To explain it a little more, connective tissue includes tendons and ligaments—but it also wraps around and cushions organs and joints, attaches muscles to bone and other structures in your body, and provides the supporting framework for organs, blood vessels and skin. The cartilage between bones, intervertebral discs, and joint capsules is also a type of connective tissue, as well as adipose (fat) tissue. When one considers the extensiveness of connective tissue in the human body, only then can one begin to fathom the true implications of this condition. The best way to describe it is to imagine your body is held together with worn-out rubber bands!

My daily life since childhood has consisted of frequent spontaneous subluxations and dislocations of not just my joints, but of my spinal column and ribs as well. This has led to many other issues including Degenerative Joint Disease, osteoarthritis, bone spurs, and, needless to say, chronic pain throughout my entire body. This disorder affects the Autonomic Nervous System as well, which impacts my heart and aortic artery; I experience constant low blood pressure and frequent orthostatic hypotension (i.e., my blood pressure drops suddenly and drastically when I go from sitting to standing), neuropathy, fatigue, and frequent spells of dizziness and occasional vertigo. I've also suffered with migraines since I was 4 years old, which we now know are related to this condition.

The main reason I started wearing a corset was that I had tried every other possible treatment modality suggested for this incurable condition, which will only become worse with age. Wearing a corset helps keep my entire body in better alignment, decreasing the chance of dislocations and subluxations. It has helped "retrain" my body, even when I am not wearing one. I have become more aware of my body mechanics, which have been completely ruined by the EDS. When all your tendons, ligaments, and joints are like rubber bands, you have no awareness of when something is out of whack, and so injury occurs often. Once one thing is out of place it affects the alignment of the rest of the body.

Wearing a corset also helps maintain a better blood pressure, thus fewer dizzy spells and less dramatic orthostatic blood pressure drops. I've realized when I go too long without wearing a corset, I start to experience a worsening/exacerbation of my symptoms and everything falls apart on me: my body becomes twisted and wracked with extreme pain.

I really enjoy feeling the "corset hug"—and it keeps my ribs and spine in place, protecting them from dislocation and subluxation, which is a huge added bonus. I am in less pain and am able to function better in daily life thanks to my corsets! Thanks to my corsets I now see my chiropractor a lot less often. I'm also excited to say that my primary care physician as well as my rheumatologist are in full support of my corseting.

Because of the major and positive impact corseting has had on my life, I decided to start a local group to help others, near and far. When I started with this venture I could not find anyone locally who knew anything about corsets. I was shocked by this, considering that my area has a thriving burlesque scene and "alternative" lifestyle scene as well. I thought for sure I'd find someone who utilized "real" corsets, but alas, I exhausted every avenue I could looking for a resource. Thus, I knew I had to do something about it: and Cleveland Corseters was born.

THE CORSETED BIOANTHROPOLOGIST

REBECCA GIBSON, PHD.

I still own, and wear, my first corset. It's beautiful—an overbust, longline corset, double-sided: green-on-black brocade on one side and silver-on-silver brocade on the other. I found it at the Silverleaf Renaissance Faire in Galesburg, Michigan, when I was twenty. It's been fifteen years, but I still love it just as much as the day I bought it—a cloudless, dry, Midwest summer day. This was long before I knew of the problems with which corseting would help me, but that was no matter—I just loved the shape, the color, and the way it held my body—a boned satin lover clasping me tight in its embrace.

Now, at thirty-five, I own eight or nine corsets of various styles and materials, and I spend my life studying the cultural phenomenon that is corseting. At the time that I am writing this, I am working on a PhD in bioanthropology, and my dissertation will focus on how corsets affected women's bones in the years between 1700 and 1900 CE.[1] While the subject is much too large to get into here, it definitely influences my thoughts on the personal decision to wear a corset.

Some might see the choice to wear a corset as contradictory to studying the harm done to past corset wearers. And indeed, there was harm.

I believe, however, that we should use the past as a tool to focus, sharpen, and reevaluate our behaviors. That we should make educated decisions, and do what ends up being best for our own personal situations. We should keep what works, adapt what does not, and create new things from the knowledge of what has come before. Which is why, although I do not advocate for daily use, you will often see me wearing a corset to work or to class.

I have a medical condition that results in loose joints that easily slip out of place. It first manifested as what I called "falling off my shoes," where my ankles would suddenly let go and I would lose my balance, trip, and twist an ankle. Now, it can be ankles, knees, shoulders, fingers, or ribs. Only one set of joints has dislocated so far—the rest have done what's called "subluxation" where the bone slides from the joint and slides back, and you're left with pain, some bruised or torn ligaments, and the subtle embarrassment of having fallen all over yourself while not having actually done enough damage to warrant medical attention. The joints that have dislocated—for long enough that they needed to be popped back into place manually—have been my ribs.

It's fascinating, really, to think of the rib as it sits in the body. Your vertebrae form a column that encases the spinal cord, and on each side of each one of your twelve thoracic vertebrae, a rib snugly nestles between the bottom of one and the top of the next. I've often said that the human skeleton is a jigsaw puzzle, with each piece only matching to its neighbors. You can tell where one rib fits at the side of two vertebrae by matching the articular facets, the places where bone has rubbed against bone. They are unique to the person, to the very bone. And things that rub together can come apart. And when they do, it is exquisitely painful.

Rib dislocation is a relatively new development for me, and I did not know what was going on at first. It turns out that the rib dislocated at the back (or the "head," as it's technically termed) and ended up sliding far enough forward that it was poking me in the kidney. Once I figured out what was going on, however, I knew exactly what was called for to help on days when my joints felt like stretched rubber and I needed to try to avoid another dislocation: corseting.

The corset has a history that is tangled up in the words and opinions of doctors; some felt that it destroyed the natural female form and beauty, while some have accepted it only as a strictly medical device. While fashionable corsets, or those used to undergird fashion-related clothing, demonstrate beautiful, detailed, exotic, and sometimes erotic natures, and can be the most delightful expression of self and style, past eras of medical corseting have seemed considerably more like torture contraptions—all metal bolts and bars, with plastic bodies and Velcro straps.

Yet there's no reason the two concepts can't merge. If well-constructed, a fashionable corset, with its satin and ruffles, can provide the support needed to ensure that my ribs stay where they should be. And though I am now thinking about them and using them in a much different way than I was that hot summer day fifteen years ago, I still love them for their beauty, their form, their way of holding and binding me; a comfortable, brightly colored, smooth barrier between my body and the world that completes my outfits and promotes both inner and outer strength.

---

1. Gibson, Rebecca. "Effects of Long Term Corseting on the Female Skeleton: A Preliminary Morphological Examination." *NEXUS: The Canadian Student Journal of Anthropology*, vol. 23, no. 2, Sept. 2015, pp. 45–60., https://doi.org/10.15173/nexus.v23i2.983.

LIBERATION FROM JOINT PAIN

CLAUDIA E.

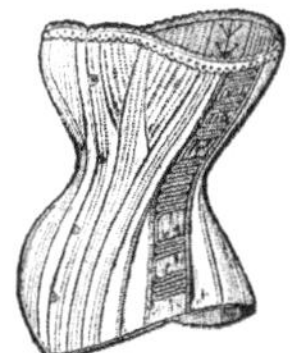

I've struggled with chronic pain since my early teens. I have hyper-mobility, which causes my joints to bend further than they are supposed to, causing greater wear and tear on them, primarily in my knees, hips, and back. This can be counteracted if the muscles around the joint hold it in its proper position, but this requires my muscles to be engaged at all times to prevent strain on the joint. Due to my joints hurting from over-extension (for example, my knees bending in the wrong direction) and my insufficient attempt to correct these issues by keeping my muscles constantly flexed, I also suffered from tension headaches.

I had tried one or two standard-sized, off-the-rack corsets out of curiosity, but, as I am naturally curvy, I did not like the fact that these corsets actually made me look less curvy.

Finally, I decided to purchase my first made-to-measure corset. When I put it on for the first time, I noticed immediately that it put my hips and back in the position they were supposed to be: my hips were ever so slightly tilted forward, which restored a proper arch to my lower back—not too much of a curve, and not straight as a plank.

The new positioning of my hips also shifted my legs, making it more difficult to overextend my knees. While I was wearing this new made-to-measure corset gently for the first week, not only did the pain in my joints lessen, but also my headaches became milder.

This was such a liberating feeling for me! The old corsets did not cinch my waist very much, but they were more restrictive, whereas the corset that was made-to-measure did not restrict my movement much and was quite comfy to wear. I purchased the corset to visually accentuate my curves, but as a bonus it actually relieved me of the daily companion that I called pain.

Since then, I have purchased one more made-to-measure corset, and I have started to make my own corsets. I don't need to wear my corsets all the time; I can wear them quite erratically in fact, and the benefits remain a long time after the corset is removed. Over time I've trained my body to hold the posture that the corset gave me, and now it just comes naturally for my core muscles to hold me that way, thanks to the corset. Due to my awesome posture, I look and feel more confident.

There are many ways my corset has boosted me, aesthetically and mentally, but it can all be summarized as: it has made me a happier person overall!

A SOLUTION FOR MY UNUSUAL PELVIC TILT

DAWN T.

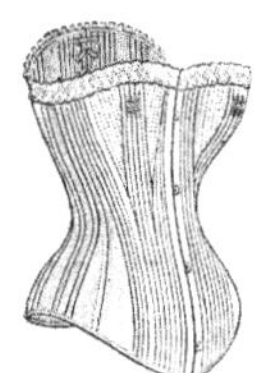

After a childhood of seeing doctors for ankle, knee, and shoulder issues, I was eventually diagnosed in my teens as having Hypermobility-type Ehlers-Danlos Syndrome (EDS).

For the first few years, most of my treatment tended to concentrate on the joints of my body that were the most unstable, and the therapists largely ignored the other parts of my body. The treatment kept me on my feet, but had limited benefit.

Around the time I started university, I discovered corsets. At first I was interested purely in their aesthetic; I loved the hourglass figure they gave, and bought my first off-the-rack corset. Up until that time, I'd been experiencing progressively worse back pain, which was further aggravated by public transport, especially on the newer curved, slouch-inducing seats now present on most UK buses and trains. I discovered quickly that wearing a corset relieved much of that pain during my daily commutes.

Around the same time, I found a different physiotherapist in my new city. This therapist was the first one who tried to treat my whole body rather than just the most problematic areas. He found that much of the instability in my leg joints was exacerbated by an imbalance from some overly strong and tight muscles in my lower back (a rather unusual issue for EDS patients), which resulted in my pelvis tilting too far forward. This also explained why it was so painful to slouch even the slightest bit, or to try and engage my abdominal muscles—they opposed the tight muscles in my back. My therapist advised me to wait to make sure I had stopped growing before wearing corsets full time, but then gave me the go-ahead six months later.

I can barely describe the benefit of that first off-the-rack corset, despite its not being quite curvy enough, and its flat steels warping slowly over time. Nowadays, I wear a custom-made corset, which, along with regular physiotherapy and tai chi classes, has really helped take the strain off those muscles and allow my back and pelvis to realign. I love my corset because of the confidence it gives me, the comfort of living with less pain during normal day-to-day activities like traveling, and the benefit of having a much more normal, or even "good," posture.

Although I can't wear my corset during my work hours due to the nature of my job, my back and hips have improved enough for that to be much less of an issue, and I still wear it as much as I can outside of work because I've grown used to the comfort of wearing it.

I'm currently sewing my first corset. I'll be the first to admit it's proving to be a challenge, but I'm enjoying every moment of it.

PART VI

OTHER PHYSIOLOGICAL DISORDERS

A HOME FOUND IN CORSETS

C. EDWARDS

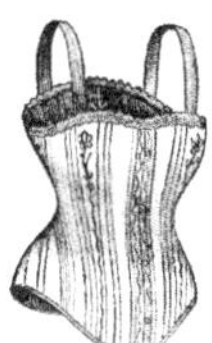

It was 2008. I'd turned 14 the week before, and my father had agreed to take me out into Sydney to choose a birthday present. I'd been into that particular shop a dozen times with my mother, who thought the whole thing pointless, and a few times with friends when we made the three-hour-if-you-were-lucky train trip from our country town, starting before the sun came up.

My dad sort of poked around in the shop, amused at the clothing on sale. Occasionally he'd pick something up, call my name, and point to it, then laugh. Just dad things, you know?

Before long, I found something I really, really liked.

It was a Gallery Serpentine waspie in red velvet; it was probably the first item I truly loved. It was over $200, and the velvet was plush and thick, a deep jewel tone. Back then, I wore a minuscule size 20″ (51 cm) corset with ease. While these days the corsets they sell aren't as curvy, back then some were quite extreme. At least, on a 5′1″ (155 cm) tall fourteen-year-old, it probably looked it.

My dad wasn't sure about it. He looked at me as if to say, "Please, something else, something less expensive; please something less outrageous," but all I had to do was ask again and he sighed and agreed. He should have known that I couldn't possibly ever pick something less provocative once I'd laid my eyes on something like that. It was the first expensive thing I'd ever owned. It also spurred a bit of an obsession.

Seven and a half years, ten house moves, forty kilograms, a collection of over a dozen corsets from several continents, and rapidly degenerating health later, I still maintain this expensive habit. Even after I lost the ability to walk and got a wheelchair, I still kept wearing them.

I have been experiencing dislocations and subluxation of my joints the majority of my life. I can't think of when I might not have had this problem. My hips only started fully popping out when I was a teenager, but my ribs and other joint dislocations, and the associated joint pain, have been lifelong. Additionally, I have chronic fatigue, asthma, and a growing list of other bodily ailments.

To combat pain, fatigue, and multiple-times-a-day joint dislocations, I found a home in corsets. The support of steel bones keeps my organic bones in place. Even under an almost ten-inch (25 cm) waist reduction, my otherwise unruly and painful body holds together. My back stops aching. My ribs stop dislocating (a point that the unaware public is always chagrined to acknowledge, as they always want to claim that my corsets will break my ribs, when ironically they've achieved close to the opposite). Even my hips, arguably my worst problem area—the only thing my ribs are second place to—stop sliding around in their joints. I sit taller with my corset, which places less stress on my respiratory system so I can breathe more easily. My fatigue is lessened (although I'm sure it's more psychological), and I feel more focused and less confused.

When your body fights you at every turn, it can be difficult to find the will and the energy to take care of yourself. Corsets, more than anything, seem to give me a sense of control over my body—something I've never had, due to my poor health and lifelong chronic illnesses. They gave me a sense of self that I otherwise would have lost. The minimal effort put into donning my corset in the morning makes me feel inspired, mentally preparing me for the day ahead—even if the day ahead is just writing. It takes my mind off the constant stabbing pain in my back and shoulders, and allows me to concentrate. My corsets are an investment in the maintenance of my physical constitution and an aspect of my independence.

An obsession that started when I was 14 has led to a world of freedom for me. Beyond the physical benefits, it's given me control over my body, the ability to manipulate it to be whatever I want it to be.

Disabled bodies are, invariably, seen as freakish, sexless, and tragic, and the media's message is that we are sad backstories, depressing side-characters with fates that bad characters "deserve." We are sad-eyed, staring out of windows, badly dressed, promoting pity to the people "forced" to "put up" with us. People are always going to stare at me, due to my wheelchair. With my corset, I might as well give them something to stare at.

CORSETS CORRECTED MY WALK

DEVON M.

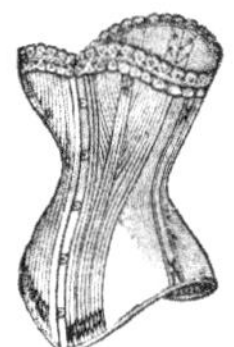

A few years back, I was preparing for my last set of midterms of freshman year. I had been sitting in a chair for hours earlier in the day, and I just had to move.

I had been bouldering the day before—low-to-the-ground climbing without the use of a rope. I had been working on a short but difficult route for a few days and it was one I knew well, but its final move kept stumping me. I was so tired from climbing the day before and from studying, I initially intended on just working out in the traditional gym room next door. I really should have stuck to that plan.

But I just couldn't help myself! I loved climbing, and after hours of boring studying, I needed something to make my heart soar. I decided to work on the familiar bouldering route I had been having trouble with. But my muscles were more tired than I had thought, and I fell twice in the first few moves of the route. That should have been my signal to get off the wall and do something else, but I didn't pay attention.

After a couple minutes of warm-up, I got to the last move of the route—the one that had been giving me so many problems. I reached for the final hold, but the tired grip of my right hand—which had been writing and typing all day—just couldn't get a grasp. My grip slipped and I fell. I remember being serene and calm: I had fallen from here a dozen or more times before and I didn't feel that this time would be any different. It was.

I broke both ankles and one of my elbows in that fall. One ankle took the brunt of it, and had to be fitted with plates and screws, which are still in place to this day. My recovery went faster than the doctors expected, and everything had healed, but one consequence was that my foot turned out. When walking further than just around my house, my out-turned foot caused knee and hip pain, but if I forced my foot to line up properly, the bones in my ankle began to hurt and the arthritis I had from the accident made walking impossible.

When I started to wear corsets, I wasn't expecting any tangible benefits—just a new hobby and another reason to keep my core muscles strong. Once I started to wear them out of the house, I noticed something wonderful. Somehow, the posture that corsets keep me in corrected the alignment of my leg, and I was able to walk properly again. Because of this I can now walk longer and more comfortably in a corset, which is really helpful since I do not own a car and I walk everywhere.

Corsets have been with me through the discovery of my scoliosis —my physical therapist encouraged me to keep wearing them to keep my back in alignment. My condition causes chronic pain, and lacing down relieves it. I am so glad that I discovered corsetry when I did.

CORSETS AND SENSORY PROCESSING DISORDER

MOLLY C.

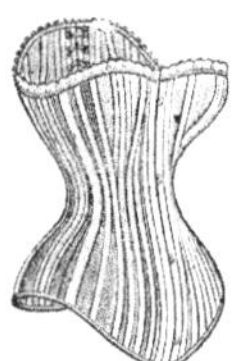

Corsets are a safe haven for me. They almost block out the noise and lights and sensations of the world, the stimulants have often overwhelmed me. Corsets help ground and stabilize me.

I have two disabilities: one is Apraxia, and the other is Sensory Processing Disorder (SPD)—previously known as Sensory Integration Dysfunction (SID).

Apraxia is a motor sequencing disorder, which essentially means that I have difficulty doing anything that requires more than one step. With Apraxia, my brain doesn't function as fluidly or efficiently as others', and has to work four times harder than everyone else's just to do basic things, such as eating, moving, talking, and thought processing.

This takes place on a neurological level. Messages going to different parts of my brain or my body get mixed up or not sent. This results in poor hand-eye coordination, poor math skills, and sometimes jumbled words when I speak. I have a tendency to trip over my feet or trip over my words because although I know what it is I need to say or how to move, my body and brain just don't work efficiently enough. It's almost as though my brain takes the scenic route whenever it's supposed to be doing things.

Sensory Processing Disorder (SPD) is a less tangible neurological disorder. In a nutshell it makes me highly attuned to any sort of external stimuli, e.g., lights, touch, smell, noise, taste, and even my sense of balance, or proprioception: where I am in relation to things. For example, I don't like light touches at all. I'd much rather have someone grip my wrist in an iron hold than very delicately.

I also have sensory episodes wherein I become unable to filter excessive or background stimuli, and everything becomes overwhelming. It's similar to a migraine in the aspect of being unable to handle noise or touch or light, but without the debilitating headache.

Over the past three years I've worn corsets more and more regularly, as I found that I have better days when I wear them. I originally bought my first corset because I wanted to see if it could help with my sensory issues (as weight and pressure on my body calms my nervous system). Even whilst breaking in the corset I felt extraordinarily happy. It gave a consistent pressure all around my torso without being constricting, and it provided a barrier against any light touch. Even though it was too long and didn't fit my body perfectly, I felt happier and more comfortable as a whole. Over time I bought a few more corsets of varying styles.

I feel more "normal" when I wear a corset. I've noticed they even help with my Apraxia: I can think more efficiently, I trip over my feet and my words less. I even experimented with how I do on school tests when I do or do not wear a corset; I do so much better with a corset. It keeps me grounded and makes it easier to focus.

I've also taken to wearing corsets every time I have a "sensory" day. (It's a day where I'm more hyper-aware of stimuli. It's a sort of prolonged sensory episode with varying degrees of intensity.) If I rate my sensory episodes on a scale of one to ten—one being I could go around the world in eighty days and ten being I'm practically comatose—I can knock down a number or two on the sensory scale just by wearing a corset. I usually don't like people touching me, but in a corset I'm more okay with it.

I still get excited when I think about how amazing it is to have something that helps with my sensory disorder. It's so hard to find sensory related information. I hope that perhaps other sensory inclined people will find this resource and learn that information and help is available.

This story is dedicated to Christina,
March 17, 1983 - February 7, 2016
She never stopped living.

PFFD AND CORSETRY

SIMON W.

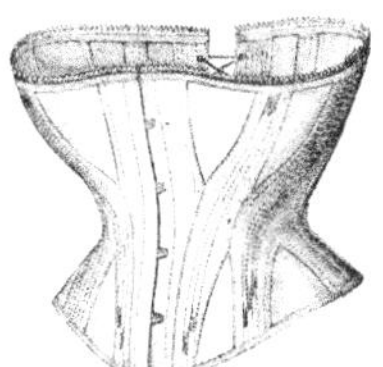

I am a young non-binary person with disabilities and a love of corsets. I was born with a rare birth defect called Proximal Femoral Focal Deficiency (PFFD). In my case, my hip joint and femur were underdeveloped. I've had several surgeries to modify my leg to be more functional, the main surgery being a Van Ness Rotationplasty. Since my right leg is so much shorter than my left, the Rotationplasty turned my leg around 180 degrees, so the foot on my shorter leg now points backwards. This allows my ankle to work as a knee joint inside of a prosthetic. It's very effective—and to be honest, it's very disfiguring.

I am very self-conscious about my body, so finding clothing that feels flattering is important, and sometimes difficult, for me. I've discovered that wearing a corset helps tremendously with my body dysphoria, and also that it helps support my achy back and counteract my bad posture, which is due to my asymmetry.

Another, much smaller, issue corsets help me with is mental illness and trauma from past abusive experiences. The pressure from corsets can sometimes offer relief from anxiety attacks, and provide a cocoon to tuck myself away into and feel safe.

While these are all lovely effects of corseting, my original interest in corsets was in their history and visual appeal. It was sparked as a young child by watching the 1999 *Sleepy Hollow* film by Tim Burton. I was so taken with the costumes and how detailed they were (in all of his films, really). But it was the incredible shaping undergarments of the women that really held my attention. It molded them so delicately, tapering their waists and pressing their busts flat.

Years later I spent much time researching to find as much information on corsets as I could. I would daydream about owning a corset, coordinating it with all of my clothes, imagining how elegant and dignified I would feel. Not knowing that there are still people who created authentic corsets, I eventually stopped looking around.

Luckily, after graduating high school, I stumbled across Lucy on YouTube, whose videos focused on my favorite subject: corsets! I binge-watched as many as I could, learning everything I wanted to know and more. I was elated to learn that functional corsets were still made, and in practically any shape, color, and design you could think of. Naturally, I got my hands on one as soon as I could.

I'll be honest, the first corset I picked was a terrible choice. My decision was based mainly on aesthetics: it was a longline overbust, perhaps a size or three too big (I am a short, tiny person)—and yet, I loved it. I could only comfortably wear the corset while standing, so naturally I bought five more corsets in different cuts and styles in order to find some I could wear and enjoy more often.

Most people ask why I spend so much time and resources on something so restrictive and (in their opinion) uncomfortable. Personally, I find being cinched up to be comforting and empowering. I feel protected and safe inside my corset, as well as fierce and beautiful. There's nothing like looking in the mirror to see deadly bombshell curves while still feeling safely wrapped inside clothes. Wearing a corset is a reminder that I am strong, powerful, and beautiful (and hey, feeling that I could stop a man in his tracks with a single side-eye glance is a fun bonus).

CORSETRY IN STROKE REHABILITATION

ALICIA M.

In June 2013, I suffered a severe brain stem stroke (although it wouldn't be until July 3rd that I knew that it was a stroke). All I knew was that suddenly I felt odd, my right limbs felt heavy and uncontrolled, and I could hear my speech slur but no one else could. These strange feelings came and went for a few days. I'd spend 2–3 hours feeling "off," then another 2–3 hours feeling completely normal. I thought I'd pinched a nerve in my neck. After three days it disappeared. I was relieved to say the least!

After two normal days, I woke the third morning having a slur and feeling off yet again. But I was headed several hours out of town to see my son pitch in a championship baseball game during a tournament. Throughout the day I felt worse and worse. By the time I got home, my husband was worried, and when he checked my symptoms on WebMD, the site told him to call 911. We drove to the ER as a compromise, as I was convinced I was fine.

I spent a total of one hour at the hospital before they released me, telling me to call my family doctor in the morning (it was a Sunday) because, "You've not had a stroke. It's quite likely you have Multiple Sclerosis." I left feeling like I wasn't sure if I was relieved at 37 years of age to not have had a stroke, or scared to possibly have an awful disease. I just knew my life was going to drastically change and I didn't want it to.

I fell asleep on the couch around 11 P.M., and when I woke at 4:15 A.M. I was completely paralyzed on my right side. The right side of my face had fallen, I couldn't speak, I couldn't swallow, and I could barely breathe. I lay there terrified and crying until my husband found me 15 minutes later. I had no way of telling him what was wrong.

At 8 A.M., we called the doctor and told him that I was to be seen immediately. My doctor also felt that with my age, and with how things had come and gone for the first week, that it wasn't a stroke. He also explained that there were so many parts of my body affected that had it been a stroke it would have had to be so large that there's no possible way I could have survived it. That was July 1st. He started testing that day. Everything pointed to MS, although he wasn't ruling stroke out completely.

I remember the feeling I got when the phone rang late in the evening of July 3rd, a day I knew my doctor was not working due to the holiday, yet it was his number showing on my call display. Turns out I had had a stroke. But no one, not even the doctor, had come close to preparing for this: I'd had a very rare stroke, a type that less than 5% of stroke sufferers have. A stroke across my brain stem, called a Pons Infarction. And out of those unlucky 5%, an even lower percentage survives. I had a long road ahead.

Over the next 2–3 weeks I recovered so fast that the medical team was baffled. My body seemed to have returned to normal, with only a slight limp when tired. My husband then worriedly returned to work, as I was on bedrest until they could find the cause of the stroke. The doctors said I wouldn't survive another, but due to insurance concerns, testing approval was slow. I was happy I'd recovered, but knew that any minute another stroke could take my life.

The first day my husband returned to work, I was in the office lying on the couch, and my son was behind the couch talking to me, when all of a sudden I felt odd. I didn't want to panic my son, but when I spoke (or tried to speak), it was obvious that it sounded and looked as if I was having another stroke. I thought I was going to die while my son called his father and begged him to drive home faster as my body shut down again, bit by bit.

Three days into a hospital stay, I had had every vein scanned, had an ultrasound on my heart (as well as my legs to search for vein narrowing), and my entire body scanned through MRI and MRA from top to bottom. They took 37 vials of my blood for various testing, as the staff was still worried that I might be having an onslaught of MS in addition to having suffered the stroke.

I asked them if I'd had another stroke. Their answer was no; it was just that because the stroke was in my stem, my brain spent a few weeks "shorting in and out" in layman terms, and this is what landed me back at struggled speech and a mostly paralyzed right side. The reason for my stroke, after countless tests, scans, vials of blood, and torture, was a complete medical mystery. They had no clue why it happened. How could I avoid another episode when I'm not sure what caused the first?

I have recovered a lot thanks in part to more than a year of therapy, although I have my share of issues. I use a walker as my right leg drags, and my arm isn't 100%. I have some dexterity and cognitive issues, amongst other things. Because the infarction ran the total width of my stem, it affected everything internally as well as my limbs. Six months after my stroke, the core muscles on my right side weren't responding to treatment very well—my abdominal, back, and side muscles didn't engage—so my doctor had me fitted for a garment originally designed for post-liposuction patients. It was like an extremely tight, uncomfortable girdle.

After too long wearing that awful piece, I asked my doctor if I could switch to corsets. I knew that if I used the correct corset, with proper steel boning, it could keep me upright and better balanced than a spandex garment could. My first corset was a Black Iris beige longline underbust with hip ties. It's so much more comfortable than the spandex garment.

My corset gives me the ability to stand properly and not lean so drastically, which in turn helps my balance enough that I don't need my walker when I'm around the house on good days. My ability to breathe is drastically improved as well compared to being in the post-lipo garment. And if feeling fun, I can use my corset as outerwear, and others think it's simply an accent piece to my outfit, and it helps draw attention AWAY from the awful walker!

I had always been fascinated by corsets and stays—I just never had the time for corset or waist training. But now, not only can I wear corsets because I love them and the history behind them, but it physically helps me have a better day in a lot of ways. I love my corset; as simple as it is, it's beautiful.

My corset has changed my life and I just hope anyone who loses the ability to have working torso muscles can recognize that a corset can help change their life too in many positive ways! And the silver lining is that it gives great curves to my now expanded figure, and makes me feel a bit sexy. It's very hard to feel attractive when suddenly you're using a walker and your limbs only work partially. Feeling unsexy and self-conscious became a big part of my life, but my corset helps bring back that sexy feeling within myself. I just can't say enough for what it's done for me.

A CORSETIÈRE'S CALLING

MELANIE TALKINGTON, CORSETIÈRE ~ LACE EMBRACE ATELIER

Thinking back over the last 20 years of my corsetry career, I have fond memories of all of the people whom I've helped with their medical needs. It brings me great joy to be able to assist them to live more comfortably. I'm very honored when they come to me via doctor's referrals or because they're desperate and unhappy with the orthopedic supports they've received in the medical system.

While I was in business school, one of my instructors asked me if I would visit her brother and see if I could create a brace for him. **Ross** was quadriplegic and needed a brace to hold him upright so that it was easier to breathe. He was quite slim; the brace he had been fitted with was too big and did not offer enough support. We discussed his needs and created a properly fitted brace based on the principles of his original support. He would call once or twice a year for adjustments or repairs to his brace. The last time I visited him, I brought his brace back to my atelier to make some routine repairs. Shortly there after his caregiver called to say he had passed peacefully in his sleep. It was very sad to hear but I was grateful that I was able to see him one last time. I asked what I should do with his brace and they told me to keep it. I held onto Ross' brace for a number of years, not sure what to do with it until this past year.

Our 92-year-old client **Patricia**, who is on a fixed income, visits our shop to have her braces repaired. She has polio and needs corsetry for abdominal support. I remembered Ross' brace and knew it would be helpful to her. I was grateful to pass it along, and she was happy to have it.

I received a call from **Dr. Gomez**, a plastic surgeon, who wanted to see our corsets to prescribe for his patients after liposuction surgery. After we discussed the compression needs, I sent him a sample of our Edwardian corset. He reviewed the corset and requested I make a few changes. He then began to place orders for our design and prescribed clients to wear them 24 hours a day for three weeks after surgery, and then 12 hours a day for an additional three weeks.

A **lovely young lady** in a wheelchair came into our store dressed very fashionably with high heels. She has spina bifida and had been wearing thick and heavy plastic medical braces since she was five. She begged her mom for a corset, but her mother was concerned about wearing a corset while her body was still developing. Finally, on her 16th birthday her mother conceded, and we were able to create a lovely corset that combined the medical support she required and the fashionable beauty she desired. I admired that even though she was unable to walk, she chose to wear the most amazing shoes.

Linda first came to visit me after being in a serious car accident. She was in a great deal of pain and had difficulty walking. I was quite nervous fitting her because I didn't want to cause her any more pain. I carefully laced her into the corset we had been making for Dr. Gomez. After gently lacing her in, she screamed, and I braced myself for fear that I had caused her more pain. Her scream was not one of pain, but of joy, as she raised her arms above her head. She exclaimed, "I haven't been able to move my arms in months! I can walk without pain!" She's been wearing our corsets 24 hours a day for the last 14 years.

Dr. Jantzen made an appointment for a custom fitting. She wanted me to make her a back brace to support her lumbar spine at L2 and L3. I fitted her with the corset style we make for Dr. Gomez and made slight modifications per her recommendations. She now writes prescriptions and sends her patients to us for medical braces. I was very honored when the first client came in and gave me a doctor's prescription for one of our braces!

I had **a gentleman** come to see me with a hereditary, neurological movement disorder called dystonia. This disease caused his back to bend backwards at extreme angles, making it difficult for him to walk. He had a custom, heavy, plastic, medical brace made, but it did not support him well enough to walk and it was hot and bulky. He wanted me to build a brace that would allow him to walk. It was quite a challenge to understand his condition and work with him to create a brace that did the opposite of what they are normally meant to do. He wanted something that would try to force him to slouch forward because his body was constantly arching backwards. We worked on a few prototypes and were able to create a brace with dual lacing, wide, rigid back steels, and leg straps to force his body into the proper position.

It's been memorable thinking about all of the medical braces I've made over the years and all of the lovely people I've met along the way. These stories are just some of the many people who have added to my career. There have been countless others who have come in wheelchairs, or with scoliosis, or work-related injuries, or general back pain. I enjoy taking the time to understand each of my client's needs and building something that is lightweight, comfortable, and functional. It gives me great pleasure seeing their smiles and helping them to live a more comfortable life. I am touched by each of them.

CORSETS FOR ORTHOSTATIC HYPOTENSION

H. ASPINALL

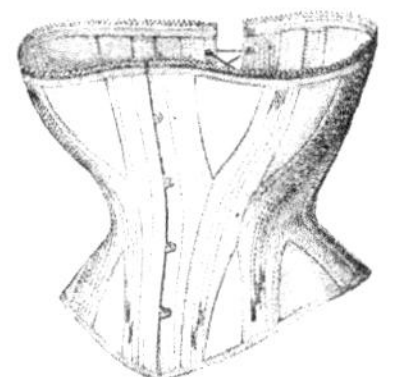

"Optimistic" was always a description attributed to me. Although I would have to agree, it often perplexed me as to how that could be. Aged 27, I'd been chronically ill for 20 years with a mystery illness that left me incapacitated. I was healthy-looking, but had a laundry list of horrendous symptoms. The doctors couldn't help, many often believing that I was simply making it all up.

I lost opportunities to enjoy my young life or succeed in a career, so I turned to private study. I had all the time in the world to figure out what was wrong with me and how to better myself, yet with every day that passed I felt my youth slipping away. Though I was motivated to heal myself and others of this terrible "invisible disease," I still faced bouts of hopelessness and suicidal thoughts brought on by relentless physical and mental suffering.

One symptom, long-enduring back pain that was worsened by three car crashes, eventually reached such heights that I knew I couldn't continue living without doing something to ease it. I was skin and bone, but too sick to gain the supportive muscle required to help my situation. Upon seeing the spinal specialist I was pushed to tears by his angry dismissal of my request to fix the root cause; he offered me only drugs as treatment.

Physical therapies failed, and medical back supports provided no relief. Filled with desperation, I took to Google, which finally revealed corsetry. From there, many dozens of hours of research lead me to Fran at Contour Corsets. She was a kind and helpful lady. After discussing my situation, we decided upon a front-lacing corset that offered no reduction to my natural waist of 24 inches (61 cm). The corset was finished in pink cotton with blue grosgrain ribbon binding. When I pulled it from the battered courier box several weeks later, I marveled at its beauty and exquisite construction.

Putting it on, staring at my reflection with wonderment, I witnessed a transformation from sickly mess to refined beauty. It was a magical experience. From then on, I wore it most of every day, even for many a night, finding reprieve from the pains of my condition.

After a couple of months of moderate relief and surprising comfort, I realized that a new corset was in order. I needed a back-lacing corset, with a more pinched-in waist to hold my rib cage up. I ordered a new one from Fran, this time a 20-inch (51 cm) black mesh corset with purple grosgrain ribbon binding. It fit like a glove. From the outside, my new 22-inch (56 cm) waist was quite shocking to those who saw it, some remarking that I must be causing more harm than good. I didn't feel that way at all. In fact, I felt more comfortable and energized than ever before.

Many months passed, and the new corset became staple of my daily life. I couldn't imagine living without its snug hold around my body, supporting and invigorating me. I began to wonder why I felt more energized by the compression, so once again I turned to the internet for answers.

I discovered "orthostatic hypotension," a form of low blood pressure in which a person's blood pressure falls when standing up. I bought a home blood pressure monitor to perform some basic tests. I discovered not only that my blood pressure was dropping, but also that there was a massive increase in heart rate upon standing when uncorseted. Yet, this effect was not as dramatic when corseted. It seemed that the corset was compressing my body, increasing and stabilizing my blood pressure just enough to account for the change in orientation. This simple, timeless garment was allowing me to live a more normal life.

I couldn't leave my research there, so I kept digging deeper and deeper until I discovered something quite unexpected. My healthy vegan diet of grains, legumes, and nightshades all contained proteins called lectins. Lectins are a form of agglutinins that can thicken the blood, causing the heart to work harder to maintain circulation. After a life as a moral vegan, I decided try a new diet in order to save my life. I changed to a paleo-style diet, and within weeks I miraculously felt like a normal human being!

My new-found lease on life allowed me to leave the safety of my home to explore the world. At first, this was quite exciting. I had finally achieved my goal, although it seemed that my discovery would not be of much use to others, as it is quite unbelievable to most that veganism could cause such health problems. I remember staring out of my kitchen window and suddenly realizing that I couldn't face the outside world. My identity as a sick person was gone, and now I had to step into truly being. I felt my inner child calling out, and with contemplation my true inner self was revealed to me. I was a male-identified person who had been trapped in a sick girl's body. I'd been unable to explore this reality with the more important task of healing at hand, but now that I had finally healed my body, it was time to heal my mind and soul.

I chose to follow my heart and transition to living as a man. I chose to put away my corset, my trusted friend and armor, which I no longer needed, and pursue a new and empowered life. I have gained muscles to run and lift, dance and play, but I will never forget the time in my life when I was supported by threads, metal, and determination.

MOBILITY AND MORALE

GINNINA S.

I was born with cerebral palsy and scoliosis. When I was young child I had to wear braces on my legs to stabilize them. As I grew older, my conditions worsened to the point where I was unable to walk without falling down, and I required surgery on my hips, legs, feet, and in the near future my spine, so I could walk for a longer period of time without needing an aid or wheelchair. I was 11 years old when I received the first of five surgeries on my feet and legs.

As the years progressed, my spine began to shift to the left, causing compression on my lumbar area and making it hard to walk or stand; in some cases even sitting was unbearable as well. When I turned 15 I had to wear a back brace to manage the pain and keep my spine from shifting further. The back brace that was issued to me was horrible and very uncomfortable. I remember trying to hide the brace by wearing four or five shirts over it, as well as wearing shirts underneath the brace to make it more comfortable. Imagine going to public high school with a back brace that made you look like the Hunchback of Notre Dame—it was a nightmare.

When my cousin turned 16 years old, I was invited to her Sweet Sixteen birthday party. I remember going to the mall with my grandmother to find a dress that would fit over my brace. We went into many stores and finally my grandmother said that I would have to wear an adult's dress. I was so upset that I couldn't wear a dress that was made for a young girl my age, but I started trying dresses in the junior's department hoping to find a decent dress that would fit me. I had to step outside of the dressing room to look at myself in the mirror, and as I stepped out, I saw all the other young girls trying on dresses as well. Their dresses fit them so nicely, meanwhile the dresses I tried on were all three sizes too big to accommodate the brace. I thought about not wearing my brace—but without it, my spine would shift, the pressure would cause my legs to go numb, I wouldn't be able to walk, and the pain would be unthinkable. I finally decided that I wouldn't go to my cousin's party because I feared that I would be the center of the jokes that evening.

My grandmother (a seamstress) and my grandfather (a coat maker and carpenter) decided to take matters into their own hands and make me a corset. That night, they took pictures, measurements, and they even wrapped me in plastic wrap and tape to create a model of my torso. My doctors were astonished by the construction of the corset; they couldn't believe that my grandparents had made it themselves. One of the doctors gave my grandparents a hard time about the idea.

That was my first introduction to corsetry—in the mid 90s. The first time I wore the corset, my grandma said I had to break it in so that it would fit my body perfectly. That was time consuming; my grandfather put so many steel bones in the corset that I thought maybe this was a bad idea—but as the time went by, I was able to wear it without any problems. All I can say is that the corset they made for me changed my whole life. I was able to move around more in my corset than when I was wearing the plastic back brace, and the constant pain started to decrease as well. I was also able to wear many more outfits, my self-esteem was boosted, and people didn't make fun of me as much.

It's funny to think that I've been wearing corsets for close to 20 years, and all this time nobody has walked up to me and asked if I was waist training until now. People are very misinformed and uneducated about the different uses of corsets and what they can do, especially for someone like me. I've only recently started hearing about negative myths and urban legends concerning corsets—if they were true, my doctors would have put a stop to me wearing a corset as a back brace a very long time ago. My corset helps me to be much more mobile. I wear my corset 23 hours a day and sleep in it every night, because without it, I would not be able to walk the next day and I would have to use my wheelchair. There are some nights where I do get lazy and don't feel like sleeping in my corset, and I pay for it the next day.

My corset changed my life for the better. Without it, I would still be wearing that old ugly brace and I would be miserable. Most of all, I wouldn't be able to explore and enjoy life as the happy and blessed person that I am.

I'm very honored to be a part of this book and to help people understand that corsets are not just for fashion—they can also save and improve lives.

PART VII

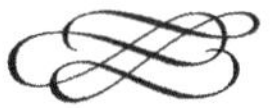

FIBROMYALGIA

A BRIDE'S TIPS ON PACING

ADELINA F.

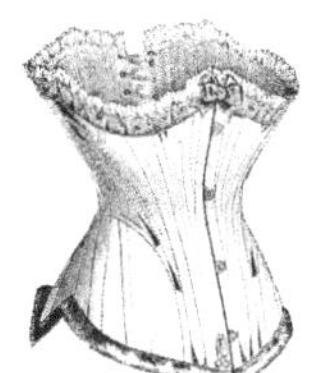

I fell in love with corsets just four months before my wedding. I was desperate to find a comfortable alternative to the standard white wedding dress, and I preferred a smaller, fun wedding as well. When you suffer from intense, all-over chronic pain, every clothing-related decision must consider comfort, with risks of being in agony for weeks afterwards if you make a bad choice.

I decided to try corsets partly because I'd tried all other dress options (to no avail), and also because I dreamed of a Steampunk-themed wedding.

Having tracked down a corset shop in London, I was blown away by how comfortable a corset can be and how good I felt about myself when I was wearing it. It turns out that wearing a corset helps me manage my chronic pain, which helps me do more of the things I love.

I'm still astonished by how quickly I can turn down the volume of the pain just by putting my corset on. I feel as though the pain in my back, ribs, shoulders, neck, and head become light enough to be put in a backpack I can carry with me, rather than in a heavy suitcase with broken wheels. For a few hours I feel relieved and energized, as though my body is working with me. There are so many more things I can do when I'm wearing a corset than without! I love that even once I take it off and the pain returns, it remains weaker than before I put on the corset.

After the first week of wearing my corset, I started to notice that it made me feel safer and less anxious. It only works if I'm relaxing and nothing too scary is happening, though. (For instance, having 50 people stare at you standing at the altar, hoping you're not going to get your new husband's name wrong!)

As my husband slowly tightens the corset, I can feel my back muscles relaxing and gently stretching. Because of the extra support, my posture improves and my shoulder and neck muscles don't need to work so hard, so slowly my headache gets better, too. It also keeps me nice and warm, which relaxes my muscles, and means I don't have to wear as many layers to stay warm. I love that I don't need a bra as I find them too painful to wear regularly.

I have trigger points, which are hyper-irritable spots of taut muscle that are tender and sensitive to slight pressure. These trigger points cause specific referred pain to other areas of my body when stimulated. I find that acupuncture and acupressure into my trigger points work well for relaxing my cramped or tight muscles, which means less pain and greater mobility. I normally go to a physiotherapist for this, as I can't do it on myself.

Because of the way the corset is built, it applies an even pressure similar to acupressure. The trigger points near the steel bones are the first to loosen and I feel less pain. Also, supporting my breasts in an overbust means the weight of my chest isn't pulling on my shoulders and neck. The rest of the muscles in my torso are also supported, so after some time they relax because they no longer have to compensate for the cramped muscles.

Being in a lot of pain all the time turned my life upside-down. The pain started after a major car accident; then improved for a bit, then got worse again. As the pain got worse, my life became more and more restricted: I couldn't cook, or sit at a computer for more than 15 minutes a day, or walk my dog. After two years of desperately trying to find the reason for my pain, I was happy to finally be diagnosed with fibromyalgia syndrome. Officially it's known as an autoimmune syndrome mainly characterized by widespread chronic pain and fatigue.

It sounds like quite a descriptive diagnosis, doesn't it? It describes the two worst symptoms, not the cause, or the many more fussy symptoms thrown in for variety (seriously, even bladder infections and ADHD are on the list).

Considering that chronic pain can lead to insomnia, depression, and Irritable Bowel Syndrome, the list of possible symptoms seems infinite. The cause of the syndrome itself isn't well understood, and there is no cure. The recovery goals are to reduce symptoms and improve your quality of life.

My current treatment is a mixed bag of painkillers, prescription medication, improving sleep, light exercise, healthy diet, learning to relax and—most importantly—pacing myself. The painkillers help reduce the pain, as long as I don't do things that will aggravate it. Unfortunately almost everything can aggravate it. Learning to pace myself is the most difficult thing I've ever had to do, but it's worth it because it means I can take care of myself most of the time. I will probably continue to learn how to manage it for the rest of my life.

I asked my doctor and physiotherapist if wearing a corset regularly would be bad for me. They were very open-minded and supportive, and said as long as I didn't wear it all day and I continued with some exercise, it was perfectly safe. After a few weeks, my doctor and physiotherapist both noticed my back muscles were more relaxed and not as sensitive to pressure.

When I wear the corset regularly, my posture improves; even after I take it off, it's a bit easier to sit up straighter. It all happens in very small increments that don't last more than an hour, but over months and months it all adds up to a big difference. In combination with all my other tools for pain management, my corset can reduce the amount of painkillers I take, avoid a flare-up, improve my progress with exercise, maintain my posture when I'm too tired, make it easier to eat healthily, and increase the length of time I can sit or stand.

None of these things happened the first time I wore it. There was a lot of trial and error. Some evenings, when the pain killers have worn off but bedtime is only a few hours away, I wear the corset for a bit instead of taking more painkillers. When I have a bad headache and I'm dizzy, but I still want to walk my dog, wearing the corset reduces the headache for a bit and I can cope.

Pacing is similar to gradually seasoning a corset, just slower and with much smaller goals. The goals are what I struggled with the most, since (in another life) I used to aim high and not make any changes when it got too difficult. I just put more effort into it when I should have slowed down and readjusted my goals. I really wanted to get a 4-inch (10 cm) waist reduction with my first corset, just because I know I'm very squishy and I had read that 3–4 inches is the average reduction. Fortunately I resisted and applied some pacing techniques.

The starting point has to be what I can do on a bad day pain-wise (but not if I'm having a flare-up). At the time I was able to wear a special made-to-measure bra for six hours a day but only for three days a week. When I started wearing this bra, I wore it for 30 minutes at its loosest, every other day and built up my duration of wear from there—so I figured that was a good schedule to start with the corset as well.

When pacing, one's goal has to be realistic, and it's also wise to set a mini-goal one can reach halfway through. The mini goal is a backup in case the original goal is unrealistic or will take much longer than expected to achieve. My big goal was to wear my corset on my wedding day for 8 hours at a 2-inch (5 cm) reduction. My mini-goal was to wear it for 4 hours without any reduction.

I kept a written record of every time I wore the corset, with detailed notes about things like: how long I wore it, what my corseted waist measured, and whether the pain had increased at any point. If the pain increased at any time, I loosened the corset, or took it off. I also wrote down if my ribs or waist were sore the next day, and if they were, I then wore my corset looser the next day.

I have found that a change of 10% (in either waist size or time) works a lot better for me compared to the 50% change I initially attempted. Only increasing one thing at a time, either the duration or the waist reduction, in very small increments, makes the corset more comfortable when I wear it for more than two hours, and I feel like I'm making progress.

On my wedding day I managed to wear it for five hours at a 1.5-inch (4 cm) reduction. I did loosen it a bit before eating, and it remained comfortable. The best thing was taking the corset off after five hours and feeling tired but not that sore. And I didn't even take more painkillers than usual, which surprised me. Afterwards I had a lie down and got changed into my favorite comfy dancing outfit, and was up dancing and mingling for the next few hours.

My grandmother complimented me on my wedding day; she loved the corset. The compliment came completely out of the blue, as she had always told me I'm fat and didn't give me any kind of praise as I was growing up. She also told me she used to wear a corset made by her mum (my great-grandmother), on special occasions—which explains the family story of her having such a small waist that my granddad could encircle it with both hands. I always assumed it was make-believe, but maybe it did have a little grain of truth in it.

These days, as I learn to manage the pain and slowly increase my activities, I can even resume some of my old hobbies, like playing the piano, writing (for more than 15 minutes), or being able to sit and play video games. Who would've thought that wearing a corset would allow me to be more active, manage the pain from my chronic illness, and help feel more in charge of my body? Having the choice to do something I love (without having to "pay" for it for the weeks to follow) is such a relief.

MY JOURNEY BACK TO HEALTH

LEIA T.

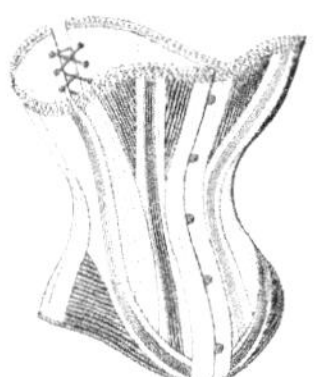

Several years ago my body decided, for various reasons, to start falling apart. I had dislocated ribs on both sides of my rib cage (those ribs acted and still act like floating ribs and have needed special attention for years to keep them in place), a very painful herniated disc in my thoracic spine, a less painful but still quite uncomfortable bulging disc in my lumbar spine, and, eventually, one of the worst cases of fibromyalgia my doctors had yet seen.

In 2011 alone I went through several treatments, including four different spinal injections, and a Radio Frequency (RF) burn—in which a hollow needle with a heated wire inside is injected into the body to burn out and deaden the nerve that is pinched between the spinal discs. That was the most painful thing to wake up from; it took weeks to recover! In the end, all the procedures did was over-stress my body until I developed fibromyalgia.

My narcotic doses and other "helpful" medication and treatments were at a rather high level, but my torso was still so weak from the damage that I could not hold myself up for more than 20 minutes (on the bad days, more than 3 minutes). It didn't matter if I was sitting, standing, or walking—supporting my upper body was excruciating! In the fall of 2011 I had to quit working, and in the fall of 2012 I was awarded Social Security Disability benefits.

Several years before this, my chiropractor gave me one of those elastic back supports with Velcro closures. I decided to give this a try since I could tell that I needed something around me to take the stress off my torso. The little elastic support was heading me in the right direction, but it was unable to perform the task it was given. Luckily, I remembered I'd had a corset made for me 10 years before, and since I happen to be a bit of a packrat, I still had it and knew exactly where it was.

My family was skeptical about my theory of the corset helping vs. hindering, but I had a feeling it would work. So, with much awkward fuss and disbelieving helpers, I was laced into my old corset.

The results were apparent to me within moments!!! For the first time in almost a year, I was able to sit in a chair as opposed to sitting on the couch with a mountain of pillows strategically placed around me! I was able to walk around the house without practically melting into a puddle of pain after being up for mere minutes! I could ride in the car again, and hold and lift a water bottle to my lips to drink! My little old corset opened the world to me again!!

The first year of wearing my corset, I wore it almost 24/7. My body was so damaged and weakened that I truly could not hold myself upright. I acquired more corsets and wore them as tight as I could; the tighter the corset, the more support it gave, and the better I felt.

My chiropractor and Chinese medicine practitioner were not that pleased about me wearing corsets, especially as much and tightly as I did. Oddly, most of my Western medicinal practitioners didn't mind my corseting; they actually thought it was an interesting idea. They cautioned me not wear it all the time and told me that I needed to do exercises to not lose the muscles in my core—but there was no way I could do that if I couldn't even hold my phone up. So, the corset it was, and it worked better than I could ever have hoped.

Fast-forward three years of nearly daily corseting: my core began to strengthen and my pain finally became manageable. I have been able to cut back on some meds, which has been very helpful in increasing my activity. Oxycodone, Exalgo, and Lyrica are the meds I was able to decrease. Not only does that help keep my bills down, but it is also better for my overtaxed body.

As my meds decreased and my activity increased, I finally felt strong enough that I decided to try horseback riding again, as I had been an avid equestrian for over half my life, but had given up my horse because of my health. For almost a year of riding I wore corsets, until eventually I had gotten strong enough that I no longer depended on them every day for every activity. Now, my corsets are for my own personal enjoyment instead of being a necessary medical apparatus.

There are still days that I have to spend on the couch, heavily medicated because of pain; days when I still need my corsets to help support me. I still work with my set of Eastern and Western medicinal practitioners on a regular basis, but we have all been blown away by the proof right before our eyes ... corsets have been an integral part of my journey back to health. It frightens me to consider where I would be today if I hadn't turned to corsets back then. Today, I'm still on disability due to pain and cognitive issues, but my quality of life has increased tenfold and I am finally, truly happy again.

FROM SUFFERER TO STEAMPUNKER

ABIGAIL B.

My name is Abigail and I live in the Netherlands. I am 27 years old; however my story begins when I was an energetic, 15-year-old soccer fanatic.

I have always been small, but I was an excellent goalkeeper; the only problem was that while I kept my mind on the ball, I wasn't looking out for myself. I jumped on the ball wherever I could in order to "save the goal," even if it frequently resulted in injuries. Concussion after concussion, I still didn't listen to my body … until I got a rather silly kick to my knee, after which I was unable to walk properly for the next couple of years.

My body told me, in its own way, to knock it off and rest: I developed post-traumatic dystrophy. A year after my knee injury, the doctors said my leg had healed, but I disagreed. To this very day I experience pains in that particular leg; it feels like it's burning on the inside, while the skin on the outside is freezing cold to the touch.

Since then, my body has been slowly forgetting how to work properly. Everything below my lumbar back became more sensitive to pain: if something fell on my foot, the pain was disproportionately stronger and lasted longer than before. Then, five years ago, the one thing I dreaded came true: the dystrophy had spread through my body. Not only did my lower body hurt, but I also started to feel pain on the insides of my elbows, wrist, and fingers. My arms became so sensitive that if I leaned against a doorpost, it felt like I had rammed against it. My entire body became tired. As it turns out, I had developed fibromyalgia too. Since I know there is no cure for fibromyalgia, I have to learn how to adjust my life and find a new normal.

But back to corsets: I learned about them in primary school. I remember how horrified everyone else was by the pictures of deformed bodies, but I could only stare at the garment. It was a thing of beauty. Although I felt sorry for the tragic fate of the whale that was killed for its baleen (and other parts), there was something magical about the idea that part of the corset came from the mysterious depths of the sea. I loved to look at old drawings of corsets; they made me wish I could just peel the corsets away from the paper and try them on.

In my mid-teens, I started going to fantasy conventions and I was surprised to learn that corsets were still made and that people wore them to these conventions. I eventually bought a standard-sized, purple velvet underbust from an off-the-rack company. When I wore it, it caused an additional weird pain in my leg, but since I loved corsets, I stubbornly wore it anyway.

I am a Steampunker now, and I have a couple of friends who are just as mad about corsets as I am. Last August, my friend and I were dressing to go to the fair for the day and I put my beautiful purple velvet corset on. After 15 minutes I complained about my leg, but I thought I simply had not laced my corset properly. My friend peered at me and said, "Your corset is too tall for you. Take it off; I will let you try my corset." This friend has the same build as me (only thinner), but she had broken her rib prior to the fair so she didn't plan on wearing her corset that day.

She laced her custom-made corset on me and my mind was blown. It fit like a glove. The chronic pain in my back that I was so accustomed to had diminished. I felt supported. She herself has the same history as I have (post-traumatic dystrophy and fibromyalgia) and she knew from the expression on my face that her corset did me good. "Wonderful feeling, is it not?" she said.

She told me to look in the mirror and I was speechless. I had an hourglass figure! For once, I felt sexy and strong.

The dress I was wearing that weekend was one I had made myself and it was too big in the waist, but with my friend's custom corset, the dress suddenly looked far more elegant than before. The one side effect was that I giggled when I had to sneeze, due to the strong hold of the corset!

I learned the difference between a standard-sized OTR corset and a well-fitted custom corset: I feel supported by wearing one, and it makes my days easier and less painful.

I am currently saving my funds to purchase my own custom corset instead of borrowing my friend's, but I hope that day will arrive soon. I find it a shame that so few people understand what a corset can really do to help alleviate pain.

THE TOOL BECOMES A TRADEMARK

ROSALIND GUDER ~ ROSALIND GUDER PHOTOGRAPHY

All my life, I have suffered from fibromyalgia. At different times, it was diagnosed under different names, from Attention Deficit Disorder to Chronic Fatigue Syndrome to Epstein-Barr Disease, but now, in hindsight, I know it was fibro all along!

One of my main symptoms of fibromyalgia is muscle and tendon pain with painful, hard lumps distributed primarily in my back, but occurring elsewhere in my body as well. I remember having these when I was a child and practicing piano for hours each day. I had thought that the terrible "knots" in my back were due to my posture at the piano.

In addition to the fibromyalgia pain, my spine went out of alignment. It's not quite severe enough for the doctor to call it a slipped disc; however, my doctor said there's nothing short of surgery that can be done for it. What this means for me is that any time I walk more than a few steps, I get numbness in my legs and feet, and pain in my lower back. There was one particular incident during a family trip to China where I was suffering so much pain that I was unable to move—an emergency acupuncturist had to be summoned!

To add to my litany of physical ailments, I have terrible anxiety, which might also be a symptom of fibromyalgia. It's another condition that I've suffered since childhood. It too has reached crippling levels at various times in my life.

During my teen years, I always wanted to wear a tight belt around my waist. I would buy fashion belts, which weren't meant to be worn tightly, and I would tighten them to the point where the belt holes were stretched and torn. I felt a little less anxious when I wore those tight belts, but I didn't make the therapeutic connection until very recently.

My second child inherited his anxiety from me. He was also diagnosed as having Sensory Processing Disorder (SPD), and often feels the need to wear his shoes and belts tightly, even to the point of cutting off circulation. According to his occupational therapist, this proprioceptive stimulus of the tightness helps a sufferer to self-regulate.

All of this came together in my head when I saw a documentary about Temple Grandin, the autistic genius who revolutionized animal care. She was the inventor of the "hug box," a device that calms those on the autism spectrum. Seeing my son's anxiety decrease with proprioceptive input got me thinking about trying something similar with my own anxiety.

I set about researching everything there is to know about corsets online. I was lucky to come across Lucy's website right away. During those first few days of research, I spent upwards of 10 hours per day watching videos and reading up on every aspect of corsetry. I bought books, Sarah Chrisman's *Victorian Secrets: What a Corset Taught Me about the Past, the Present, and Myself*, and Ann Grogan's *Corset Magic*. After digesting this wealth of knowledge, I ordered myself two Josephine corsets from Isabella Corsetry, and one Vamp corset from What Katie Did. I was hooked!

From the first wearing, I felt my anxiety dissipate. And on the days when I forgot to put the corset on in the morning, I would certainly notice my mistake by noon. With corsets, my condition has improved to the point that anxiety is no longer a factor in my life!

The other major benefit to me is spinal/postural. I had been resigned to the numbness, tingling, and pain that accompanied a walk of any length. With the corset, that is gone, too—I can walk pain-free! I can only assume that wearing a corset realigns the slip in my spine.

I cannot wax lyrical enough on how corsetry has positively changed the quality of my life. It has also given me a trademark look that attracts attention everywhere I go!

OF 'CORSET' MAKES ME FEEL BETTER

JENI C.

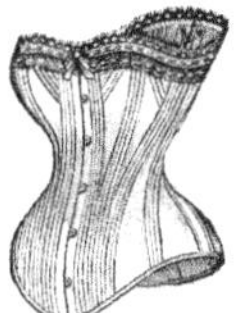

Here is a little write-up about how, in the twenty-first century, I came to wear corsets on a daily basis, and how they helped me regain my health.

I am in my mid-30s, and of average height and build. I have three children and two of them are very close in age (a little over 16 months apart). I had to have physical therapy when the littlest one was about a year old; my muscles had not contracted properly after the last baby and I had extreme flexibility in my core because I didn't have the muscle tone necessary to function properly.

To make matters worse, my tailbone was actually slipping downward and making it painful even to sit. My posture was horrible from spending nearly two years pregnant. (Pregnant women know how we hunch to accommodate the weight, walk duck legged, or—well, let's face it—have less lady-like movements due to the additional person we are carrying.)

It took 18 months of physical therapy to learn how to balance and sit again without crying in pain. During this time I wore a medical brace/support to keep my body in the proper position. It was scratchy, synthetic, elastic, very uncomfortable, and difficult to wear under my clothes. I hated wearing it. I stood a lot instead of sitting, as it was easier than explaining why I was in pain.

My grandmother told me about her own mother who wore a corset until her dying day; how much my great-grandmother had loved them, and how much they helped and were a part of her daily life. Many women threw off the corset for less restrictive garments, but not she. She still felt as though a proper lady should always wear the appropriate undergarments (and they helped with that extra pound or two and kept her clothes fitting nicer).

Okay, enough with the nostalgia—how did I come to find (much less wear) a corset? All I can remember was when the stomach pain started: crying at bedtime, not knowing what was wrong; doctors not knowing what was wrong either. Joint pain, stomach pain, headaches, anxiety, muscles giving out ... I felt like I was unraveling.

The stomach pain started while on a trip involving lots of hiking (and other outdoor activities), but nothing, I thought, was too much to handle. I went to bed early and slept for hours. I seemed to stay tired longer than most other people; when I was feeling well I was fine, but when I got exhausted it seemed I was down for the count.

This had always been difficult for me. Even as a child I would fall asleep on the floor getting ready for school in the morning. It would take weeks, sometimes months, to feel spunky and motivated again. As an adult, I struggled with my job and home responsibilities (dinner, kids, house work, life). So for the rest of this hiking trip, I tried to hide my struggle—but my family could tell something was not right.

After we had finally come home after our trip, I set up appointments with multiple doctors. The first with my family doctor/ GP ... tests were normal. He sent me to see a neurologist next ... tests came back normal. Next referral, Center for Disease Control ... non-conclusive. Referral again to a rheumatoid arthritis specialist ... I was diagnosed with fibromyalgia and chronic fatigue. $5000 out of pocket, and every test you could imagine. I was reassured that I didn't have MS, French Polio, or malaria. No tumors, no obstructions, no internal brain hemorrhaging. I felt like the doctors labeled me simply because they didn't have a clue and got tired of seeing me.

In the meantime, I needed my life back. I was still a wreck. It was like experiencing a hangover every morning: I ached all over my body, and my stomach pain was the worst of it. I constantly pushed on my stomach with my hands to alleviate the pain. It felt good to sleep on my front with a pillow under my abdomen, but my neck couldn't handle it. My posture started to become horrible again from constantly bending over. I tried hiding the discomfort during the day, but the silent tears at bedtime took a toll on me. There had to be something I was missing, and I felt that no one was there to help me.

I had been referred to a fibromyalgia specialist; still, though, some doctors consider this a made-up diagnosis. My family doctor was impossible to work with, as he told me all I needed was exercise and that I was just lazy.

The fibro specialist helped, but they wanted to prescribe drugs and those seemed to make things worse; the medication they prescribed caused depression as a side effect. Drugs were not helpful in the long run, so we stopped them completely.

Welcome internet! I would have to find my own solution. I tried elastic cinchers at the beginning of my search, although I felt more like a tube sausage wearing those—and since they are made out of plastic, my skin suffered badly. Here I was in pain, discomfort, depressed, and feeling as though the weight of the world was on me to just "suck it up and stop being lazy." I was at an all-time low and I don't think anyone realized it but me.

Then it happened: in the process of looking up my own remedies for fibromyalgia (or whatever this thing was), I found women online who had commented and blogged about how corsets had helped them. I read everything I could find on corsets and their effect on the body (both good and bad). Remembering what my grandmother said about corsets, I sighed with relief. This might actually help! At a minimum, it was one more thing I was ready to get off my list and say I had tried.

Obviously it would a big change in my daily routine though, and would not be not something I could hide from my husband. I told him my crazy idea that I wanted to try corsets and see if they would help me with my severe stomach pain. I talked with my aunt (who is a historian who studied textiles and clothing over the centuries and is an amazing seamstress, often making costumes for museums). She thought I was nuts. Growing up in the 60s and 70s, the idea of wearing corsets was something similar to self-inflicted bondage to her.

It took a little while, but I eventually ordered my first corset. It took a few days to figure out how to wear it comfortably, but when I put the corset on, immediately the pain in my bloated stomach subsided and I found relief. Aesthetically, it gave me a defined waist and made me feel more feminine. I loved my amazing posture and actually felt graceful in it after I had seasoned it.

Some fibromyalgia sufferers say that if I really did have fibro, then the pain of the corset against the skin would be too much to bear. All I can say is I already had pain everywhere. When I started wearing my corset I began to get some amazing relief. I even wear my corset when I sleep, albeit loosened. I take it off for some outside activities and wear it under my clothes most days. I have better posture and can function now at work.

I've changed my diet a little, I take good vitamins, I try and get good sleep and all those things fibro patients are supposed to do; but my biggest relief has been my corset.

My kids don't always like my corset because they can't come up behind me and tickle me, but they love that I don't cry from pain, as I used to.

My specialist has actually called me to ask questions about what corsets have done for me, and started offering it as an option to some of her other clients. It's funny, now my grandmother talks about how her mother and her granddaughter both love their corsets and she is so happy I that have found something that has helped me.

My corset is my little secret. It's my favorite undergarment, hugging and supporting me through the day. There are so many things I love about my corsets, but what I love most is how they took away my pain and gave me the chance to have my life back.

PART VIII

GASTROINTESTINAL DISORDERS

CHAGAS AND CORSETS

HEIDI J.

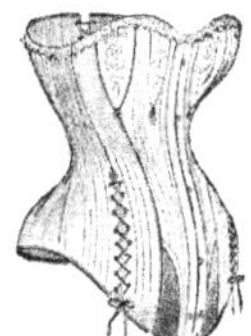

There is something very basic about "protecting" or "constricting" the gut. One of the things you see always in the Old Testament is about "Girding your loins." I loved that phrase, and used it on myself to face, say, a chemistry test. Most people think it has something to do with private parts, but your "loins" are your back muscles. The fighter wore armor similar to a kidney belt or a back brace to protect their gut and back, and to also support the weight of their sword. This idea of "girding your loins" goes back even before the Romans, and for the fighters, it sure wasn't about fashion. But I think it gives courage too. Even a simple off-the-rack back brace for heavy lifters: you put it on, and you feel braver.

I have a disorder of the gut, which has been well-documented by X-rays and experts. The large intestine is supposed to be a simple loop of about five feet long, held in place by the mesentery—mine unfortunately isn't. The surgeon described it as "just a big pile of guts."

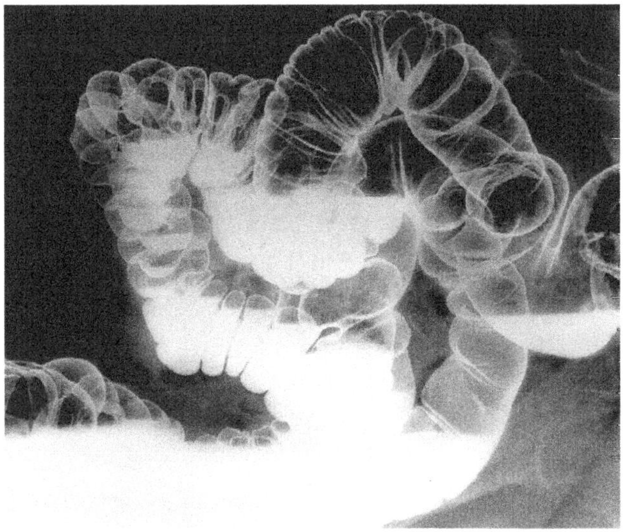

X-ray of Heidi's large intestine. White fluid is barium to help better visualize the lower GI tract.

You are looking at my large intestine—which is also doubled over itself in length, totally in the wrong place, and not held down at all. There are around 15 feet of large intestine (not all of it can be visualized in any one picture; I have several pictures in different views).

It really is amazing how much "slop" is in there. The radiologist took a lot of pictures in the barium study, and everything pretty much slops from one side to the other when I turn.

Neither I nor my doctors know what is going on exactly. There aren't many known causes for overgrown colons or cardiomegaly, and even fewer for people who recover at all. The primary theory is Chagas' disease, which is endemic to much of the world. In my youth, my family travelled throughout Mexico. I used to collect bugs as a hobby as a kid—and one particular bug I remember, which I now recognize as the "Kissing Bug," transmits the protozoa that causes Chagas.

I have the rather classic symptoms for the disease, including huge gut overgrowth and heart issues. But—I don't test positive for Chagas antibodies. I've been tested for all the weird types of cancer, bacteria, and autoimmune disorders that the doc could think of as well. Anti-protozoa drugs seem to stop the episodes though, so possibly it's a similar bug.

Whatever the cause may be, it acts like an infection of some kind; it causes my white blood cell count (WBC) to go high and then makes me rather sick, and seems to cause things like blood clots and heart issues: the high WBC always predicates the illness, and anti-protozoa drugs usually get rid of it.

To be clear: I'm not in danger of dying from this. I've had this for over 30 years now and my body is pretty used to it.

Where corsets primarily help is with my gut—as mentioned, my gut is too overgrown and becomes distended, which causes digestion issues and hernias. Keeping my bowels compressed solves the digestive symptoms I'd otherwise get, and also indirectly helps with the symptoms of my heart and lungs.

Before I first tried abdominal compression, I had been holding down my stomach away from my lungs so I could breathe. Which felt great, but you can't exactly go around holding your stomach down all the time.

A core issue there turned out to be pleural effusion ... a physician saw it 2 years LATER in an X-ray, but the doc at the time didn't tell me so I didn't know what was going on. My lung had actually partially collapsed, so the extra pressure on it from my gut felt worse than it would have otherwise.

Then I saw my bowel X-ray, and it showed how the ascending loop of my bowel fills with gas and presses UP on the diaphragm like a balloon underwater, leaving less space for expansion of the lungs.

The doctors basically didn't want to treat me much because they decided I had "heart failure" ... I could barely walk or think really.

So where does a corset fit into all this? Having a fix that I could easily order was a very good thing. Without any abdominal compression, my waist measures close to 50 inches (127 cm). Most of what is in there is gas and stools ... not fat or fluid ... and without the proper pressure, my intestine twists and turns and gets blocked by big pockets of gas.

But—if I place pressure on my gut, the expansion goes away

quickly. After I got tired of holding my abdomen down with my hands all the time, I started wearing a back brace, and it really did help with the gas—my waist went down to 32 inches (81 cm) or so in very short order.

Removing the air and distension from my bowels and taking the pressure off the lung let me breathe, and eventually the pleural effusion got better. Removing the upwards pressure on the diaphragm also helped with the hernia symptoms. I was having pain when I swallowed, like something was "caught" or it was kinked—with the pressure gone, my esophagus started working right again.

My heart also started working again sometime after that … partly by getting the pressure from the diaphragm off of it, and partly by treating the infection with medication. A series of echocardiograms showed a modest improvement in my ejection fraction by up to 10% between March and November. In that same time frame, my BNP levels (a hormone made in response to heart damage) also went from 1400 down to 180. Now a few years later, it's 120 or so.

However, the back braces just would not stay in place. The one I used for years dug into my upper torso and caused sores, and basically didn't fit well. I found it difficult to find any size that worked. If I get a size to fit my 32″ compressed waist, it doesn't expand far enough for proper adjustment. If I get the size that expands to fit my 50″ distended waist, it works for a week and then it's too loose.

Corsets were the next part of the equation—and they got me really curious. There is so much science to getting corsets to WORK, and given that corsets were worn daily at a time when all the work was hard labor … the fact that everyone wore them says that the corset was more than a rich-people's fashion statement.

The first real OTR corset I tried wasn't anything very special, and worked when I re-strung it so I could get it on originally. But my gut function totally stabilized, and I stopped having any trace of IBS or bloating or gas or ANYTHING. Although I am more interested in durability than about looks, my corsets seem to hold up pretty well with the nice Jacquard fabrics.

I've found this venture to be really interesting when introducing my corsets to my medical team. My docs were surprised that my corset actually did any good. I was surprised no one had actually tried it before!

The docs were rather accepting, which surprised me, but the idea of a medical device that is also, well, loaded with all kinds of historical and emotional issues, not to mention attractive … they were worried about my gut possibly getting twisted and causing fecal impaction. However, the opposite is true: what happens WITHOUT the corset is that my gut gets full of air, part of it becomes a kind of balloon, and it acts as a block. But if my gut is compressed, it can't bloat and can't rise up to affect my lungs either. My gut works fine IF I wear a corset.

Mostly the docs thought it was a good idea. It's kind of along the lines of what compression stockings do for veins in the legs and feet: by compressing a "tube" it actually works more efficiently and keeps circulation going.

The doctors don't really have a treatment for super-colon except surgery. And actually, I am glad I didn't try that first. I consulted with surgeons and their basic take is: "You need surgery. But if the corset works … it's way safer." I tend to agree. When I wear a corset I feel wonderful.

I've worn corsets for a few years now, and a big part of it now is that it makes me feel empowered. I mean, it doesn't cure the issues with my heart or gut, but overall things have gotten better. My muscles don't have "lumps" and are stronger, I stand tall and have plenty of stamina, and my digestion is great. My gut is still way too long, but it all compresses very nicely with a corset, doesn't take much space, and it works normally. Recall, I was diagnosed with "heart failure" several years ago, with a "below normal ejection fraction." Now it's "normal ejection" and my heart function has stayed in the normal range for 3 years or so. I have another echocardiogram soon and I'm curious to see what it shows. I'm more active and healthier than I have been in years, so I'm thinking the next echo will be better. Basically I still have "whatever it is," but it seems to be in stasis for the moment.

My goal right now is to find a well-fitting custom corset that adjusts wide enough to accommodate the distension. What impresses me about corsets is just how good the fit is! But even with OTR corsets, I'm happy to do anything to promote the whole idea of corseting or even gut health in general.

Point is, corsets may be important for some of us, beyond the attractiveness issue. At 58 or so, it felt odd to be going corseted, but my daughter thought the whole thing was fun, which was helpful. At the age of 62, I'm starting to feel like the grandmother on Downton Abbey ... old and upright and sassy.

I really believe we are onto something in terms of empowering women, and it is an important message. It's beyond just being "comforted" ... it's about being strong and "upright" and awesome. Women in corsets is now very empowering for me as an image. Like Wonder Woman, it's that strong figure that they capture so well. Like looking into a mirror of "the me that could be."

"Solaced" really fits for me.

JOURNEY TO DISCOVERY

S.M.

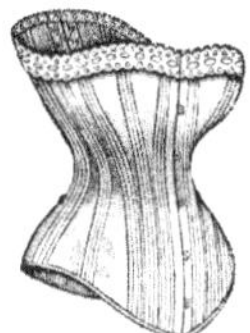

I initially became interested in corsets in 2008, when I had to have a lightly boned one made for an 1840s living-history event. A seamstress agreed to make me a custom corset. I had prepared for stricture but was pleasantly surprised how comfortable it was. I enjoyed historical reenactment, but saw corsets as an accurate article of clothing that I needed to wear for authenticity. When those events ceased, I put away the corset.

Several years later, in 2011, I was surfing YouTube and stumbled upon a channel devoted to modern corsetry: Lucy's Corsetry. I had no idea such a subculture existed. Her videos were incredibly informative and I developed a thirst to learn all I could about corsetry. So I followed her book recommendations and I learned even more.

I really wanted to try a "modern corset," and so I ordered an off-the-rack, Victorian-style underbust corset. It was six inches smaller than my waist, as recommended, but it was so stiff that I could not cinch down at all. Moreover, it seemed rather long for my very short torso. Whenever I sat down, the busk would dig into my crotch and the sides would jam into my armpits. Ugh! It felt like a body cast, not something I would like to wear. Too many OTR corsets have busks much too long for a 5′1″ (156 cm) woman.

I did more research and found a custom corsetiere who happened to live nearby, which meant I could get several mockups and fittings. This gorgeous custom corset fit perfectly, hugging my curves and feeling comfortable enough to wear for extended periods. Custom corsets reminded me how important the fit is for a garment designed to embrace the torso closely for hours. I wore it while at home but was yet too shy to wear it outside.

By 2014 I began to experience upper gastric pain that impaired my ability to eat much. This scared me into thinking that perhaps corset wearing somehow caused this abdominal pain. Were the horror stories about corsets injuring women true? Oh, how I wished not. Still, I was now hesitant to wear corsets for fear they would exacerbate the problem. At about the same time my pre-existing fibromyalgia and chronic fatigue were getting worse. I was spending more and more time lying down, preferably on my stomach as this alleviated some nausea. Corset wearing faded into the background.

Then one day in 2015, after a morning of nausea and fatigue, but having promised to join others on an excursion, I donned the Victorian corset to see if it brought any relief. After 15 minutes the nausea left and I felt energized. With minutes to spare, I met the group, wearing my corset (underneath my clothes) since I felt so much better.

My abdominal pain though seemed to return with the corset off. My doctors had not known of my corset wearing. I was too shy to admit a practice that some could consider injurious. I was very concerned of potential stern lectures of how corsets were the cause of my discomfort, so yet again corsets faded into the background.

In the fall of 2015 my pain intensified. In desperation for relief, I donned my loosest corset and the inward pressure of the busk provided relief from pain and nausea. This time I wore the corset to my gastroenterologist and related my findings. To my relief, he did not lecture me about the evils of corsets, but in fact told me to wear it if it helped. Unfortunately, he had no medical explanation as to why wearing a corset helped me.

However, all this would change when, in a few months, the abdominal pain and nausea intensified and not even a corset provided relief. It turned out I had adhesions which caused a small bowel obstruction, and I was operated on as an emergency case. Following surgery, a latex waist belt was wrapped around my torso as a pressure brace. It was uncomfortable, too long-waisted, scratchy, hot, and abrasive. A proper corset, I thought, would be so much more comfortable. So, at my one-month appointment, armed with a new custom underbust corset, I asked the surgeon if I could wear THIS, demonstrating exactly what I meant by "corset."

"It helps the pain and nausea," I added. "I only cinch two inches (5 cm) right now." (It must be said that I am NOT a tightlacer. I have only ever cinched 2–4 inches.) Much to my surprise he said, "Sure, whatever makes you feel more comfortable." I could not believe it. I asked point blank whether corset wearing caused the adhesions.

"NO," was his definitive answer.

"And they will not cause adhesions in the future?" I followed.

"No," again he answered. Then he added, "It [the corset] won't prevent them either."

I floated out of his office feeling so relieved. I could honestly respond to naysayers that the corset did not cause the GI problem and that it would not in the future. Following that positive response from the surgeon, I decided to allow myself to embrace the corset as a daily garment. I was still recovering from abdominal surgery so cinching amounted to only 1-2 inches. In a few days something remarkable happened: not only did the persistent nausea subside, but now I had loads of energy, which I had not experienced in many years. Now, I am not saying the corset is a miracle garment restoring health and vitality, but the diminished symptoms were not a coincidence. I cannot deny that the days I feel best are those when I have worn a corset.

As time goes on, I am learning to love myself more by discovering a powerful inner strength and innate feminine identity long suppressed to fit into culture's obsession with the emaciated form on the catwalks. For me, corset wearing is not oppressive at all, but rather freeing. Personally, corsetry is not a matter of my achieving the smallest waist; it is about emphasizing my natural hourglass figure, proclaiming the woman that I am, and having confidence in my body.

My corset journey has changed with time. Initially, I was attracted to corsets purely as costume. Then the more I researched and studied, the more I appreciated the sheer beauty and artistry of this garment. After that, I discovered medical benefit though as yet inexplicable. Lastly, I found pride in my curves and could claim the femininity of my shape. This empowers me.

PILL FREE AND PAIN FREE

STEPHANIE E.

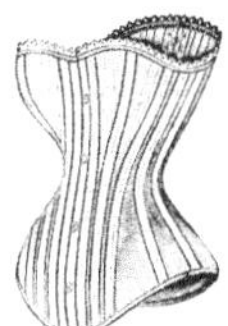

Corsets have helped me so many ways that I barely know where to begin.

When I was 19, I became pregnant with my first child. I am petite, with a tiny frame, and weighed 102 pounds (46 kg) before pregnancy. During the entire pregnancy I had constant back pain, and even after I had given birth, nothing helped except pain medication. I became heavily addicted to the pills, but I didn't notice how bad it was until I landed myself in the hospital from them.

One of the side effects from the medication was constipation. I had gone almost three weeks without going to the bathroom, and it led to sepsis. When I arrived at the hospital, the doctor told me if I had waited just few more hours, I wouldn't be here today.

That week was one of the hardest times of my life. I had terrible withdrawal symptoms, and all I could think about was how much I wanted and needed the meds. It was only after a week of recovery that I began to feel better. I took a good look in the mirror and saw what those pills were doing to my body, and I knew I had to find a different way to cope. And I have lived through the pain.

Losing weight helped a little; I lost 40 pounds (18 kg). I happened upon an article about a woman who wore corsets. I can't remember her name but I showed my boyfriend the article, which reported that she experienced dramatic weight loss from her corsets. He gave me a budget and told me to get one for myself. Exploring the options online, I was lost trying to find the perfect corset for me, but I soon found Lucy's YouTube channel, which helped tremendously, and then I purchased my first corset.

I started wearing a corset with the intention of losing weight, but what I found instead was relief.

Wearing a corset alleviated my back pain. For the first time in years I was able to sit and stand for long periods of time without hurting. I was able to hold and play with my son longer than I was ever able to before. I considered it a miracle.

I also have mind-crippling social anxiety. Vomiting before I have to go somewhere due to nerves was an everyday occurrence, and my psychiatrist prescribed pills to control my anxiety. I still have a hard time just talking with a stranger or going to the store by myself, but wearing a corset has helped me stay calm and in control.

Before I would always wear a rubber band around my wrist and would snap it on the inside of my wrist if I were close to a panic attack; it would bring me back and help me concentrate. Now when I'm out and about, I don't need that rubber band. I still get nervous around social settings, but wearing a corset has helped me far more than the anxiety medication ever did.

Another unexpected benefit from corsets: I don't get as constipated as I used to! I know that seems silly to say, but somehow my back pain would constantly freeze up my bowels. Now I can evacuate easily.

The corset has also improved my posture. When I was growing up, I always used to slouch when I walked. I would always look down at my feet with my shoulders hunched. But the corset forces to me stand and sit tall. This has given me so much confidence—I feel empowered, as though I can do anything. I never felt that way before.

As for my original intention of using the corset to lose weight: It has helped me lose inches. Before corseting I had a 32–33 inch waist (81–84 cm), and after the first year of use, my waist shank to 28–29 inches (71–74 cm). Corsets gave me the hourglass I wasn't born with; moreover they changed my life.

A MILLION REASONS FOR CORSETS

ELLE W.

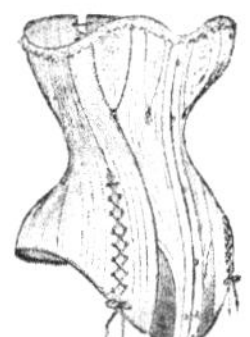

My name is Elle, and I live in Oakland, California. I've been wearing corsets for over two years, and I own seven corsets as of now.

What first attracted me to corsets was simply the way they looked, and how they changed the way clothing hung on the body. When I was growing up, my grandmother and great-grandmother both wore compressive undergarments, as was the custom at the time. Back then it was flexible girdles, which was the norm.

Today I've noticed that fashion has changed to more casual clothes. People today seem to have a misconception that human bodies have evolved greatly in the past 70 years; that now we have a body shape different from those in the past, and that only famous people or those who bust their behind in the gym are capable of coming close to having that vintage hourglass silhouette.

I'm quick to tell others that no, bodies haven't changed all that much—people back then wore undergarments and corsets that made their outfits look a certain way, and some people wear corsets now just as they have in the past.

Inspired by the older generations of my family and the recent return of the corset in fashion, I decided to try a corset. I looked at the prices of custom corsetry and they were out of my budget, so I purchased my first corset off-the-rack from Orchard Corset to see if I would like it—and that's when I noticed the benefits.

When wearing my corset, my back didn't hurt so much. The corset encouraged my body to engage muscles I hadn't used in a while, but it wasn't an uncomfortable soreness per se—it trained me to stand and sit up straight.

The way my clothes fit changed almost immediately with the corset. And after a while I noticed I was truly dropping pant sizes as well—my body was changing because the corset was changing my eating habits. It didn't allow me to eat too much, or eat too quickly. I stopped finishing everything on my plate at mealtime, and I stopped drinking soda while corseted, because the carbonation made me feel as though my head would pop off.

My corset also helps with my Irritable Bowel Syndrome (IBS). I can avoid flare-ups in part by using corsets to discourage me from eating the wrong things that originally contributed to the flare-ups.

Obviously, it's not healthy to drink soda or eat large portions of heavy meals. Even when I eat a small serving of processed food (like a candy bar), my stomach complains—and these symptoms can be even worse when I'm wearing a corset. However, I can eat healthy salads all day long and feel totally fine in my corset. I became accustomed to eating more healthily with a corset, and the healthier habits have in turn eased the symptoms of my IBS.

When I do experience a bad flare-up, it's not only the inside of my gut that is painful, but the skin on my abdomen also becomes sensitive to the touch—so I choose not to wear my corset on those bad days. But with mild flare-ups, however ... Hmm, come to think of it, I haven't had mild cramps in a few years, so it's possible that the pressure of the corset helped alleviate them without my realizing it. These symptoms are not quite as noticeable in a corset, if I notice them at all.

Corsets have taught me a lot more about my own body and my own figure, made me more aware of which fashions work with my body and which don't, and all in all, I'm enjoying my experience.

The reactions and commentary I've received on my corset have been mostly positive, and always interesting. As a woman of color who unabashedly wears a corset, I've heard quite a bit of interesting commentary from other people of color, who say that corset training is what "white people do." I wish that people would take the time to be more accepting of others—as long as you're not being explicitly lewd or blatantly offensive, one should not be so concerned by what someone else wants to wear.

Living with a large bust, it is also challenging to others to see me standing tall and proud with my shoulders back, because some assume that I'm trying to stick my breasts in their faces. Some have asked me "why is your chest protruding so much, why is it so high?" I explain to them that this is my natural chest, and I'm finally able to sit up straight with my corset. Before my corset, I used to slouch—not only because of the heaviness of my chest, but also because I tried to hide myself, and that's not how anyone ought to be. This is my body—I have a big chest, and that is not going to change. I tell others that it's okay to be different—I like corsets and it doesn't mean you have to like them; I'm not trying to force my practices on others.

Other than that, it has been a positive experience. It's interesting when I run into someone I haven't seen in a while and they comment on my figure and ask what I've been doing. I love to tell them that I've been wearing a corset. When I allow them to try on my corset, more often than not they're surprised and say, "It's so comfortable!" and I tell them "I'm lazy by nature and I don't 'do' uncomfortable—if corsets were uncomfortable, I wouldn't wear them!"

There are a million reasons why people wear corsets; not everyone is trying to get a super small waist or participate in body modification. Although there's nothing wrong with that, it's not what I want for myself. I also don't wear corsets for psychological reasons, but I understand that many people do.

The great shift to a positive body image and self-acceptance I see in so many of the other corset wearers within the community is something I enjoy very much. Anything that can make people feel better about themselves and more loving toward their body image, I personally say to go for it.

I would like to see people in the corset community be more open, accepting, and patient toward others who are new to corsetry—either those who have misconceptions, or those who are interested and just beginning to learn about them, because we were all beginners once. The more people there are who openly share their corset experiences, the more others will realize that corseters aren't all that weird (although I believe that anyone who's worth their salt is at least a little weird)!

Hopefully more corset wearers around the world will become empowered to wear their corsets out of the house, explain to others what corsets are and what they can do, and show patience (even when the other party is not so patient), as it helps build understanding and tolerance.

I also want to encourage people of all sizes, colors and genders who are interested in corsets to become part of this growing community and to have fun with it, because there are so many types of corsets and so many reasons for corseting. Corsets are not just for one type of person, but for anyone.

ULCERATIVE COLITIS AND CORSETRY

MARGARET M.

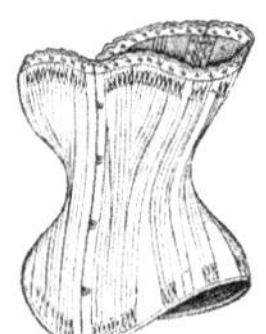

The etiology of ulcerative colitis (UC) is still rather mysterious, and the medical literature is not sufficiently conclusive (in my opinion) as to which treatments are most effective. Even my gastroenterologist seems to be guessing a lot of the time—treatment for me has been more trial and error than guaranteed relief. There is no cure for UC—only the hope of prolonged periods of remission.

I was diagnosed in 2005 and was doing mostly okay with the prescribed medications and listening attentively to my body, for ten years. In the spring of 2013, I started getting more into corseting by moving away from fashion corsets and purchasing my first custom piece from Lace Embrace Atelier, as well as many of their ready-to-wear steel-boned waspies. I would use these on-and-off for certain outfits, for the odd bit of relief for mild UC cramps (which occurred regularly), and for relief after throwing my lower back out. (Now that was night and day—no corset, I needed muscle relaxants. Steel boned waspie—I could work at my desk job drug-free!)

I do not lace every day nor do I lace regularly; I lace up when I want to add "wow" to an outfit, or when the cramps come.

During the spring of 2015 I had my worst UC relapse, essentially bringing me back to square one—the entire length of my colon was ulcerated. The cramps during a relapse are horrendous, and I was at my wit's end because I did not want to become addicted to pain medication; however it takes months to heal from a full relapse.

Cortical steroids (not to be confused with anabolic steroids used by certain body builders) were required to keep me out of the hospital and are part of the standard treatment to get the bleeding under control; however I still had to function day-to-day as my body healed. Chronic pain is a reality.

Corseting saved my sanity and improved the quality of my life, and I wish more people knew about it. The pressure of a well-fitting corset seems to alleviate the relentless pain associated with my brand of cramping.

My unexpected psychological benefit is the security the "day-long hug" of a corset offers, which is very welcome considering that physical pain just increases anxiety for me. I have a 30″ (76 cm) natural waist and I find that wearing my corset at a 4–5″ (10–13 cm) reduction for 8–10 hours works wonders for me on the bad cramping days.

I've wondered why squeezing my waist helps with cramps, but I do not have an answer. Since my gastroenterologist is very conservative and traditional, I doubt I will ever mention corseting to him, which is unfortunate. My family doctor seems less stuffy than my specialist, so I may mention it to him one day. A medical opinion can be useful, provided it includes some research related to corsetry. I doubt he would be well informed on the effects of corsetry; though it's worth a shot, I suppose!

PART IX

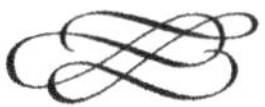

DYSMENORRHEA & ENDOMETRIOSIS

A GENTLE SWADDLE FOR ENDO

A.

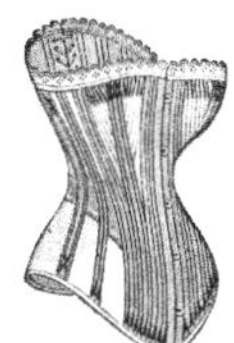

In my early teens, I experienced painful menstruation that frequently confined me to my bed. From age 14 into my early twenties, specialists told me the cause was everything from burst ovarian cysts to severe constipation. I was prescribed an arsenal of painkillers, sedatives, and hormone therapy to control this severe pain. What I was experiencing was not simply "typical" period discomfort, but rather aching and bloating so severe that I looked like a doubled-over, weeping pregnant woman. These episodes lasted for weeks at a time because of my irregular cycles.

After years of poorly controlled pain, I was referred to a new gynecologic specialist who suspected that I had endometriosis. The Mayo Clinic defines it as a "painful disorder in which tissue that normally lines the inside of the uterus—the endometrium—grows outside the uterus … most commonly [involving] ovaries, bowels, or the tissue lining the pelvis." The endometrial tissue continues to respond to hormonal changes regardless of where it has migrated to. During menstruation, these endometrial implants (tissue that has migrated outside the uterus) become inflamed and can bleed, but this tissue remains trapped in the abdominal cavity.

Endometriosis can only be confirmed by a surgeon. During my

first surgery, at age 22, the amount of endometrial tissue that had to be scraped from my abdominal cavity was staggering. I was in surgery for several hours as the migrated endometrium was scraped or cut away from my abdominal wall and organs. I would later learn that this had been the cause of my irregular cycles and debilitating pain all along.

In the years since my initial diagnosis, I have had four separate surgeries to remove endometrial implants, adhesions, and general scar tissue from my abdominal organs and walls. Multiple surgeries of this nature are common for women with endometriosis. I awoke from my most recent surgery with my distended belly swaddled in a soft cotton and elastic belly binder. The binder acted as a support garment and felt like a pleasant hug. The gentle pressure provided noticeable relief immediately.

After I healed fully, I spoke with my surgeon about gentle corseting to help manage my pain, and she gave me the go-ahead to try it out. I own three off-the-rack underbust corsets that provide gentle pressure. This helps manage not only my pain, but also the severe bloating that often accompanies endometriosis. I do not lace down to extreme reductions, but find that at a 2–4 inch (5–10 cm) reduction, the corsets provide support and comfort on even my most difficult days.

Physical intimacy can also be exceedingly painful for women with endometriosis. There has been much research into ways to manage the physical and psychological effects of this aspect of the condition. I am fortunate to have a partner who is supportive and understanding of the issues surrounding my experience of frequently painful intercourse.

I have found that the use of a corset as part of a lingerie ensemble helps me to feel womanly even in times when my body does not.

Currently, I am in the process of saving up for a custom-drafted polymesh summer Contour Corset from Fran Blanche, which is especially useful during the hot months in my desert home. I am grateful to Lucy for her YouTube channel because it helped me to understand the benefits of corseting.

RECLAIMING CONTROL OF MY BODY

C.T.

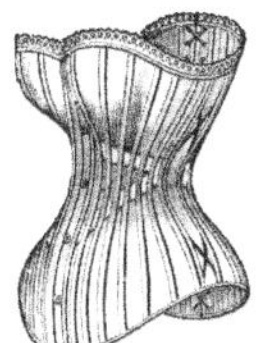

I first noticed corsetry after following the marvelous Georgina Horne, of *Fuller Figure Fuller Bust* fame. Seeing photos of her in a corset made me start to explore the idea of purchasing one myself.

As I started to look into it, I stumbled across anecdotal evidence about other uses for corsets, particularly for back pain, anxiety relief, and even for conditions like Irritable Bowel Syndrome (IBS). I have endometriosis and fibromyalgia, so I have pain in my pelvis, tummy, hips, back, and shoulders. I have a lot of burning and aching back pain, especially in the evening, which can be bad enough that I have to lie on the floor, as sitting is too painful. Because I have had many surgeries (including a midline incision to remove endometriosis) my tummy muscles are weak and my back muscles have to work extra hard to keep me upright.

As I read and learned about corsets, I started wondering if the back support they offered would help with my back pain. After a false start with a cheap, off-the-rack corset, I found Lucy's videos and began to understand more about the way corsets work. I decided that, with my 12″ hip spring, I needed to get a custom corset. I approached

Geraldine of Valkyrie Corsets and now I have a beautiful teal blue underbust. It's truly a work of art.

As well as looking gorgeous, it helps with my pain levels. The back pain almost vanishes when I have my corset on. It seems to offer enough support that the muscles aren't overworked, and so the awful burning sensation vanishes. I'm keen to build up muscle strength, and I see a chiropractor who gives me exercises for home, so that I won't end up relying solely on the corset for support. But, in the meantime, it's providing me symptomatic relief.

My corset also helps with endometriosis pain. I naturally press my hand onto my tummy when it hurts, as the pressure and warmth seems to relieve the pain, and I've found that the corset does the same thing in a more controlled way. It provides a really deep, firm pressure, and because it is consistent all over my tummy, it doesn't hurt in the way my jeans' narrow waistband does; it actually seems to help my tummy muscles relax too.

I didn't expect the corset to help in this way, and was even a bit dubious about trying to wear it when my endo pain was bad, so it was a very pleasant surprise to find it actually helped. Endo pain can be anything from intense period pain, with cramps and aching, to intense twisting and pinching pain. I find the corset most effective at combatting deep, aching pains, as the pressure seems to counteract and soothe them.

I don't wear my corset every day, and whenever I develop a chocolate cyst (an endometrial deposit on the ovary that is filled with blood) I don't wear it, as the pressure aggravates the cyst. But when I have my usual endometriosis pain, I find the warmth and pressure really soothing. The term "corset hug" seems very appropriate, as the corset is providing an all-around pressure and its extra layers keep the area warm. It will never cure my pain, but it certainly helps with it.

I was able to man a stall at the Victorian Christmas Fayre, standing up all day, something I could never usually manage.

Between the endometriosis and fibromyalgia, I have often felt very out of control with my own body, especially as we are pursuing fertility treatment. I sometimes feel as though my body doesn't behave the way it should. Wearing a corset helps with how I view my body and myself. When I have a corset on, it feels like I'm taking control back from the illnesses and saying, "this is my body and I'm doing what I want to do," rather than fitting my life around chronic illness.

Most pain relief involves taking pills (with horrid side effects), or devices like a TENS machine (which is very effective, but involves trailing wires under your clothes to sticky pads). Using a corset for pain relief is amazing as the only side effects are the curvy hourglass figure, which I love, and feeling really sexy and confident. It's something I'm doing for myself, and love doing.

AN EIGHT-HOUR EMBRACE

LAUREN E.

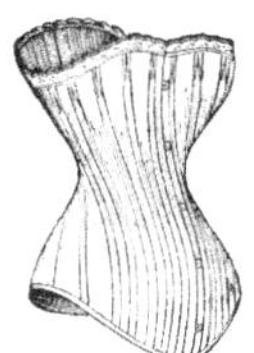

I started wearing corsets around two years ago because I had heard that they can help reduce anxiety, and I had been suffering from panic attacks for about a year prior. After going through a few "bad" corset brands, I finally got myself a decent corset and wore it every night to bed and over the weekends. As I became more comfortable in my corset, I noticed that I had fewer panic attacks—and since I am not taking any medication for panic attacks, I could only put it down to my corset.

A year passed since I bought my first corset and I was much more confident. By then I only experienced panic attacks in prolonged stressful situations, instead of at almost every social event I went to.

Around this time, I started to train my waist down more, working towards my goal of closing my 20″ (51 cm) corset. As I increased the duration and the frequency of wear, I began to notice that my periods had become a lot shorter and lighter. Heavy periods and painful cramps run in the family, and my periods usually lasted for roughly two weeks. Before corsets, there were times when I needed to take time off school as the pain and the heaviness interfered with life. As I started to wear my corsets during my periods, the cramps were less painful than usual, and as the days went on, they disappeared altogether. Also, I found that my flow became shorter and a lot lighter. I no longer have any cramps, and my periods last for about 5–7 days instead of the previous 12–14.

I've also suffered with acne for about a year and a half, and it often flares up during my periods and during times of stress and anxiety. But since I've increased the hours spent in my corset, I somehow get fewer spots than I used to. I attribute these changes to the calm, even peaceful, feeling I get in my corset due to its "hug effect." While I can't link the two for sure, studies have shown[1] that hugging someone for longer than twenty seconds aids in the release of oxytocin, an anti-stress hormone. Since I'm in my corset (which mimics a long-lasting hug) for approximately eight hours each day, I have a theory that my body releases more oxytocin to lower my cortisol levels, thus causing less stress-related symptoms, including fewer stress spots on my face.

---

1. Grewen, Karen M., Susan S. Girdler, Janet Amico, and Kathleen C. Light. "Effects of Partner Support on Resting Oxytocin, Cortisol, Norepinephrine, and Blood Pressure before and after Warm Partner Contact." *Psychosomatic Medicine* 67, no. 4 (2005): 531–38. https://doi.org/10.1097/01.psy.0000170341.88395.47.

THE ABILITY TO LOVE MYSELF

S.P.

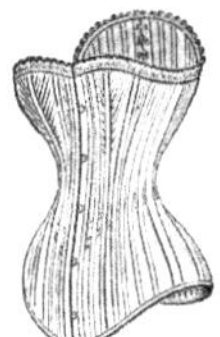

While growing up I always felt unattractive. I was the only Asian girl in a school of Caucasians. I was also incredibly hairy and had broad shoulders, so I was made fun of for looking like a boy. This continued through elementary and secondary school, where I was picked on and told I was unattractive. To add insult to injury, as a Eurasian I gained no sympathy from other Asians in secondary school, friends included, and I often felt isolated. I had attempted suicide and had little to no self-confidence.

It wasn't until the 11th grade that I became fascinated with period fashion, after reading lots of classics like *Wuthering Heights* and getting lost in Poe's fantasies. I was obsessed with the elegance of the nineteenth century, where beauty lay in the fashions. I became interested in corsetry due to this, but didn't pursue it until I had a back injury from ballet and felt the onset of degenerative disc disease.

I also had issues with my posture, which impacted my breathing, and severe pain from PCOS (polycystic ovarian syndrome) and endometriosis, which required my taking a combination of contraceptive pills and codeine to ease the symptoms. I was then diagnosed with Panic Disorder and Generalized Anxiety Disorder.

My first corset was from Isabella Corsetry. It took almost a full month to get to me because I'm in Australia, but this corset helped me tremendously. I no longer have to take codeine for my endometriosis and PCOS pain.

My posture is great, which allows me to breathe, in addition to making me feel more confident and more attractive. PCOS and endo (along with all of that teasing) had killed my feelings of femininity—looking in the mirror and seeing a shapeless blob and hearing others taunt me for not looking female enough was a regular occurrence. While I still struggle with my gender identity to this day, being able to reclaim my body into how I wish to be perceived means a great deal to me. With a corset, I am now less anxious and I'm able to leave the house, go to university, and do things I previously thought impossible, like giving public speeches and getting a job. Corsets have afforded me the ability to love myself, and now I have the confidence to embark on an overseas internship to teach at a university.

Corsets are an object of vanity, and I admit I love how I look in them, but at the same time they've helped my health improve and helped restore my confidence, allowing me to accomplish things beyond my imagination.

Now, I wouldn't advise people to go grab a corset as if it were a miracle cure. It's not a cure-all and I strongly encourage people to seek professional assistance first before seeking such alternative aids. Some people say that the pressure from a corset helps them with anxiety, but for me it can sometimes trigger a panic attack. The only thing a corset has done for my anxiety was make me feel more confident, resulting in reduced anxiety. I don't wear a corset every day, it's simply not practical for me and my lifestyle—but the pain relief and confidence I feel, and the curves I see from my 18″ (46 cm) waist, are my trophy and a reminder that I can do anything.

PART X

POST-SURGICAL RECOVERY

THE TRANSFORMATIVE NATURE OF CORSETRY

JESSE STAR

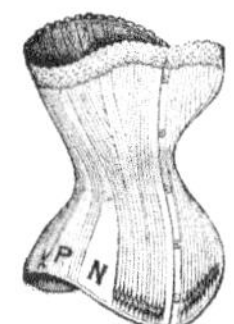

I'm a 41-year-old woman from Toronto, Canada, and corsets have literally changed my life.

It's sometimes hard for me to remember what life was like before everything changed in March of 1992. I was a brainy kid who worried about being fatter than her schoolmates, and worried even more about being weird. My parents had separated a few years prior, and we had recently moved into a house with my new baby sister. Lots of change!

I had no idea, though, that 17-year-old-me would be setting foot on a decades-long journey to be reunited with my body. I thought I was just going to the store for some juice.

I was heading home after a walk in the rain, when I was struck by a car while crossing the road. The injuries seemed pretty minor, considering the circumstances. My left leg was broken, and I counted myself lucky to have gotten off so lightly.

I had surgery to repair my leg, which led to my developing Osteomyelitis: a bone infection that turned into a brutal disease that resisted all efforts to mend the damage—as a result, I experienced things that changed me forever. Days turned into weeks, which turned into months ... then years. For a long time, things looked extremely grim.

I spent a long time in and out of many hospitals, having surgery after surgery, as my uncooperative body slowly fought the infection that came very close to claiming my left leg, and my life.

In 1994, I had a successful major surgery to repair my leg. My right side abdominal muscle (my abdominus rectus) was grafted to form the muscle of my left lower leg. After that surgery, I developed a secondary necrotic infection in my abdomen where the graft was taken. The removal of infected tissue left me with a deep, cavernous, hard scar through my center that never really healed. I bled for six years, and went through many painful treatments trying to get the skin to close.

My teens and early 20s were spent in a very different kind of self-discovery than most people have in that period: stubbornly re-teaching myself how to walk, learning how to do painful medical maintenance procedures on myself—and in the process, I lost myself a little bit.

The swelling and the many surgeries changed the contours of my body forever. For many years, I couldn't even look at myself in a mirror, and I wore shapeless clothes to hide the things about my body that I couldn't face, let alone show to others.

Life didn't stop while I healed, though.

I went through physiotherapy, re-taught myself to walk, and moved out of my abusive mother's house. I had no time to deal with what had happened, and I stayed in endurance mode for a very long time. Looking back, it's not difficult to understand how I ended up with body dysmorphia, even if it didn't manifest itself in typical ways, and I didn't understand what was happening at the time.

I had to work to support myself. I learned through trial and error that in order to survive, I would have to hide my disability from my employers, which made it all the easier to keep sidestepping my own body. People worked alongside me for years and had no idea what had happened to me. I never talked about it, I never acknowledged it, and I tried not to think about it. Hiding from yourself gets easier the longer you do it, and change becomes more difficult the more you become set in your ways.

For 20 years I didn't wear shorts, and I have never worn a midriff-baring shirt. I spent a great deal of time looking for clothes that didn't exist: clothes to cover up and hide me, rather than clothes that suited or flattered me ... because I couldn't possibly conceive of my body ever being attractive in any way. I accepted it, thought I had made my peace with it, and went on with my life with the perspective that this was how life was going to be for me: I was ugly, my body was monstrous—and I was massively disconnected from my physical self.

It was during one particularly horrific clothes shopping trip that I decided I wasn't going to live like this anymore; that I was going to do what I could to heal my body, and to work towards making myself whole.

I made the arrangements to have a discussion with a reluctant surgeon in 2007, and after about six months of waiting and hoping, there was a cancellation in his schedule, which opened up a slot for my surgery.

It was risky. He would be cutting out the old scar tissue, and attempting a "joining" of old scar tissue with new.

I was told that I might lose my belly button, and that the chances that things might not heal (given my personal track record with that sort of thing) were much higher than I liked.

The surgery went well. While healing from the procedure, I developed post-surgical hypersensitivity, so the surgeon gave me the go-ahead to use binders for dressing changes.

I started my physical shifting with elastic binders because of the damage and staining that was sure to happen from my still-draining sutures (super unpleasant)—but eventually I got a few corsets. There was certainly some trial and error (like when I figured out I should be wearing a liner underneath them so that my sweat wouldn't damage them—oops) and they were more "Camp"-like and medical-looking than the amazing constructions from talented corsetieres whom I now follow.

But any discomfort from those medical corsets was worth the

feeling of almost-symmetry. The scars I have across my midsection aren't just lines; since the abdominus rectus on my right side was grafted to form the muscle of my left lower leg, my middle section is much flatter on one side than the other. My contours are odd, and my proportions are off. I have felt uneven ever since that procedure—unless I'm wearing a corset.

Like a tender embrace reminding me I'm good enough to be loved (by me), I found that gentle shaping made a huge difference in how I viewed myself.

Not satisfied with merely throwing myself back into the pool as a swimmer, I became an avid SCUBA diver in 2006 and, despite having had abdominal surgery in 2007, went on to get my Divemaster certification in 2009.

Not only did I swim in a suit that revealed my scarred leg, the one-piece tank suit I purposefully chose exposed every weird little bump, the oddly placed divots that I had that most people don't. I no longer hid behind shapeless clothing—and I had a shape! Years of corset wear gave me a defined waist, and made me care far less about what my SCUBA buddies thought about my scars.

The freedom I felt allowed me to be confident enough to do things I never would have imagined myself capable of doing, and eventually I didn't "need" my corsets in the same way that I once did. (Although I still wear them on occasion, I am no longer a daily lacer.) I would never have taken that first step had I not been able to look at myself, and have something about myself to look at that didn't make me want to cry and give up forever.

I feel the same way about the transformative nature of tattoos. I have been lucky in that I have an extremely talented tattoo artist in my family—remember the baby sister I mentioned at the beginning of this story? She grew up to be a gifted artistic prodigy. She tattooed the scar on my leg in a personally revolutionary experience that has not only further changed how I see my body, but how other people see it as well. Instead of inspiring pity and answering rude, inappropriate questions from strangers, people stop me on the street to tell me how much they like my squid!

STORY OF A SCAR AND A SWAN

LELANIE K.

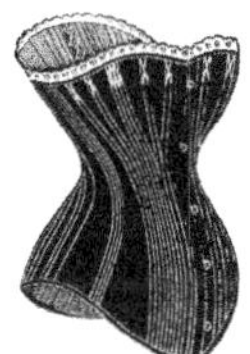

I was first introduced to corsets in 2001, when I was just 14 years old. My mother bought me a fashion corset. While it didn't take anything off my waist, I fell in love with the general look of it.

As a teenager I had to wear a medical corset for several months after I had reconstructive abdominal surgery. When I was a newborn, only a few days old, I had necrotizing enterocolitis. This mostly affects newborns and causes the bowels to die off, which can be life-threatening as bacteria spills from the intestines into the body. My case was so severe that it resulted in my needing emergency surgery and having 90% of my large intestine removed. Many abdominal exploratory surgeries use a midline (vertical) incision on adults, but as a tiny baby I was given a transverse incision from one side of my body straight across to the other.

After that I had four more surgeries to correct the previous mistakes. As I grew, the scar grew with me—and with so many surgeries, my skin had grown straight onto muscle, creating a very ugly scar. At 16 years old, I finally had complete scar reconstruction, and I was given a post-surgical medical corset to help with the healing.

Not too long after this, at the age of 17, I discovered the work of a local corsetiere, Æiden Swan. There aren't too many corsetieres in South Africa, but Æiden's work is among the best. I admired their work for a long time, but it would be many years before I invested in a quality corset.

When I was 20, I wore my first "proper" corset, albeit not one of Æiden's. This was also a fashion corset, but it took an inch or two off my waistline.

Once I started working, I realized that my office block was only a few miles away from Æiden's studio. So in 2011, a decade after my fascination with corsets began, I finally purchased my first decent professionally made corset, customized to fit my measurements.

The first benefit I noticed was a confidence boost. I have always had wide, large hips, even when I was underweight due to health issues. I had always struggled with my self-esteem due to being bullied over my pear-shaped figure. But with my corset, I now had a tiny waist and I immediately felt confident and came to love my body.

The second problem that my corset helped with was the discomfort remaining from the extensive surgeries on my abdomen. Due to my necrotizing enterocolitis as a baby, my abdomen was always more likely to give me issues, and my intestines were always very prone to IBS as well as picking up bugs. My corset made me feel more comfortable than I had been in a long time. With the right custom corset, I have no pain in my scar whenever I am corseting.

Corsets also make my periods more manageable. One unfortunate year my period was right on Halloween. I decided I was not going to miss out, and I still wore a corset. To my surprise I had no cramps at all that day. I tested it again the month after, and again there was no pain for as long as I was wearing a corset, so it makes my periods more manageable.

To add to my already bad luck in terms of health, I currently have hormone issues, which make my health fluctuate very erratically. A corset still provides a much-needed confidence boost on the bad days. I still use my corsets for back pain, scar pain, and period pain. I have also made corsets for myself and others, and through this craft I started meeting more people—amazing people with similar interests. And as for Æiden, whom I had looked up to for so many years, they've now become one of my closest friends.

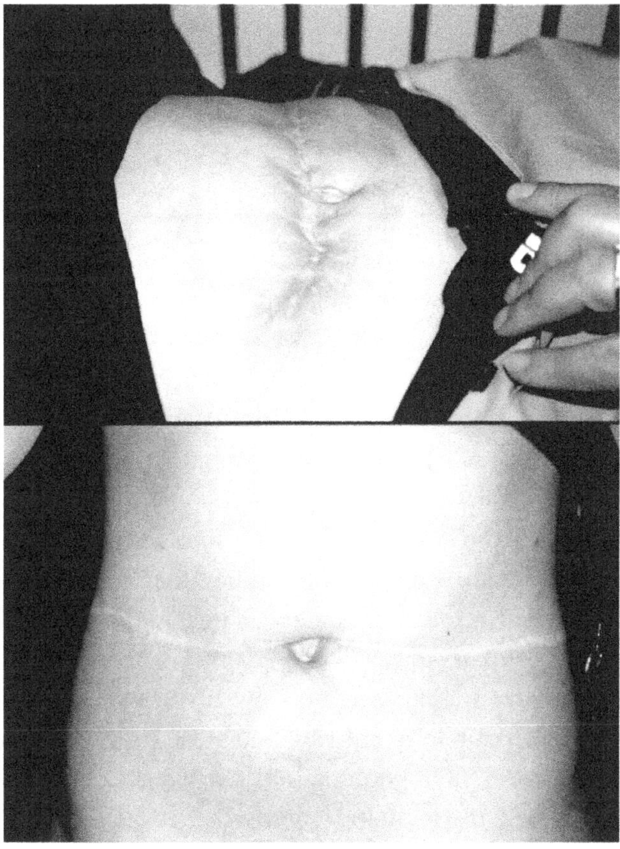

Lelanie's abdomen before (above) and after (below) her reconstructive procedure to remove the scar tissue from her previous life-saving surgeries.

STEALTHLACING VS. CANCER

STEALTHLACER

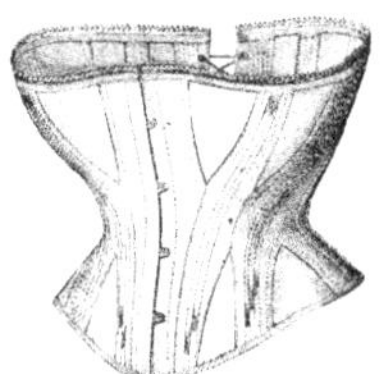

I, a non-smoker, am a lucky survivor of lung cancer.

I began corseting some months after I heard three fateful words: "You have cancer!"

The surgical team (or the "Texas Chainsaw Surgeons," as I call them) removed most of my left lung. They thankfully got all of my cancer, but caused a lot of peripheral damage. It was hell; I felt as though I had been carved up like a Thanksgiving turkey. I had five major incisions on the surface, and my insides were much worse, since they had to cut into my ribs and muscles, and damaged my nerves in the process. On good days, it felt like a fastball had hit my chest, and on bad days I felt somewhere between a piñata and a gunshot victim. Just breathing was painful, and coughing and sneezing were even more excruciating.

I used pain pills, pain patches, nerve suppressants, and muscle relaxants. I couldn't sleep in the same bed as my wife, as any slight movement would wake me, and the slightest touch would bring me to tears.

After Western medicine failed with pain control, I desperately searched for alternatives. The only thing that provided some relief was applying heavy pressure to immobilize my ribs. I tried wrapping several Ace bandages around myself, but they were just not firm enough. I was just about to seek a medical marijuana card to buy some tasty brownies when I considered corseting.

One night, in desperation, I decided to try my wife's off-the-rack (OTR) corset. I had bought it for her as a gift several years earlier, but she had never used it. I was so very ashamed and snuck off to the spare bedroom to examine it. Luckily, it was about my size. I felt apprehensive and guilty when wrapping it around me, but the desire for pain relief was the straw that broke the camel's back. I lost my inhibition.

My heart raced and my hands trembled when snapping the busk studs into the keyhole slots, and I wondered if I was doing something shameful. What would I say if my wife saw me? However, I was so desperate for pain relief that I just didn't care. When I first pulled the laces, there was no going back. It felt taboo—and yet thrilling—at the same time. I laced gently and it felt pleasant, so I slowly and carefully laced a bit tighter. It stung at first from the skin movement, but once I stopped tightening the laces, the pain suddenly ceased.

It was like the calm after a storm, and it felt wonderful! The corset helped to stabilize my skin and ribs, and provided immediate relief from the sharp stabbing pains in my skin and the intercostal muscles between my ribs. The firm pressure also provided some relief from the baseline pain in my deeper layers. The compression was very soothing, like a hug. I was content and at peace with myself. Within minutes I was sleeping like a baby, tightly laced. No matter what anybody thought, this is what I needed medically.

For the next several weeks, I rarely took the corset off except to eat and shower. I am certain that the rib immobilization helped speed my recovery. Within a few weeks I was almost completely weaned from pain pills, and within three months I was able to bicycle up a 1500-foot hill.

My first corset, which I had bought for my wife, was a 24-inch (61 cm) off-the-rack corset from Timeless Trends. My waist became very squishy and shrank rapidly from corseting, especially after I began exercising again. Soon that OTR wasn't curvy enough to hold everything in place, especially on bumpy roads. With all the extra room inside my thorax after my lung surgeries, my stomach was dancing around like a lottery ball whenever we drove, even on the relatively smooth freeway. I felt nauseated from the little bumps on the freeway that someone else normally wouldn't notice.

I searched high and low, but couldn't find an OTR corset that both fit my ribs and that also held my abdominals firmly in place. I therefore ordered a 22-inch (56 cm) custom Victorian underbust (by Sheri Jurnecka from Romantasy). The first time that I was laced into my custom corset, I was instantly hooked and have never looked back. It felt taboo to be molded into such a feminine shape, but the pain relief was real. After several months of 22/7 lacing, both corsets quickly closed.

I next ordered a 19-inch (48 cm) Bella underbust (by Sharon McCoy Morgan from Romantasy) to "stealth" in during the day, retired the OTR, and used the 22-inch corset for sleeping. I now have five custom corsets of 19–23 inches (48–58 cm) in the waist; in public, I always stealth lace, except on very rare special occasions.

I probably corseted over 6000 hours during the first year, most of it very tightly laced. I corseted everywhere, even climbing ladders all night long at work. I unlaced only for workouts, for showers, and for cool-down times after workouts. Since then, I have laced less regularly and have even gone months without lacing, after hospitalizations or for various other reasons.

After my thoracic surgeries, the left side of my ribcage was over an inch smaller than my right side. Since then, over the years, tightlacing has helped to even out the difference between my ribs and has drawn in my floating ribs a little. My natural waist shrank dramatically, from over 30 inches (76 cm) after my surgeries, down to 23 inches (58 cm). My newest corsets are larger in the ribs, as my right lung has expanded to fill the void where my left lung used to be, and my "underbust" measurement has grown. My stomach and other lower organs have jockeyed around and occupied the void too.

In addition to the pain relief, help with nausea, and comforting compression to help me sleep, I have also recently found that corseting can eliminate the dizziness that I used to encounter sometimes due to low blood pressure.

I have also corseted to help recover from back injuries. For instance, when "bouldering" recently in Yosemite, one jump was just a little too far. The following morning I felt very tender on my thoracic spine and I instinctively laced up. The immobilization was what I needed to reduce the pain and let me heal.

Corseting has also comforted me psychologically. This was a huge help for a new cancer survivor. My wife and I were BOTH given months to live in 2002 and 2003. I am in remission from lung cancer and am back to riding centuries on my bicycle. My wife has had 5 brain surgeries, many years of chemo and radiation; she is still valiantly fighting brain cancer. We continue to go to our "his and hers" oncology appointments. The comforting corset hug has helped me sleep a little easier despite such very challenging events.

Over the years I have become very attached to my corsets and feel like my armor is off when I am unlaced. Summers are the most challenging, as I must compromise to avoid showing boning lines when going shirtless. I find myself wearing a weight belt a lot when working in the yard. I love backpacking with an extra small padded hip belt and snug shoulder straps. I can cinch in tightly and no one is the wiser.

I had been fascinated by lingerie since my teens, but hadn't dared to buy any for myself. Corseting has opened the doors and helped me accept and embrace my feminine side, even if I rarely express it to others outside of closed doors. I would never have had the courage to corset, had cancer not forced my hand. During the last year I have corseted, without stealthing, at a couple of events FAR from home. It was so very liberating and very encouraging to have such positive comments and questions from many people. However, I am still petrified of being exposed in my hometown.

I am very private, and have never discussed my corseting near home except with my doctors or therapists. Not even my best friend knows that I lace. As you can imagine, it is especially hard for guys to find others to talk to about corseting. In San Francisco it would be easier to strike up a conversation with neighbors, but not in the very conservative area where I live.

I have found a few friends online with whom I can finally openly discuss my love of corsets, even boldly feminine ones in fuchsia satin, without fear of ridicule. I have posted to various blogs and social media and have even contributed to books on corseting. I hope to continue contributing back to the community that has helped me so much, both physically and mentally. I always try to help others with sizing or other corset questions whenever I can. If you see me online, please feel free to ask me a question, or just to say hello. I love chatting with other enthusiasts when I have the opportunity!

FROM TIRED SCARS TO TERRIFIC NANA

MELISA R.

I've had several abdominal surgeries throughout my adult life. In my 20s I had a laparoscopic removal of my gallbladder. I had a medically necessary hysterectomy at the age of 30. In 2001 I had what was then designated as an "experimental weight loss surgery," called a Gastric Reduction With Duodenal Switch. It is a hybrid of a Gastric sleeve and a Roux en-Y (RNY) surgery. Through this surgery I was able to keep that all-important pyloric valve in my stomach, but they removed 90% of my stomach, stapling it and wrapping it in mesh.

Two years after achieving a substantial weight loss from 328 pounds (149 kg) to 150 pounds (68 kg), they did another surgery to remove eight pounds of excess panniculus, as well as perform a tummy tuck (removing my belly button in the process due to a marked loss of blood flow to it). This surgery re-opened the original 6″ (15 cm) scar from the weight loss surgery, which was from sternum to belly button, and I now had an anchor-shaped incision over the original scar, going vertically from sternum to pelvis and out each side to mid hip.

Due to circumstances beyond our control, we were forced to change insurance companies, and I no longer had Dr. Ara Keshishian, my original surgeon. So when I started not feeling well, I thought it was the flu. Unfortunately, it wasn't. After eight months of going through more doctors than we could count, never seeing the same doctor twice, and going to the urgent care every other week, I was finally referred to a bariatric surgeon.

This doctor ran no tests, and just said that it sounded like I had a blockage—one that none of the other doctors and their myriad tests managed to find—and that he'd have to reverse my original gastric surgery to cure the issue. HOWEVER, he was going "on vacation" so I'd have to wait a few weeks.

Meanwhile my daughters and husband had been watching me get paler and weaker by the day, barely able to eat or walk under my own volition.

So after that doctor appointment, I got on my computer and went to my online support group for Dr. Ara's patients, moderated by the head nurse in Ara's office. Usually I'm well spoken, with a flair for writing and an aversion to spelling errors. But this ranting, rambling letter to my group evidently worried several people.

Shortly after going to bed, my phone rang: it was the nurse who worked for Ara. All I can remember is she kept telling me to call my husband and get to Ara immediately.

The next thing I remember was seeing flashing lights through my closed eyelids and hearing familiar voices. I opened my eyes and saw Ara and my husband who were almost running down the corridor of a hospital I didn't recognize, pushing my gurney towards the radiology unit. My husband was explaining the whole situation to Ara, and Ara was getting more furious as the tale went on.

"Hi Ara," I said. My doctor greeted me, and then smiled and said "You're okay now." I then felt myself relax because I knew he wasn't going to let me die. We found that I did, indeed, have a blockage. A simple X-ray would have shown that the blockage wasn't where anyone was looking. That gallbladder removal in my 20s had scarred over, preventing the release of bile; therefore I was not absorbing food well in my small intestine—and because of my gastric surgery, there was only 75cm (30 inches) of my intestines left for absorption of *everything* I ate. My blood work showed I was literally *three days away from dying!*

They hooked me up to nine bags of different nutrients, and I woke up the next morning having no idea what had transpired the day before.

That morning, Ara was beyond livid regarding my current condition and the major conglomerate insurance company. I also was not stable enough to have surgery yet; all the fluids they gave me the night before had watered down my blood, and I required a blood transfusion.

When the conglomerate wanted me transferred to their facility, Ara took the call and you could hear him six rooms away yelling at them, accusing them of malpractice and "trying to kill [my] patient." He refused to release me several times and they quit asking and simply paid him after he told them about my condition and how a simple X-ray would have prevented eight months of suffering.

On my third day in the hospital, Ara was able to do the surgery, reopening the same scar. He noted a build-up of scar tissue, cleaned what he could, fixed the blockage, kept me in the hospital for another week, then sent me home.

Two months later, after changing our insurance to ensure he was on the list, I was still having problems eating, keeping food down, etc. Tests were done and Ara then made note that our intestines are like skin: they are elastic to a point, but once they are stretched beyond all they can stand, they no longer return to the size they should. Therefore I had the intestines designed for a 328-pound person, in the body of a 138-pound person—so when I ate, my intestines folded over themselves, causing blockages. I was once again opened up (in the same scar, sternum to pelvis) and had three feet of intestines removed.

Four days after returning home from that most recent surgery, I found that I was unable to use the restroom in any capacity and my husband took me to the local Urgent Care. I was declined a medical helicopter flight to Ara's hospital, and my surgery was assigned to a doctor who was unacquainted with the heavily modified layout of my insides.

I woke up in the ICU with an ostomy bag attached to my abdomen and another 12-inch long incision on the same tired scar. I freaked out! Finally a doctor came in, explaining that I had an intestinal leak that had healed itself, but my duodenum had swollen to ten times its normal size; the bag allowed excess air to escape. Yes … I had a "fart bag." However, in order for that bag to be removed, it needed to scar over so as not to cause another leakage. I just knew I'd need another surgery because I already had quite an extensive web of scar tissue already. Sure enough, three months after the bag was removed, I was in Ara's operating room having my intestines unwound from that scar (re-opening the same scar again) and he inserted more mesh, hoping to contain the scarring.

Then the other issues … I'm sure you're wondering, "How could there be more?" Well, during the time between the original weight loss surgery and the removal of the panniculus, I was doing laundry and felt a painful pop in my back. A CT scan confirmed that I had herniated a disc. The doctor I saw gave me epidural injections and wrote off the injury as part of my deteriorated health from the malnourishment. I ultimately ended up in a wheelchair, unable to walk due to the weakness and pain.

Shortly after my stomach issues seemed to finally settle down, we moved from California to Kentucky. I then went to a spine institute where they discovered that my disc space between vertebrae L4-L5 was completely gone—the vertebra in my lumbar area was sitting atop the other one at an angle that jutted the bone itself into my spinal cord. This caused not only severe pain but also nerve damage and loss of blood flow to my right leg. I had back surgery—and to insert the cage, they entered through my abdomen where my right ovary should be. The surgeons were guided through my abdominal cavity by Ara over the phone. The cage was inserted and a fusion at L5-S1 was done, but ultimately failed.

Now my back muscles have to compensate for the lack of any useful abdominal muscles due to the numerous surgeries, and my back is already stressed from slight scoliosis and Degenerative Disc Disease. More recently I was diagnosed with bursitis in my hips and

Degenerative Joint Disease. I now have a spinal cord stimulator, which is a small implant in my back that sends electric currents to my spine to manage the pain.

All this brings me to corsets.

I've been wearing a corset almost every day since January 2015. It has alleviated so many issues! Before wearing corsets, I used to be able to go out but, as my husband likes to say, I had a time limit of three hours before I became lethargic. My kids and granddaughters would be bummed out because fun time was over; Nana was tired.

Now, I can outlast my daughters sometimes! I can stand straighter, have more confidence, and my anxiety is down because I don't fear someone accidentally hitting the stimulator implant in my back. I've been on 50 micrograms of Fentanyl for over 15 years, and I'm proud to say I only take a pain pill now instead of using the patch. My range of motion has improved much when wearing a corset. This was just with my OTR corset, so I could only imagine what a custom corset could do to support more of my abdominal muscles and to hold in the scar! My thoracic muscles still spasmed from lack of support with my OTR corset, so I knew it was time to upgrade to a customized corset.

I had the opportunity to have two bespoke corsets made by The Bad Button, here in Kentucky—and what a difference a bespoke versus an OTR has made! My abdomen is completely supported, my back is completely supported and my hips are also supported! I feel great and I'm able to tolerate those ten-hour-long car rides to see my grandchildren. Before trying a corset, I would be in tears from the pain after two hours of driving.

Thanks to my corsets, I have a life of less pain and anxiety—and I can be "fun Nana" to my grandbabies!

CORSETRY FOR ILEOSTOMATES

ALISON CAMPBELL, CORSETIÈRE ~ CRIKEY APHRODITE

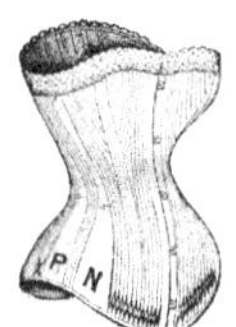

As a bespoke corsetiere, I get many unusual and interesting requests. The best ones, however, involve challenges that will really impact the client's quality of life. One of the most memorable for me was a request for a corset from a young woman with a stoma.

It's always rather nerve-wracking getting a request that relates to a medical issue. No corset maker wants to do more harm than good, obviously, and I'll be honest—I strongly considered declining the order. It's a bad idea to take on such an order unless you're very sure of what you're doing.

The thing that reassured me in this instance was that the client was a doctor. She therefore was very informed, happy to sign a disclaimer, and gave me the confidence to work with her and be guided by her. She was a rather amazing woman, completely unperturbed by it all, and had a sharp sense of humor. You've got to love someone who decides that if she has to carry around spare bags, then they'll damn well be stored in a designer pouch!

There were several main requirements, the priority being access to the bag, of course. A modest waist reduction, adjustability over the bag, avoidance of boning over the bag, and a removable, protective washable panel in case of leakage. I went away and researched, scribbled, considered and then decided the most obvious place to look for solutions was in antique maternity corsets. Such corsets usually involved various additional laced openings so the corset could be substantially adjusted. The ideal solution!

It made no aesthetic sense to only place lacing panels on the bag side, so I mirrored it on the other side. The only difference was that the non-bag side did not fully open, whereas the panel over the bag could flip right up and had an overlapping panel behind it, with a soft removable waterproof membrane attached to it. The client was very slim, so it was tricky placing the opening and giving protection from the eyelets, etc. But a combination of expandable gussets and the underlying panel gave maximum adjustability and protection. The lines of narrow ribbon laced openings also gave a very pretty effect. The client was delighted. It gave her a smooth line with no telltale bump and, crucially, it didn't look like anything other than an uncommon corset design.

Some time later I was approached by another client for a similar corset. What would the odds be you'd think! However, unfortunately the rate of stoma operations on young women in Scotland is rather high. The reasons for this are as yet uncertain, but there are approximately 120,000 ostomates living in the UK, and over 3000 operations per annum are performed in Scotland alone. It was lovely to be able to answer her hesitant query at the consultation with a resounding, "Yes! I've done that before."

This client was rather less comfortable with her condition than my previous client, and her prime aim was to conceal. It was actually easier to make than the first one. This was partly because I'd done it before, but also because she had a curvier figure and there was therefore more room to center a panel over the bag. We were able to have just one laced opening over the front hip on each side. With silver-tipped laces over the black satin, the finished corset looked more pin-up than aid—and it did the trick, smoothing over the bump of the bag, and offering a little compression, which the client told me felt good.

One of the most wonderful experiences as a maker is to see your results make a difference to someone emotionally as well as physically. My client looked amazing and I believe it really helped her cope with some events where she'd otherwise have been very self-conscious.

So, it a was huge learning curve for me, but an incredibly worthwhile one. I was delighted to have helped my clients and to have been able to add a small boost to their quality of life.

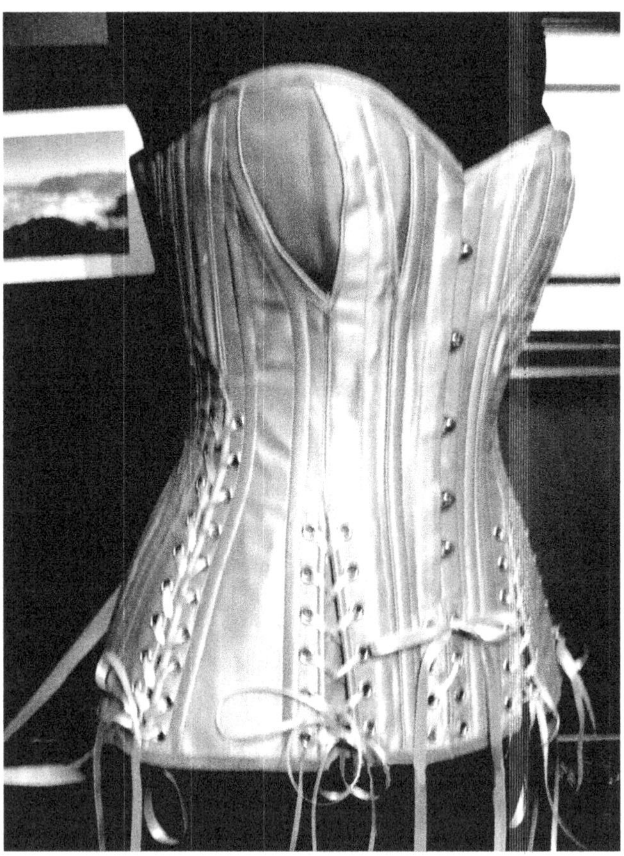

Crikey Aphrodite bespoke overbust for the physician (her first ostomy client)

PART XI

ARMOR

THE CORSET THAT SAVED MY LIFE

D'ARCY R.

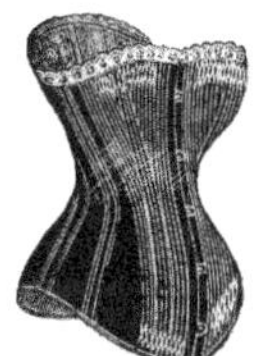

In the fall of 2010 I was visiting my hometown of Los Angeles and enjoying an evening out to dinner with friends. My outfit for the occasion was a silk 1940s New Look dress and a cotton canvas underskirt worn over my most recent acquisition: a corset by Hoss Masoumi of Hoss International. It was a custom underbust with a mid-weight cotton interior layer and silk satin exterior; eight boned panels, each containing two individually pocketed spiral steel bones, as well as four additional bones along the lacing panel; and an extra-wide spoon busk at the front.

Returning home on the freeway, a car in front of me in the fast lane slammed on its brakes, causing me to swerve to avoid rear-ending it. My car slammed into the center divider, with the steering wheel's airbag knocking me unconscious. While I was passed out, my car ricocheted off the divider and skidded across all lanes of the freeway, finally reaching the banked shoulder, where it rolled into the ditch.

I opened my eyes several minutes after my car had come to rest, unbuckled my seatbelt, and climbed out of my car (on its side, the door partially ripped off). I walked toward a group of motorists who had stopped to call 911 for me. Upon seeing me, one man shouted

"Oh my God! We thought you were dead!" I was dazed, shaken, and sore, but otherwise I felt fine.

Despite this, when the paramedics arrived, I was taken to the emergency room. The paramedic cut me out of my dress and, upon discovering my uncommon underpinning, asked, "I'm sorry, what is this?"

I was still a bit out of sorts and I think I responded, "It's a corset ... for my waist...." He started to try to cut it, immediately hit one of the steel bones, and asked, "How do you take it off?!"

I think my answer was a groggy "There's metal in there, but it's not all metal, but that part is ... but don't cut it, please, I can take it off...." I started to sit up to undo the busk, which caused every person in the ambulance to shout "DON'T MOVE." (Even with my brain working at a fraction of its normal capacity, I was STILL worried about protecting my corset!)

At the emergency room, I was examined and tested for concussion, broken bones, internal bleeding—but outside of some scattered bruises and tiny cut to my forehead that required a pair of stitches, I was found to be entirely unharmed. My corset had been, unfortunately, cut off me.

The police had contacted my mother when I was taken to the emergency room. When she arrived, I was still on the stretcher with my neck stabilized, crying. She, naturally, ran up, asking "Oh my God, how badly are you hurt?!" Sobbing, I responded "No ... I'm fine ... but they cut up my new underbust!"

The attending doctor wás beyond impressed, surprised, confused ... and as I was preparing to leave the hospital, he returned with the slashed remains of my corset, asking if he could line it up with my body to check something.

When he did, he pointed out all of the places where the bones and busk had bent and dented, places where my ribcage smashed against the steering wheel, the door to my car, and the gear shift when the car rolled. He explained that having my corset on must have been a bit like wearing a metal cage around my torso that had absorbed and distributed the various hits while protecting my body. Based on the placement of the bends and the light bruising on my body, he guessed that I would have had broken ribs without the corset.

He also asked if my corset helped with my posture. He explained that it was likely responsible for my having avoided severe whiplash and back injury during the initial impact and after I was knocked out, as I was held in proper posture by the corset and couldn't go limp and suffer the jarring movements from the crash. Shaking his head in amazement, he said "Honestly, I didn't know people wore those anymore, but now I almost feel like I should be recommending them! Why don't NASCAR drivers wear those things?"

The corset was, obviously, ruined after it was cut off me, but I still keep it in my corset drawer today, bent and shredded. Every time someone says, "Wearing that thing can't be good for you," I pull out that pile of steel and fabric and say, "Actually, this one saved my life!"

SAVED FROM PARALYSIS

LILIANA G.

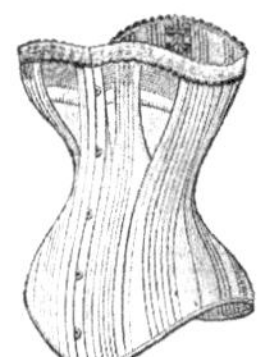

My name is Liliana, and I live in Chihuahua, Mexico. My story is about the use of corsets while driving, and how my corset might have saved me from paralysis.

I was 43 years old when the accident happened. On July 29th, 2014, I was driving on Mirador Avenue—the street is on a very steep hill, so it's necessary to step heavily on the accelerator to be able to maintain speed at the steepest spot without rolling back.

As I approached the intersection at Lisboa street, I saw that I had the green light ... but looking across Lisboa, I saw a truck that was not slowing down as it was approaching the intersection: it was going to run the red light. I repeatedly pressed the horn, and I stepped hard on the brakes and tried my best to stop the car, but the impact was inevitable.

The truck was long and took up the width of the two lanes on my road, so I could not avoid hitting it when I got to the intersection. My car's hood ended up underneath the semi-trailer.

Luckily, I had not only my seat belt to protect me, but also a corset that my daughter had lent me. I used to wear it every now and then because I have a herniated disc that causes severe back pain. The corset helps me maintain a good posture and this keeps the pain at a minimum.

The day of the accident, after the police and the insurance company finally arrived, my neck and back were both in a lot of pain. The police sent me to the medical facility in their office. (In Mexico, we must go to the police station to declare car accidents.) I went to the orthopedist and, after taking a few X-rays, the doctor told me that I had a 3rd-grade sprain in my back (which means some tearing of the ligaments).

To my surprise the specialist told me that I was very fortunate to have been wearing a corset, because the impact was so hard that I could have ended up paralyzed from the waist down. The corset acted like armor that protected my lumbar spine.

Ever since the accident, I take comfort in wearing the corset that saved me. I wear it every day, even if I am not in pain, and I am very thankful for the fact that I still can walk.

MY ARMOR, MY WEAPON

ASHANTI C.

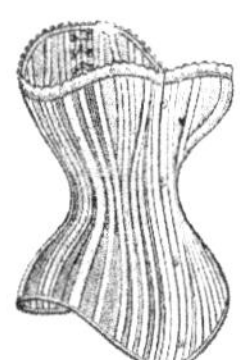

I don't remember what first attracted me to corsets. In a way, I think it all goes back to the film *My Fair Lady*, based on G.B. Shaw's play, *Pygmalion*. As a quiet, self-contained child, I was fascinated by the idea of transforming myself from an ugly duckling to a swan. That movie taught me that there is more to being a swan than just looking the part, but that doesn't necessarily mean that you have to give up on yourself.

When I wear a corset, I feel like Eliza Doolittle at the ball: I'm still a little shy behind my pretty shape and attractive walk, I'm still a bit awkward in my own skin, yet all around me others whisper and wonder whether I'm a princess. When I wear my corset, flaws of face or figure no longer exist, verbal gaffes are no longer problems, and the clumsy weird girl is transformed into a confident, outgoing woman who can do anything.

When I started wearing a corset, people started perceiving me differently. And that improved perception felt so good that I wanted to actually become that confident, outgoing person. In fact, I've worked to become her. In my corset I've been able to push myself to do things out of my comfort zone, things that I would have dreaded without it, and these accomplishments have made me more of who I want to be.

I still second-guess myself in social situations and say and do very silly things (both in public and private), but because of the confidence that wearing a corset has given me, I am a little more like that confident, outgoing woman I want to be, even when I'm not in my corset.

All of this says nothing about how corsets helped me with my back and hip pain, helped me to improve my posture, lessened the frequency of my debilitating migraine headaches, and protected and supported me after a cystectomy that led to a hernia.

More recently, my corset had played a part in saving me from a head injury as well:

On my way home from work on a rainy fall afternoon, I decided (rather unfortunately) to take a short cut by pulling my bike off the road and going down the sidewalk instead. The streets in this area were all one-way, and taking the sidewalk would save me from having to go all the way around the block just to get to the other corner. At the intersection, the pedestrian light changed, and I began to cross—only to see a large SUV exiting a parking lot in my way. I stopped to let it go by and watched the cars in the road dwindle away. When I saw there weren't any more cars but the SUV was still waiting, I assumed that the driver was waiting for me to pass, as some drivers give right of way to pedestrians and bicyclists. I crossed in front of the vehicle and was shocked to see that it was getting closer.

The next thing I knew was pain, and I was on the ground, but thankfully I was able to catch myself. I had been whipped around and my legs were useless (not broken, just sore, thankfully), but I was corseted at the time, and the stability around my middle allowed me to escape head injury in what could otherwise have been a horrible situation.

I wore my corset daily for the next month, and it assisted me in recovery from the accident. It helped me to remain stable and distribute my weight, when I couldn't put pressure on one leg. Later, when I was beginning to walk again, the corset helped me avoid significant back pain from leaning on makeshift canes, and later still from limping around on my own. My corset made a horrible situation much less stressful.

Corsets are my armor, and sometimes my weapon—and this is only the beginning.

THE ART OF BARTITSU (A THWARTED MUGGING)

BIRGIT DEADLYGLAMOUR ~ DEADLY GLAMOUR JEWELLERY

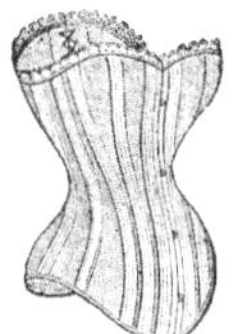

I realized recently that I own a considerable number of corsets. I started about 20 years ago, with the usual off-the-rack Vollers and Axfords purchases, and the collection grew when I started working in the same building as corsetiere Velda Lauder. I realized I fitted into her sample sizes—an advantage of having an incredibly squeezable waist. I'm not tiny by any means—I'm 1.74m tall (5′8″)—but I can lace into tiny waist corset sizes. It's innate, somehow.

Fast-forward to now, and my collection fills two sizable drawers in a chest, and contains such showpieces as two corsets by Dark Garden and a second-hand True Grace by the late Michael Garrod.

In spite of all this, I only own a single "head-to-toe" designer gown with a corset; everything else is "buy the corset and create an outfit around it." I make clothes and jewelry, and in spite of having been around for a bit, I still go out and dress up with a vengeance.

This particular ball gown was made by Wyte Phantom: it is vaguely late-Victorian looking, mostly purple and black, with a huge feather collar. Again, a lucky find: it was supposed to be for somebody else and a photo shoot, but it just fitted me, and I simply had to have it.

It was the perfect outfit for Gala Nocturna 2015. That year the theme was "Swan Lake," and it was probably the best dressed party in Europe.

The event was held in a huge chandelier-festooned ballroom in Brussels, and I think I looked quite agreeable, when measuring myself up against professional costume designers who had worked on their outfits for months. A whole night of dancing, absinthe drinking, and merriment: truly one of the most impressive parties I've ever attended, and I've been to quite a few indeed.

The evening was over, and unfortunately I was not in the same hotel as the rest of my friends, but in one which was a bit further away. No matter—I'm a Londoner, and have been living in a decidedly edgy part of town for almost 20 years. I'm not easily scared. It was around 30–40 minutes walking distance from the ballroom to the hotel, and so I put a coat and scarf over the corset and ball gown, changed my dancing shoes to athletic shoes, and set off.

A bit of fresh air is good after a long party, and prevents me from having a hangover in the morning. I do this all the time in London too, walking to the nearest spot of public transport, or even walking home (if less than an hour away). I don't like going in taxis late at night on my own, especially if I can't check where that taxi driver is going. I feel safer walking on my own.

All proceeded as planned. Unfortunately, what I had forgotten to take to the party were my glasses, as I was wearing colored contact lenses and long fake eyelashes. So, it was a bit problematic to look at road signs and the area maps dotted around Brussels and check that I was still on the right way back to the hotel.

And then I was outside a Brussels underground station, at the top of some stairs. It was well lit for a change, and I suddenly realized that somebody was behind me, mumbling something.

I turned around. It was a small young man, wearing a blue Puffa down jacket and a red hat that made him look not unlike Papa Smurf. He mumbled some more.

I do speak French and Vlaams (Dutch), but not all that well, and the brain cells were a bit otherwise occupied after having had so many drinks at the party. So I just said, "I'm sorry" in French, and proceeded down the stairs to get away from him.

He came after me. I picked up speed, so he wouldn't get to me before I was all the way down, and turned around at the bottom of the stairs, shouting, still in French "What do you want, leave me alone!" (I was quite proud of my language capabilities at that moment—it's amazing what the brain comes up with to distract you when you're supposed to think of other things).

At which point, he kicked me in the stomach with full force. I remember the thought, "Another one of those guys who has seen too many kickboxing videos; he should really practice a bit more, that looked sloppy."

And, of course, nothing happened. I didn't keel over in pain as Mr. Inept Mugger doubtlessly expected. I was wearing a fully steel-boned corset, which is as good as armor. A hard kick in the stomach did no damage to me whatsoever.

His face was a picture of surprise.

I stood my ground—running away is not a good idea, as you'll have the mugger at your back where you can't see him, you will be quickly out of breath in a corset, and there was no help in sight anyway. He tried to slap my face, and got me, a bit, on the ear. It hurt, but not too badly.

Suddenly, the adrenalin kicked in. I have been doing historic martial arts for quite a few years now, and what I do especially is Bartitsu—a Victorian style of self-defense, famously mentioned in the Sherlock Holmes novels. It shows how to defend yourself against the ruffians and ne'er-do-wells in the street, armed only with a walking cane or even your bare hands. I didn't have a cane with me, and didn't want him to get close enough to grab my bag, which I was still carrying over my right shoulder. Instead, I slammed my left arm and hand forwards, fingers straight ahead, and poked him in the eyes with full force.

I remember feeling the moisture on my fingertips, and thinking "I got you right, and this will hurt you even more tomorrow, you little bastard. And if I'm lucky, I scratched your eyeballs with my fingernails, and you will have to go to the hospital with an infection."

He tried to hit me again, but I just did a standard normal arm block, where the opponent hits your lower arm instead of your face. The "automatic training response" had obviously kicked in.

This was the point when the mugger decided it was all getting too much effort, he turned around and ran, up the stairs, and off into the Brussels night. The whole encounter had lasted probably not longer than five minutes.

I was flustered, of course. I waited a bit until I had cooled down and proceeded to the hotel, where I realized I had lost a button from my coat—the only casualty of the evening from my side. For some unknown reason, I was thoroughly and irrationally angry about this.

I slept for a few hours, met up with my friends again in the morning, told the story to one or two ("You wouldn't believe me what happened on my way home, some idiot tried to mug me...") and was thoroughly surprised that my story made the rounds in the whole group within the day, as I honestly thought it hadn't been such a big deal. I didn't even consider going to the police, as, well, nothing had really happened.

My Bartitsu group friends were even more impressed when I told them the story back home, and I'm now moderately famous around Bartitsu practitioners as the living proof that a Victorian method of self-defense can still be put to good use in real life, over a hundred years later.

Yes, a corset protects you from the ruffians in the street today too, just like it did a century ago. I bet the mugging Smurf will not consider lone women in the street as an easy target anymore. I hope he got an eye infection, too.

I'm going to Gala Nocturna again this year, but it's in Ghent this time. Also, my hotel is around the corner from the ball venue. Just in case.

Yes, of course I will wear a corset.

PART XII

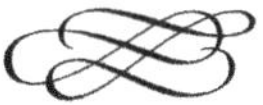

BODY POSITIVITY

A BEAUTY OF MY OWN

A. LEIGH

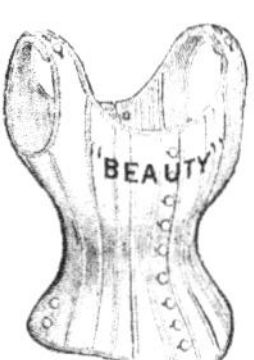

I have atypical anorexia nervosa—a little-known eating disorder characterized by restriction of food, like the better-known anorexia nervosa diagnosis, but not necessarily accompanied by severe weight loss. Because of the cyclical nature of my illness, and my PCOS (polycystic ovarian syndrome), I never became underweight. However, I have many of the symptoms of other eating disorders, including malnutrition (at the worst point of my illness my nails shredded off and I lost my hair in clumps), dizziness and fainting spells, and body dysmorphia.

Body dysmorphia is difficult to explain to anyone who hasn't experienced it. It means that what I see when I look at myself isn't necessarily what's there, and that my impression of my own body can change quickly and with no warning. It's a scary, disorienting feeling, and it's a huge trigger for my eating disorder, as I feel tempted to try to control my uncontrollable, shifting sense of myself.

I've been in recovery for about a year now. The cure for my atypical anorexia was lots of therapy, hard work, careful self-examination, and help from a nutritionist. However, none of these helped much with my body dysmorphia.

The only thing that really helped with that was corsetry. I first wore a corset for a theatre performance and loved it so much it soon became a hobby. I loved that I could finally feel some control over how I looked. I loved the glamorous silhouette it gave me, making my curves feel beautiful for the first time. And most of all, I loved the sense of self it gave me. In crises of dysmorphia, I could put my corset on and feel secure about the size and shape of myself, just the way I am. It provided a temporary relief, as well as simply being a beautiful garment I loved to wear.

I hope to one day to own a custom-fitted corset to wear regularly, but in the meantime my current corset remains both a pleasure and a necessity in my life. I went through a brief period where I wore it under my clothes on a daily basis, but unfortunately it couldn't stand up to such heavy wear. Now I save it for special occasions, whether it's when I really need to feel the sense of control and definition it gives me, or when I simply want to dress up and feel great about myself, exactly the way I am.

Corsets are often seen as a tool of oppression: a way to force women to change their bodies. However, to me a garment I can choose to wear or not wear at any time is much less oppressive than our new cultural ideal of thinness—sometimes attained through dieting that often, as in my case, approaches the point of starvation.

I expect that corsetry will always be an "alternative" form of beauty and fashion, but to me it has been an empowering way to understand and embrace my body, to have a kind of beauty that feels as if it were truly my own.

WESLEY

PENNY "UNDERBUST" BROWN

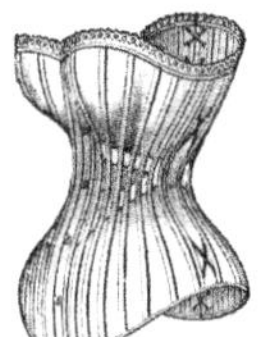

I can reduce my relationship with corsetry down to the simple concept of feeling in control of my body. There's a lot more to it than that, but the most basic, core feeling that I get from putting a corset on is control over my own flesh.

As a female in society, it can often feel as though you're not allowed to have control over your body. Everyone spends so much time telling you how it should look, or what you should do to take better advantage of your looks. But the sensation for me of placing that steel-boned artwork over my trunk, and feeling it tighten into a protective, almost armor-like shell, gives me a distinct feeling of power, safety, and complete authority over my own self. This sovereignty of my own body is what I discovered several years ago, when I first started waist training.

However, the era of my life prior to this was not particularly enjoyable. I was in a foreign country within a foreign country: an Australian woman living on an American military base, located in a remote area of Japan. I was also trapped in an incredibly small apartment, with no driver's license, in an area where walking wasn't an option to reach anything worth visiting. So, in a short time I gained a large amount of weight, and exacerbated the hell out of my social anxiety. I should also mention that I have PCOS (polycystic ovarian syndrome) and generally terribly balanced hormones, so excess weight comes to me very easily, and doesn't have any interest in leaving.

As I'm sure you know, beloved reader, our society likes to place a lot of value on our body weight (or, to be more specific, value is inversely correlated to weight). So, for me, my own perceived value went down as the numbers on the scale went up. My stress and fear of judgement steadily worsened in those eight months between moving to Japan and putting that corset on seriously for the first time.

Enter my husband's first deployment. Now, I was already trapped indoors for much of the time, but when my husband deployed to the Middle East, I was stranded and isolated in a way that was almost crushing. I hit a very low point in my mental health.

About a week after my husband left, when I was feeling especially down on myself, I decided to try to do something positive and attempt to see myself through my husband's eyes by taking some saucy photos to send to him. This inspired me to pull out of the closet an item that I hadn't worn in years: a steel-boned corset that I'd gotten from a goth shop about four years earlier. I'd only worn it a handful of times, but when I left Australia for Japan I decided to bring it with me, as it had been a several-hundred-dollar purchase and I didn't feel like leaving it behind.

My corset would soon be dubbed "Wesley." That first day of putting Wesley on, I felt suddenly entirely in control of my own body. In hindsight I should have seen it coming, as I know my own psychology quite well—but there's so much more to it than just psychology. The physical feeling of wearing a corset that fits you is a very comforting sensation to some people. I, and many others, liken it to being hugged. It's an extraordinary feeling of comfort and safety.

There's the obvious immediate gratification of feeling that your body is smaller, which is of course incorrect, but it still reflects a rather dramatic redistribution of weight. There's also a certain pride and authority gained when wearing a corset, as it automatically changes your posture to communicate dominance and confidence.

In addition, there's something that I've noticed that could be interpreted as a form of escapism: it's the feeling that the target of criticism by others is not personal. When a fat person is insulted for being fat, often it's not something they have control over. Maybe in some vague way they could take that insult and get themselves to weigh less, but lifestyle changes are incredibly arduous, and there could be a slew of complicated underlying health conditions.

But when someone insults you for wearing a corset, or notices you for it, or makes you feel weird for it … it's easy to view the attack as on something external, and not part of you as a person. It's so much easier in general to take an insult about something that isn't an identifying part of your existence. I should have known this about myself, as it's the precise reason I started dressing as a goth in my teen years. People would insult my clothing instead of insulting my interests, such as reading or playing video games.

Not only that, but there existed this whole social group built around the persecution we faced for our clothing: the goth community accepted me into a culture of people, some of whom were facing very similar difficulties as myself. Corsetry was precisely the same. The corset community is one that is much smaller than the goth community, but it's also far more tightly knit.

That first time I put on Wesley, I underwent a massive metamorphosis in who I was. I lost many of my uncomfortable fears of the world. My social anxiety took a back seat to my personality for once, and I was able to reach out to the people in my world. Needless to say, I didn't much want to take Wesley off after experiencing this. So … I didn't.

For about four months, while my husband was deployed, Wesley stayed on my body at all times, apart from when I was showering or at the gym. My diet adapted by necessity to suit that of a waist trainer, and my lifestyle changed too.

The lifestyle and diet of a waist trainer is one I would liken (not in practice but in theory) to that of a body builder. You have guidelines that you follow, and if you deviate you lose a bit of progress, but overall, if you stick to the lifestyle you start seeing results. Some people have a predisposition to success and they progress more quickly, others see far slower results. The people, like me, with that predisposition tend to feel more encouraged to stick to it; so let's just say that my body felt like it was designed for waist training.

I started going to the gym religiously, every single day, sometimes twice if I was bored (remember, my husband was away and I had no social life). So along with my waist getting smaller, my entire body started to transform as well. I quickly got too small for my corset, so I altered it by hand as I shrank. Wesley shrank with me, and I modified it into more of an hourglass shape rather than the tube it had been before.

I realized that for me to be healthy (healthy as in getting physical activity, not losing weight—I do not directly correlate the two), I needed to feel good about myself to begin with. If I have low self-esteem, I don't feel inspired to fix myself, and I feel miserable and that I don't deserve to be happy. So for me, putting the corset on and feeling that confidence was a direct step towards getting my body into shape.

There is also a direct tie between weight loss and waist training for me, as continually wearing a corset has the effect of allowing less space in my abdomen for food.

Sadly, Wesley finally expired. It had been modified too much; its original waist measurement was 36 inches (91 cm), and its eventual size was 23 inches (58 cm). I had reduced my corseted waist circumference by thirteen inches in four months, and Wesley finally breathed its last breath. Too many steel bones broke, and its stitching had fallen to shreds. This coincided with my husband returning from the Middle East, so finding a new corset became less important than just enjoying being with my husband.

For me, feeling in control for that period of time changed my entire view of myself. I am no longer hung up about my body weight. I work out because I enjoy it, and I love looking at myself in the mirror, in a corset or totally naked. There's no fear for me there anymore. The truth is that I always found myself beautiful, but I was always so scared by the way the world viewed me, and I took that fear out on my body.

Corsetry genuinely changed my life in an incredibly positive way. I still frequently wear corsets, but as of writing this I no longer wear them 23 hours a day. Maybe someday in the future I'll do so again, but it's hard to find the time to strictly live by any lifestyle.

Something else that changed was that I now view corsets as part of my identity. So when someone attempts to put them down or spread misinformation, it's no longer something I can laugh off as just being something outside of me. They are important to me. They stirred a passion and a positive change in me, for which I am grateful.

I've met some of the most amazing people in the world thanks to corsets; my career began thanks to the confidence corsetry gave me; my mental and physical health has greatly benefited from them. Honestly, it seems a little astounding to me that an article of clothing that garners such hate within society could be so beneficial to me, but it's the plain and simple truth. Corsets for me are nothing short of lifesaving.

THE WOMAN WITH TWO WAISTS

MISS OYE

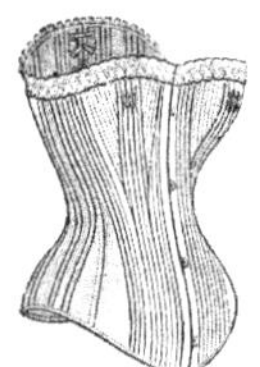

I've suffered from back pain from muscle imbalances for years. I would throw out my back several times a year, and the pain was often so bad that I was frequently unable to perform the exercises necessary to relieve the pain. When I was able to do my exercises, I could only do them lying down.

A great deal of my pain and discomfort was relieved while I was wearing a corset, and the more often I wore it, the less pain I was in, even when I wasn't wearing it! I could work longer hours, I could actually stand up for extended periods of time, and recently, I started taking dance classes and I'm happy to say I plan to continue dancing. I had given up taking lessons years ago because I thought I would never be able to dance without pain.

I haven't thrown out my back since I started wearing corsets; this is due to the muscle-strengthening exercises and the many measures I've taken against it ever happening again—but without my corsets I would not have been able to even begin such measures.

I have loved costuming since I was a child, so my fondness for corsets existed from an early age. But it wasn't until I started taking costuming and costume history courses in college that my apprecia-tion for different types of corsets and silhouettes was fully cemented.

It was through learning about the differences in popular silhouettes over time that I began to understand why everyone around me loved to try to convince me that I hated my own body.

You see, I like the way I look uncorseted. I'm muscular, and bulgy, and boxy, and curvy. I also like the way I look corseted. I can shape my body in ways that aren't possible without a corset, no matter how much weight I gained or lost. But we live in a society that wants people to have a single body image. The "you" that a person shows the world must be the ultimate and only "you" that exists or that is considered real. So for years I thought, because everyone would tell me, that if I sometimes wanted to look the way I do corseted, I must not want to look how I do uncorseted. I couldn't want both. But I did.

And then I did my research. The first day I spent hours double-checking to make sure I could lace myself tightly without permanently altering my size. I was worried that I had found myself in a "have your cake and eat it too" situation and that it was too good to be true.

I wanted a well-made, sturdy corset, so I thought a waist-training corset would be necessary. But whenever I looked them up, the results were about the process of waist training. No general information on waist training either—it was mostly people blogging about their personal experiences.

I didn't want my waist to change permanently! I wanted two waist sizes not one! I was discouraged, but thankfully I really liked corsets, so I persevered.

Eventually I started finding genuine corsetieres. Most corsetieres I've seen online are very open to giving out information, and for that I am eternally grateful.

Many people, who don't know better, think corsets are a magical and/or evil item that instantly begins to permanently mold or destroy your body. Many people who hate the idea of corsets are invested in creating an air of mystery around them to make newcomers nervous and wary.

But real information about corsetry is now open and readily available, significantly more so now than it was when I started my journey. There is no veil of mystery. The veil does not exist!

Looking at the way corsets are made and learning about corset wearing showed me that real waist training takes years of dedication and work. I also saw that many occasional corset wearers enjoy corsets for the exact reason I sought them out myself. I learned that liking two shapes for my body is not a paradox. It isn't even uncommon. It is possible. More than possible. Now it is my lived reality.

A MENTAL SHIFT

THAO P.

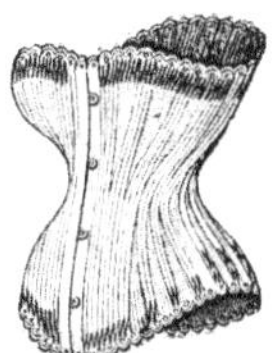

I had my first corset experience in mid-2015. That doesn't sound like long ago, does it? Still, I want to show others who are new to waist training that one doesn't need to wear a corset for a long time to see its benefits.

I was always aware of how my body looked in my teenage years. The reason is simple: women in my family are well-known for their curves. My mom and my sister often received compliments on their wide hips and round bottoms. So of course, I couldn't help but feel excited to hit puberty and see similar changes in my own body.

But as it turned out … nothing happened. I remember many times my aunt looked at my flat butt and teased me: "Owa, it seems like you don't possess any genes from your mother's side, my poor baby!" Then my mom laughed at her joke. We live in an Asian culture where people often comment on one anothers' appearance (and on many other personal issues), so I pretended to be chill and act normally—but inside, I felt like an outcast in my family.

So as soon as I entered college, I started dieting with the hope of slimming down my body and getting a "perfect" figure. Those extreme food restrictions led me to binge eating later on, and eventually to bulimia. While my parents slept in their room upstairs, I hid my dinner to eat alone at midnight, and tried to avoid noise during times of binging and purging since I didn't want to wake them up. It was a smooth act; I wasn't caught the whole time. But I got so tired of my sneaky behavior and the way my entire day revolved around food. Giving up this lifestyle was necessary, yet I didn't know how.

Then one day, I was randomly surfing on the internet and caught a video of some girl sharing her past three years' experience of wearing corset. At that point, I thought it could be the answer for my figure transformation. After speaking with Orchard Corset and asking for their suggestions for corset styles to fit my body, I bought my very first corset: a CS-301 waspie.

One thing I noticed was that whenever I wore my corset, I couldn't binge as much as I used to, which was good, as it helped me with reasonable portion control during meal-time. Even if I wanted to throw up, the compression from my corset made it impossible to do so unless I loosened its laces. It was a mind-blowing and extremely pleasant discovery.

I decided to wear my corset up to 16 hours a day to avoid the binging-and-purging temptation. I learned everything I needed from Lucy's website, from putting a pillow under my knees while sleeping to powdering my skin in order to minimize chafing. The fact that she put both videos and written articles on her website helped me to understand, since English is not my mother tongue.

There are still times when my emotions beat up my reasoning and I fall back on the old track, but they are becoming less and less common. Now I'm learning to control my urges—and I know it will be a long process that requires much patience and discipline, but the only way not to quit is to think positively.

Once I chose to wear a corset most of the time, I received many concerns and questions from other people. The first time my best friend grasped my waist and noticed something tough under my clothes, I was embarrassed and didn't quite know how to explain it to her, since a corset is such an unknown item in Viet Nam. I told her everything, from A to Z, and nervously awaited her criticism. Fortunately, she supported my decision and said there is no need to worry of what people think about me.

This reinforced my belief so much that I even wore my corset outside of my shirt as my Halloween costume last year. Of course, my classmates were very curious about it and some showed negative reactions, but hey, my best friend said I shouldn't care, so why should I?

The most incredible thing was that I decided to tell my mother the secret about my eating disorder. I wasn't sure why I did that; maybe I yearned for someone to sympathize with my feelings. She said nothing while I confessed to her, and it took her a while to understand what I was trying to say. This illness is not well understood in Southeast Asian countries and there are no real therapy centers to treat this in Viet Nam.

I burst into tears when I saw my mother's facial expression change, as I felt that I had indirectly blamed her for my bulimia, as well as the shame I felt from hiding it from her. We sat down, hugged each other and cried in silence that night. It was an intense moment but I felt released at the same time, as my secret was gone and my mother showed such compassion and forgiveness.

Sharing this story is also a way for me to open my heart to others and perhaps help someone who is going through the same problem.

I really love wearing a corset, not only because of how my body has changed (my waist has sized down and I look curvier even though my weight has stayed the same), but also because of the shift in my thinking. Thank you for reading my story!

UNCONDITIONAL BEAUTY

PHOEBE L., CORSETIÈRE

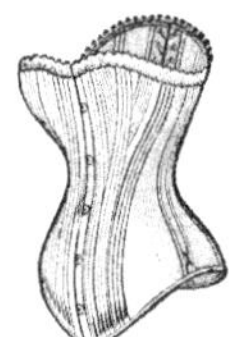

There are a few things in this world that, when you put them on, make you feel insanely feminine and sexy: a sassy pair of high heels, that perfect shade of red lipstick, luxurious stockings ... and a genuine, well-made corset.

I tried on my first authentic steel-boned corset only a few years ago. I borrowed it from a friend for an event. She taught me how to loosen the laces all the way up, fasten the busk, and lace myself into it. The process and garment itself were both fascinating and exhilarating. In fact, it was life-changing. I wore her corset for only one night and just a few hours. For that short time I was laced up as tight as I could possibly stand, yet I felt fabulous. When the night was over, I really didn't want to return my friend's corset.

So, of course, I had to have one of my own. However, after researching handmade corsetry for the next few weeks, I decided that, instead of purchasing a handmade corset, I would try making my own. And so I became a corset maker. For real: it's what I do. I've been making corsets for a little over three years, and I have been in the business of making corsets for two of those three years.

When I sewed my first corset, I was attending college for something entirely unrelated. I had no intention of becoming a professional corset maker. So why did I change my whole life-plan for corsets? What makes the job of corset making so special?

When I decided to sew for other people, my reasoning at the time was that I wanted to share with my friends (and the world) that special feeling that wearing a corset gives a person. I wanted to see people look in the mirror and smile at themselves, and I wanted know that I was a part of that little ego boost. It's the most amazing feeling to see a client put on her corset and see herself for the first time in it. It's indescribable, and so rewarding. Every stitch, every broken machine needle, every finger prick is worth it in that moment.

While the benefits of being a corset maker are numerous, probably the most profound and unexpected benefit is my recently found confidence. Not only have I gained confidence in my skills as a seamstress and designer, but I have found a body confidence that I never, ever had. I always lacked confidence when it came to my body. I grew up extremely skinny. I was bullied from a very young age and always felt insecure about my weight when I was young and thin, and again insecure about my weight as I grew more plump after having children. I was never happy with how I looked. Honestly speaking, I used to look in the mirror and see something I hated.

The corset wearing community on the other hand is extremely body-positive. People often think that others wear corsets because they are unhappy with their shape, but that is far from the truth. The women that dominate these communities are strong and confident individuals who celebrate their curves.

In my corset making work, I do consultations and fittings, and I see bodies every day. I see bodies of all shapes, sizes, and genders. I see how people view their bodies, in and out of corsets. It may sound strange, but the more bodies that I see, the more I realize that my own body is just as beautiful as the ones that I am building corsets for. Every person I work with has a unique shape and proportions; and I can honestly say that I have never worked with a client that I didn't find beautiful. Corset making has opened my eyes to individual beauty in others ... and subsequently, individual beauty in myself.

I wouldn't trade that for anything.

KNOWING ONE'S WORTH

KIKI

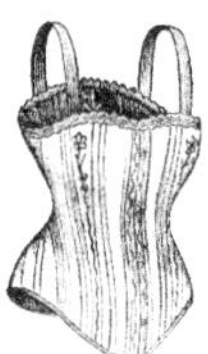

Corseting has become something very precious in my life. I've been lacing for nearly three years now, and I've become very insistent about lacing up at least every other day for a good number of hours. I love the corsets I own, I love the feeling of wearing them, and I love the way they make me look.

I struggle with depression, body dysmorphic disorder, and an eating disorder every day of my life. They're things I've dealt with for the better part of a decade, but only in the past few years did I start seeking treatment for it.

When I started researching shapers 4–5 years ago, I was only looking for something that would cinch my waist in a little bit. I was looking for something closer to the spandex undergarments that are sold abundantly, and I thought, "Huh. Maybe I could buy one of those stretchy things and it could hold in my tummy and make me feel a little bit better about my body image."

But then I found pictures of corsets. Real corsets. I knew, to an extent, that some people still wore them, but I didn't know why. Costuming? Back support? I was curious and decided to read a little bit about them. I knew only as much as most other people did about corsets, and I was highly aware of the social stigma against them: how some people consider them tools of torture to oppress females.

I fell in love with corsets nonetheless. I fell in love with the way that they look, with the craftsmanship that goes into making each and every piece, with how people who wear them seem to love them in spite of the stigma. Everyone that I've seen who owns a corset seems enthusiastic and positive about them. And I love that it is their choice to wear a corset—our choice to wear a corset.

After a year of drooling over those gorgeous pictures, I broke down and bought a corset from Dark Garden in San Francisco. Even though it took a bit of maneuvering to get there on my free weekend, and I ended up spending most of the money I'd made over the summer, it was extremely important for me to buy my first corset in person.

My favorite feature about my corset is that outstanding curve—you know the one I'm talking about—that hip shelf. My cinched waist accentuates everything above and below and makes me look like a pinup.

I try very hard to not let my corset become a crutch in my battle with mental illness. If I genuinely feel terrible about myself, or even just sick, I won't wear it. The corset hasn't solved all of my body image difficulties; there are still days where even when I wear my corset, I'm still not happy with myself; but that's something I'm dealing with and I take it day by day.

But the days when I do wear my corset, it gives me the biggest confidence boost in the world, one that I wouldn't otherwise have. And even just owning the two corsets in my collection makes me happier than anything. They were absolutely worth the investment, and they remind me that I'm worth it too.

BREAKING THE CYCLE

ANA L.

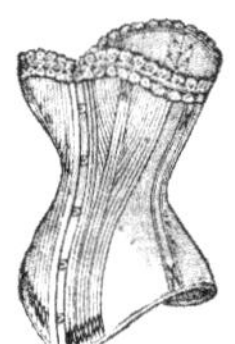

As strange as this sounds, corsets have helped me with my mental health and allowed me to love myself again.

To put it frankly, I've always had a very bad body image. I recall spending far too much time sitting in front of the mirror, staring at everything I hated. Because of this loathing of my body, I had a tendency to believe that people passed judgment on me as well, which consequently led to my distancing myself from others. My self-induced isolation was the beginning of a very lonely period, and this loneliness deepened my depression.

It was a vicious cycle. As my body image worsened, I distanced myself more, and this was followed with more depression, and downward it spiraled. As the condition progressed, I began to self-harm. To this day I believe that the self-harming was a consequence of this untreated cycle of depression, isolation, loneliness, and self-hatred.

One day I was surfing on YouTube and I stumbled across some videos about corsets that sparked my interest. I quickly became very intrigued by the whole concept of corsetry in general. Not long after, I decided to purchase my first corset online, hoping that it might be able to help improve my body image.

I cringe when I look back on it, but naïve as I was at the time, I purchased a plastic-boned corset. Nevertheless, from the moment I put it on, I was in love. I instantly looked shapelier and, as I looked at myself in the mirror, I felt happier than I had in years. It may sound incredible, but I stopped self-harming. My body image improved and I wasn't afraid to take my jacket off in public anymore. Gradually, I began to get closer to people again. At last, there was an end to the cycle, and life began to improve.

When the plastic boning in my corset started to kink out of shape, I decided it was time for new one. Armed with more information, I decided to purchase a genuine corset with spiral steel bones. Now, being used to twisted plastic boning, the first moment I put on the smooth steel-boned corset, the comfort was a revelation. I couldn't stop grinning. I instantly felt amazing!

With my new genuine corset I felt much more confident than I had ever been before—especially since I am required to wear tight pencil skirts most of the time, the corset gives me a very flat abdomen. My tummy used to be one of my most hated areas, and now I no longer feel that I have to hide my tummy under my blazer.

One last benefit: Whenever I wear my corset, I always feel like I'm getting the tightest, warmest hug. It may seem strange to some, but I love it.

No matter how much you may hate yourself, or how lonely life may seem, or how deep into the darkness you seem to be, know that there is hope. Your cycle can be broken, and it may come in a most unexpected way.

OVERCOMING VULNERABILITY

DAKE K.

My name is Dake, and I'm 19 years old. As a student I spend much of my time sitting and writing; sometimes in uncomfortable chairs or with an unpleasant posture—which has eventually caused me back pain. I am also suspected of having hypermobile Ehlers-Danlos Syndrome.

I decided to give corsets a try, because my back pain was becoming excruciating and I knew I needed something to support my posture. I purchased my first corset a year ago. I do not consider it a waist-training corset, as it has the same waist measurement as my natural waist.

Before buying my first corset, I made sure to research the subject as much as possible, to compare information about different kinds of corsets, and to read other people's stories about how corsets helped with their back problems. Equipped with this knowledge, I then felt ready to buy one when I became a legal adult at 18. I am happy that I took the time to research as much as I did, and also glad that I made the purchase.

My posture is much improved and my back pain is gone. I don't even need to wear my corset around the clock. I wear it only when I need it to avoid back pain, especially when I know I will be required to do things in unpleasant positions.

I also have an anxiety disorder and, interestingly, my tummy is the area that causes most of the anxiety. Before discovering the world of corsets, I got severe anxiety if I felt any kind of pressure on my waist and tummy, even from high-waisted jeans or a belt around my waist. The tummy is such a vulnerable part of the body; I found it very uncomfortable and scary to feel anything against it. I couldn't hold my own hand to my abdomen, because even that caused me anxiety.

When I bought my first corset, I made sure to get one that was the same size as my natural waist, so that it would cause as little pressure as possible. I will admit, even that gave me a hard time as I tried to get used to the firmness against my tummy. I wore my corset during weekends, when I was a little more relaxed, because I didn't want to deal with any extra anxiety on top of school and other stressful things going on.

It took three months to be able to feel confident and comfortable in my corset, but I can say that it really did me a favor. It helped me to overcome my anxiety. I still have some anxiety about things, but I'm getting better day-by-day. I've even been wearing my corset outside my house. It was a huge step for me to feel the corset braced against my tummy as I went about my day and not feel anxious or have a panic attack.

The last way the corset helped me was with my body image. As with many other teenagers, I struggled with my weight and appearance. At the age of 17 I had decided that I wanted a perfect hourglass figure and a tiny waist, but I thought I had to lose weight to achieve this. I was already a skinny girl, but it wasn't long before my weight dropped to 42 kilos (92 pounds)—and even after all that, I still wasn't happy with myself. I realized that my body is naturally pear-shaped and I could never naturally create an hourglass figure. That is when I stopped the madness and started to restore my health by going back to my previously healthy weight.

After getting back to a healthy weight, I felt somewhat self-conscious and dysphoric because I could never have what I considered the perfect body for myself.

I had been interested in corsets for years thanks to Dita Von Teese, but between my lack of information and my tummy anxiety, I couldn't find a quality corset. But when corsets became more popular in recent years, I was finally able to research and buy a quality corset for myself.

Even though it did not reduce my waist, it still created curves. I saw myself in the mirror with a perfect hourglass figure and finally felt happy with what I saw—and I didn't need to lose weight to achieve it.

PART XIII

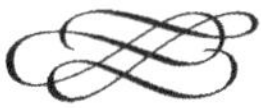

PREGNANCY & POSTPARTUM

FINDING MYSELF AGAIN

JULIA E.

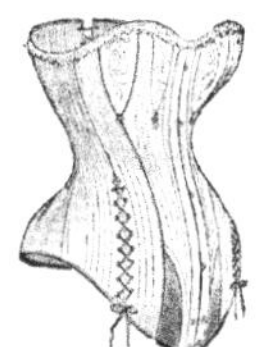

My first pregnancy took its toll on me. I had pelvic pain (Symphysis Pubis Dysfunction), which prevented me from walking more than absolutely necessary. I was depressed, constantly in pain, and constantly had food cravings. I was reasonably fit before my pregnancy, but once the baby was born I didn't have the muscle strength to lift her. Breast-feeding was a nightmare and I had constant headaches for the first three weeks.

Slowly but steadily I started walking again. The first time I went for a walk, it lasted only three minutes. Over time, I was able to walk for five minutes, then seven, then ten ... for the first time in my life, walking was a real means of working out. I got help from a physiotherapist, who helped me strengthen my core and adjust my posture, and my life improved dramatically. But after several months I still couldn't stand at a concert (which I loved to attend) or sit in front of a computer to any meaningful extent.

In addition, I never felt pretty. I had lost about half of the weight I had gained at the peak of my pregnancy, but I still was 10 kg (22 pounds) heavier than before. I love food and I easily get blood sugar drops. Portion control has never had any effect on me other than causing headaches and grumpiness. But this time I tried something else: I allowed myself to eat as much as I wanted, but chewed at half the speed. The food is just as delicious, but I took in fewer calories and I was full for the same amount of time!

I have a beautiful corset that I had used for clubbing before I was pregnant. One day I tried it on, and found that I could still squeeze myself into it. So the next time I had a party to attend, I laced it up and felt that my clothes fit me again. And I also realized that the pain in my back was gone, even after I took it off. It was great to give my muscles a break. It complemented my core fitness sessions and also made it easier to find the posture that my physiotherapist tried to teach me. I now had a better idea how to sit and stand even without it.

I started wearing corsets most of the time that I needed to sit or stand for long periods of time: at concerts, parties, in front of the computer, or just socializing while sitting at a table. At this point, I also realized that I became less hungry while wearing a corset.

After half a year of daily walks, I went running. The first time, I ran for two kilometers without stopping (and then I hit "the wall"). I used to run before, but I never found joy in it. But now, with better posture, a stronger core, and a slightly higher weight, it was fun. It felt empowering! My body was finally mine again.

It took two more years for my back to be mostly pain-free. I believe that the pregnancy caused my body permanent damage, but it also gave me an incentive to really invest in my body and deal with physical problems that had bothered me for years. I'm now five kg (11 pounds) lighter than I was before the pregnancy, with a toned body that can sustain a triathlon Olympic distance. My ten-year goal is to do an Ironman triathlon! I know, it sounds insane that corsets could help me with that, but I believe they have helped already.

These days, I no longer need to wear a corset for pain. I have a rectangular body shape, and sometimes when I want to feel more curvaceous I still choose to wear a corset. It's comfortable when I do a full workday sitting, or when I travel, but I no longer depend on a corset to feel like a normal person.

OUT OF THE DARKNESS

JANELLE

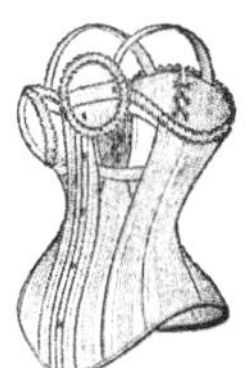

The physical problems that I deal with on a daily basis can be summed up as … "interesting."

My support system when growing up was inconsistent at best: the "support" was more in the form of criticism on how to be better, and I rarely received praise of any kind. I was already naturally shy, but I retreated into myself further because my parents' treatment made me feel beaten down and cowed at times. Because of this, I struggled with confidence issues, coupled with depression, into adulthood. My outside reflected my inside, as I physically shrank and slouched.

Fibromyalgia also runs in my family, so I'm in chronic pain every day. The pain starts in my back, running up into my neck and all the way down to my pelvis and through my legs and feet. I deal with oversensitive and irritated nerves all over my body, migraine headaches, and horrible fatigue which makes it an effort to even breathe some days. On top of everything else, I was dealing with postpartum depression. This was all prior to getting my first corset.

I originally became interested in corsets because I love the fashion and style of the Victorian and Edwardian era. My husband knew that I loved corsets, and he probably thought I was a little crazy, but he loved me in turn and said to go ahead and pick one out. When I put my first corset on I probably tightened it slightly more than I should have (beginner's mistake), but I was a little shocked at how I felt. I felt nervous, energetic, and slightly out of breath (since I was used to breathing more in my abdomen instead of higher in my chest). I took the corset off after ten minutes because I didn't know how to make sense of my feelings, and the rush of this new experience. But what I realized when I took it off was that I felt lethargic again, and—in some way—let down.

Later that day, I decided to give the corset another go. I put it on again (a little looser this time) and again felt more energetic and surprisingly happier. The nervousness from tying it too tightly was no longer an issue, and all I could think about was how ecstatic I was that my back and hips didn't hurt as much as they normally did. I always loved the look of corsets, but when I was buying my first one I had no idea that I would love the back support and the energy it gave me.

As the weeks went on and I was breaking in my corset further, I started noticing that I wasn't as grumpy or unhappy as I had been. I rationalized that since I was so insecure all my life and always wanting to be held, the corset was giving me the constant hug that I needed to feel secure and loved. Intellectually I knew I was loved and cared for, but the physical pressure of the corset, simulating a hug that lasted as long as wanted, was the reassurance I needed to hold me together during that time, especially during the darkest moments of my postpartum depression.

I ended up getting a second corset, and for quite some time I wore one or the other almost daily. I wore them under my clothes, as I didn't want to draw attention to myself. But as I continued to wear them, I started holding myself up a little straighter. When I went out, I no longer avoided conversations with other people outside my family, and I began feeling more confident in general. I almost never left the house without wearing one: wearing a corset made me feel close to invincible and capable of handling anything! I felt stronger, more self-reliant, and supported (in more ways than one). It was exactly the confidence boost I needed to finally start growing into myself. This self-realization may have started a little later for me than for others … but as I always say, better late than never!

At the time of this writing, we are expecting another child, so my corsets have been put away for now—I look forward to the day I can hold my new baby, and I also look forward to wearing my corsets again. I know that they will not only help with any postpartum depression, but I'm curious to see what they can do for my diastasis recti as well!

DIASTASIS RECTI CORRECTION

TABITHA R.

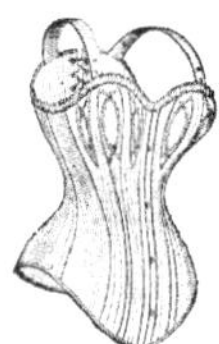

I had not heard that corsets helped with diastasis recti (abdominal separation) until many years after I started wearing them, when a friend with a much more severe case asked me if corseting helped. Both before and after my pregnancy, I wore my corset simply for the sake of wearing one.

I was an active-duty Marine for nine years, and bought my first corset the same year I joined. While in the Marine Corps I was a welder, which limited how often I could wear my corset. Wearing anything metal that has the potential to touch the skin is a serious safety hazard. This includes the steel bones in a corset. So my usual routine was to wear my corset during the first part of work, usually between 7 A.M. and noon, and then remove it at lunch before welding.

My comfort, activity level, and the type of work I did were the only factors that determined when and for how long I wore my corset. I did not notice any advantages or disadvantages of corseting from a purely physical perspective, but I enjoyed the aesthetics of wearing them.

I continued this routine for four years, until I became pregnant. I stopped wearing my corset, but continued my active Marine duties. My diastasis recti from my first child was a relatively mild case, measuring three finger widths between my abdominal muscles. It was only visible when I did yoga and performed any physical activities where my feet were planted and my abdominal muscles flexed. In those circumstances it was possible to see a mound on my stomach, because the muscles tensed at an upward angle.

Given my active duty status and the way that prenatal care is handled, I did not have a consistent doctor to consult regarding any aspects of postpartum corseting. Rather, my care was in the hands of the entire team of doctors at the Naval hospital. As such, I did not divulge my corset wearing to them, as I felt that it would be viewed unfavorably by at least one of them. The last checkup I had was at six weeks postpartum. I waited two months before resuming corset wearing, when I was sure that the pressure would no longer be uncomfortable on my pelvic floor.

In addition to my corset wear, I participated in a very strenuous workout routine, with special exercises for my mid-section during the recovery period from the pregnancy. This usually included running between 3–7 miles (5–11 km), then performing at least 45 minutes of calisthenics. Approximately ten months after the birth of my child, when everything was healed properly, I shifted my workout focus to distance running (at least 10 miles or 16 km), and strength training.

While I wore corsets for the enjoyment, with no therapeutic motives, I felt much better about myself while wearing a corset, especially when I first resumed after delivery. I was very thin and petite prior to my pregnancy, so the changes in my abdomen were very obvious on my frame, and I was not used to carrying extra weight on my body. Add into that the fact that I did not have a curvy shape to begin with—the pregnancy ended up making my waistline bigger than my bust, underbust, and high hip, and the same size as my full hips. Corseting, in addition to my workout routine, helped to restore more balanced proportions to my body.

I do still have a small gap in my abdominal muscles, but it did not get any worse from my second pregnancy, from which I am currently recovering. Now, a few months postpartum with my second child, I've recently resumed wearing my corsets for occasional enjoyment, and I look forward to being able to wear my collection of smaller corsets again.

AS MEDICINAL AS THEY ARE FASHIONABLE

HALLE E.

I was 12 the first time I went into a lingerie store. My mom and I were doing ordinary shopping at the mall when she decided to go into a store that was a little more risqué. She told me to wait by the fitting rooms and keep to myself while she looked around. I was entranced by the sea of black lace and sumptuous satin. What truly caught my eye, however, was a green brocade corset that wrapped its mannequin in elegance.

I saved for a year before I could call that corset mine. My cousin and I convinced our parents that we were mature enough to ride the bus to the mall alone. After casually browsing a few stores, I went for the kill. I chose the one that looked closest to my measurements and went to work convincing the sales girl that it was a bridal gift for an older relative. A few minutes later, it was mine.

I went straight to the bathroom and laced up. I felt glamorous and free. It was if I had matured right in front of that mirror. I wore that corset every day under my jeans and tees: a little secret that had a huge impact on my confidence.

Of course, at the time, I was inexperienced as to what a proper corset was. Once I started lacing, I set out to learn everything that I could on the subject. I quickly realized that mine was a fraud—a plastic boned, cheaply made knockoff meant more for the boudoir than for tightlacing. Luckily, I was blessed with a crafty mother who had been teaching me how to sew since I was two years old. I doubt that she intended for me to use the skills she imparted by sewing controversial undergarments, but that did not stop me from checking out every drafting book at the library and getting to work.

My second corset was simple, but sturdy. Around this time, my dad's boyfriend also bought me the book *The Corset: A Cultural History*, by Valerie Steele. I took it as a sign that this was my calling. Armed with more knowledge, I began gradually reducing my waist. This was before social media, so the only people who knew about my lacing lifestyle were my best friend and my cousin. Both were supportive, but uninterested in the science and history behind the lingerie I loved. I longed to meet others who shared my obsession and would "grow" me.

It was not long before I took a job with the same company that started me on my corset journey. I knew that the corsets they sold were a lie, but I felt oddly loyal to the brand that introduced me to this passion, and I hoped to meet others who shared my enthusiasm. I wore my real, self-drafted corset underneath my suit every day. I have scoliosis, so aside from making me feel confident and sultry, my corset also supported me when I felt as if my back would give out. I worked sixty hours a week and could not have handled those long hours otherwise.

Within the first few months of working there, I found out that I was pregnant—and quite far along. I had inadvertently laced throughout the first eighteen weeks. Panic set in and I was certain that I had subjected my baby to harm. Thankfully, I had a mindful, progressive doctor. She assured me that I was fine since I was carrying small and never felt pain or discomfort when in my corset. "Stress hurts babies more than a little pressure," she said.

I stopped wearing the corset, and the effects on my body became quite noticeable. I went from feeling confident to anxious and achy. Only then did I realize how much of a difference that corset made in my life—not just cosmetically, but physically and mentally as well. I packed a new corset in my hospital bag to wear after I gave birth—a freshly made underbust that would fit my larger hips and allow for breastfeeding. After the birth of my child, it took longer than expected to lace comfortably again, but it was a welcome diversion to help me adjust to my new life as a parent and deal with the postpartum depression that followed.

I had a bit of an identity crisis when I became a mother. I had always been comfortable in my own skin and advocated feminism and sexuality. Was I still allowed to be a sexy young woman with a no-nonsense attitude with a baby now on my hip? I had some soul searching to do, but I refused to give up my corsets in the meantime. They were as much medicinal to me as they were fashionable.

In the years that followed, it became clear that my relationship with my son's father was not going to work out. He had become bitter with the balancing act that was our lives. Trying to run a handmade clothing business, work a full-time job, and spend as much time with our son as possible had left me spread very thin. There was not much time to be a wife on top of all this. His resentment soon turned to jealousy, which led to abuse.

As most domestic abuse victims do, I blamed myself. I knew I had not really been present, so I felt that I had earned my mistreatment. I began to dilute my personality to quell his jealousy. Corsets and skirts became yoga pants and tee shirts. Red lipstick and victory rolls were replaced with no makeup and a messy bun. For the first time in eight years, I made the decision to ditch my corset for more "practical" undergarments. I no longer stood upright. It was a metaphor for my existence at that time.

When he left, I simultaneously had a panic attack and breathed a sigh of relief. I had begun to realize my worth, but was terrified of being alone. While packing boxes to move to my new home, I came across the corset collection that I had carefully tucked away. I felt frumpy, frustrated, and damaged, but I put one on anyway. As I tightened the laces, I could feel the stress leaving my body. It was the hug I had been longing for all those months.

I spent the next year building a life for my son and me. Back to working long hours, I started investing in more corsets so I could rotate them daily. I even started sleeping in one. When I was without my corset I was just another person, but with a corset I felt powerful. It became my armor, guarding me against my own insecurities and limitations.

I eventually found a partner who is not only accepting of my body modification lifestyle, but encourages and appreciates it. He understands that it is not about being provocative or providing a fetish, but feeling empowered. Together we have been through more than most people care to imagine; from a cross-country move to a car accident that left me unable to resume a normal life for over a year, let alone lace.

I had managed to keep waist training a part of my daily routine until that accident. Unlike the first time I stopped lacing, this was not a decision I made for someone else. I did not quit, I did not give up—but my body simply could not handle being laced into a corset. I was sad, but kept moving forward. I attribute the difference in mentality to having more of a community. Social media has opened up some wonderful channels of networking that were not previously available.

When I reached out to my corset groups, I was met with encouragement. Many wonderful members shared their stories of needing to hang up the laces for a while too. I did not feel that I had failed. It was amazing to have people there to say, "You are doing your best; you'll get back on your feet one day." In the meantime, I was able to see their progress and stay motivated for my own healing.

In fact, writing up my corseting timeline for this book has encouraged me to start lacing for the first time since I received my doctor's clearance. Feeling the tug of the laces was like a visit from an old friend. My waist has grown by several inches and I have to take it easier than I used to, but I am confident that I will be back to my old schedule in no time.

It may seem silly to put so much faith in an undergarment—surely someone wouldn't write this much about their bra or panties—but my corset is more than underwear. It is my back brace, my armor, and my stress blanket. It makes me feel self-assured, feminine, and disciplined.

Occasionally it even holds up my stockings. My hip spring gives my toddler a place to rest while clinging to mommy. Designing gives me an outlet for my creativity.

Others may not understand, but when you take something ordinary and give it a chance to be fluid and fill unexpected roles, it changes your perspective on what being resilient is. I feel as though that is a good metaphor for my life right now.

PART XIV

GENDER IDENTITY

MY WORLDS, UNIFIED

Z. KHAN

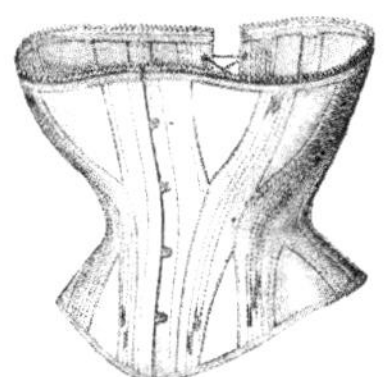

My desire to try on a corset began several years ago, when I discovered Lucy's YouTube videos, but I never had the time, money, or (so I felt) reason to do so. The thought rarely crossed my mind, and was not acted upon for years.

Then, my whole life essentially collapsed. By some odd twist of fate, my parents discovered my three-year relationship with my boyfriend at the time. Coming from a rather conservative Pakistani family, being gay meant I was threatened with everything from disownment to loss of college funding. My then-boyfriend repeatedly assured me that he'd be there for me and that I'd have a place to stay in case I did end up leaving my family behind.

As you might imagine, six months after our relationship was discovered by my family and I was beginning to come to terms with all that had happened, he unceremoniously dumped me.

I was back to square one. I managed to land a job and, with my newfound financial independence, I ran away from home. It was not my wisest choice, but my apartment was paid for in full already and I had friends that I could rely on. This apparently shocked my parents enough that they finally realized that I was serious.

With the money from my job, I began to research the off-the-rack corsets available. After purchasing a Timeless Trends underbust, I discovered how corsets had a calming effect on me. My inner resolve was all I had left to rely on, and corsets helped me keep a level head and stand tall in the many arguments and disagreements that have occurred with my family through the last year. As my waist got smaller, I felt better about being proud of who I am, and standing up (literally at times) for myself and what I stood for. This calm confidence helped me to begin to patch things up with my family and, I believe, save my college career as well, as I did get them to agree to not cut me off.

Additionally, I use corsets to cross-dress, and they've helped me realize that there is nothing wrong with wearing what you want. Men have worn corsets of various styles throughout history for various reasons: in the military, on horseback, for medical reasons, etc. My reason, apart from the confidence, is for dressing in drag. In fact, it helped me meet some of my drag idols, but that's another story altogether.

Before I found corsets, I can only describe myself as being withdrawn when it came to standing up for myself. With that little bit of steel down my spine and a cinched-in waist, I could rebuild after losing my relationship and nearly losing my family. I found the strength to wear what I want, get what I need, and do it all with shoulders back, waist nipped, and head held high.

And that's where I stood for another year or so. But life never stays as stable as we'd like, and another storm was coming. I discovered that corsets not only helped me with my confidence and posture, there was something else: the hourglass silhouette of the corset resurfaced many long-repressed feelings about my gender identity.

As I approached college graduation, I thought I'd had it all figured out—but of course, there's a large gap between college and the real world. Upon graduating, I decided it was time to sort through the previously buried emotions and ideas surrounding my gender. It's a journey, and it's not always an easy place to be. Hourglass figure aside, most people still treat me as a man. People may give me a sidelong glance, and I'm still to many folks just "that guy in a corset."

On top of this, I once again found myself kicked out of the house. My father took a look over my gender non-conforming clothes, corset and all, and told me to get out. So I did. This time, though, I resolved never to return. The only things I brought with me were my corsets, laptop, and clothing. During this tumultuous period, I found myself in yet another problematic relationship.

Here, again, corsets became another odd, yet key, tool. I'd always found myself drawn to the BDSM subculture (which of course corsets are often associated with). But here again I felt intimated and apprehensive. Upon seeing my well-trained waist however, the people of this community reacted far more positively than I could have imagined, and Cleveland's Leather and BDSM communities accepted me as a person more openly than those I knew in my past.

I find that corsets unify my many worlds in strange ways. While I no longer identify as a man, corsets have stayed with me through nearly all of the large events in my life, whether they have been catastrophic or ecstatic. I am still on a long journey regarding my gender, but the shape and compression given by a corset continues to help lift some of my long-repressed dysphoria. I do not know where my journey will end up—but wherever it goes, I'll keep the corsets.

FINDING HER IN ME

ANDREA M.

A corset gave me hope that I could be the person I knew I always was.

I am a thirty-something trans woman, and I have struggled for over two decades with my gender identity. One could say I've always been a great actor, because nobody ever suspected the lumbering oaf that I showed the world ever worried about his gender identity; I even fooled myself for a good number of years. Despite feeling more comfortable in women's clothing, my body steadfastly refused to yield hints of femininity to me, hiding behind weight and body hair—a nigh-formless lump of supposedly male flesh.

For a long time, I thought of myself as a cross dresser, and I found myself reading up on all the tricks for cajoling my body into presenting as feminine. As much as I preferred women's clothing, something always rang hollow for me in these tips—sure, I could get breast forms to give me a larger bust, or padded panties for fuller hips, or a wig to form curls tumbling down my shoulders ... but at the end of the day, those would all come off, and I was left feeling stripped of my temporary femininity.

The idea that I had to add something to my body in order to look like a woman spoke to my fears that my own body wasn't enough.

As Halloween approached one year, I found myself—as many cross dressers do—fantasizing about going out in public dressed as a princess, or a succubus, or a superheroine—anything that screamed feminine. I was still in the closet about myself though, and the fantasies would stay unrealized—as much as I wanted to appear in public as a woman, I didn't want to make a mockery of it. I didn't want to look like a man dressed in a woman's costume, but my body let me know that it would betray me should I ever test it.

And yet the lure of a sexy Halloween costume drew me into a store that sold corsets. I had concocted an elaborate story for my interest in the corsets; that I had lost a bet to some friends and that I was there "reluctantly." The saleswoman saw right through my tale and smiled knowingly; even in my small city, cross dressers were not unknown. I was in and out of the store for a couple of weeks, hmming and hawing —checking every sizing guide on the internet, trying to figure out what size to wear.

There was nothing particularly special about the corsets stocked by this shop. Mass-produced by some generic company, I'm sure. In my mind though, these simple corsets seemed a door to another world ... a waking world where maybe I could actually be me instead of in this fugue plane. Of course, I was too afraid to step up to that figurative door, let alone through it. Until one day the saleswoman asked if I wanted to try a corset on.

I was gobsmacked.

I don't think I would have ever summoned enough courage to ask for it myself, but she smiled sweetly and helped me figure out which one might fit. She laced me up just tight enough to feel secure, and then she let me look in the mirror.

I cried.

For the first time ever, my body let me see a hint of the femininity that I always felt. All the stereotypes and myths about corsets—the pain, the inability to breathe, the inability to move—were blown away in a moment by the soft but firm embrace. A small, but noticeable, bust appeared on my chest. A defined waist separated my upper and lower body. Hips, while far from child-bearing, topped my legs. Even with my men's business casual outfit, the corset made me look like the woman I felt I was—more womanly than I ever thought possible.

I never did dress up in a woman's costume for Halloween, but I did buy the corset. I learned how to tighten it myself, and I wore it whenever I could—even under my men's clothing. From that point on, whether I was wearing a corset or not, I knew my body could be feminine.

That was a few years ago, and that corset has long since fallen into disrepair, although I still smile and cry when thinking about how it made me feel. Since then I've come to know myself not as a cross dresser, but as a transgender woman, although I have yet to start transitioning. I know I'll start on hormones someday, and my body will reveal the beautiful woman I know it will be—I've seen her, staring back at me in the mirror, wearing a corset.

PARADOXICAL LIBERATION

PHILIPPE KOPLJAR

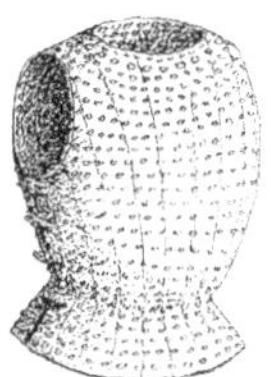

I was fourteen when I bought my first proper, steel boned corset. It was an off-the-rack number in satin with both frills and a bow at the front, oozing femininity over my entire presence. I did not even try it on before buying it and so it took only minutes before it was pinching at my hips. My breasts were squished together so high I could almost rest my chin on them, and my waist sat right below my bosom.

Buying that corset, costing me less than a new pair of shoes, was a final, desperate attempt to hide my identity. It was a mask covering my true self by forcing my body into a form so unnatural to me that it physically hurt. I was hiding in the open, blatantly pretending to be someone else, and painting layer upon layer upon layer of femininity on the boy within me. Having gone through puberty early and quickly, I did not realize what felt wrong until my hips had already grown and my fat redistributed to create one of the most feminine figures I have ever seen.

Growing up as a girl, I was taught the same thing as so many other girls: that being beautiful was more important than being me. I lost a lot of weight in my late teens and as my body shrunk so did my soul.

Every morning, as I laced up tighter than the day before, a little piece of myself was numbed, pacified, and chained away. The pain, physical and emotional, took my focus away from accepting who I was, but ultimately I could not escape. Every evening as I slowly unlaced, I felt one more layer of denial fall away, whether I liked it or not. As my breasts fell down against my ribcage and my posture bent forward, the lie became unavoidable, but there was no one else but me to see it.

That person was so deep in denial of his own existence that he hardly felt alive at all; captured in a false smile, a short dress, and an abusive relationship. No one could suspect at that point that I was not a girl.

At 20 years of age the abusive relationship came to a drawn-out and crippling end, but the traumatic experiences of that relationship stripped away my ability to deny my own emotions.

As I was clearing out the physical remnants of my ex, I also cleared out my self-denial. Among my corsets there was only one that did not look like it came straight out of a burlesque show, and that was the one I kept. It was an underbust corset almost eight inches too small, but with my hopes up I laced it tighter and tighter. During the process I became spiritually stronger with every pull of the laces, feeling confidence rising with my strict posture.

Then I looked at myself in the mirror and was disgusted by what I saw. The contrast between the tiny waist and my huge bosom made me feel like I was looking at a blow-up doll. My soul was contrastingly deflated. I quickly unlaced and threw the corset over the back of a chair, where it came to hang for weeks. In my mind I was done with corsetry at that point.

A friend who was visiting asked if she could try on the corset, and I thought why not. It looked comically out of place on top of her t-shirt and jeans, but the figure it created on her was drastically different from the figure it created on me. The corset that, on me, created hourglass curves from out of this world, on her created a boyish and slim figure. In looking at my friend's low waist and flattened figure I saw the possibility to use corsetry not as a shield and a disguise, but as a weapon in refusing to hide my inner self.

I realized that in order for my body to be shaped into a masculine figure, I needed someone to expertly craft a corset that did the opposite of what most corsets are designed to do. I wanted to flatten my chest, lower my waist and create the illusion of square shoulders. Is it really possible to create a corset to give a more angular, rather than curvy, silhouette? Yes.

As of now I am waiting in line for surgical and testosterone treatment. I may wait for months to come, being that so many are now coming out as trans and seeking treatment. I have never been comfortable wearing binders, partly because of my fat creating creases at the edges no matter how covered it is, and partly because they tend to make me hyperconscious of my own body and thus increase feelings of dysphoria. It may seem strange that corsetry does not have the same effect on me, but since it stiffens me and corrects my posture it actually serves to retract focus from my body. The layers of fabric numb any sensation of touch or pressure, and the pressure from other clothes that otherwise might pinch, such as from tight trousers, is distributed evenly while wearing the corset.

My chest is flattened, but instead of having pressure surrounding my ribcage, the compression is loose around my back and stiff across the front. The corset holds my tummy in and presses the fat up and sideways, helping to even out the difference between chest and waist. It fits snugly around my hips but does not press down on my iliac crest; instead it creates a square hip with a sharp waist that tapers up over my sides. Shoulder straps pull back my shoulders, creating a square silhouette. Even after surgery and hormone treatment I will wear corsets to help shape me.

I no longer use corsetry to hide who I am, instead I use it to make what is inside me visible on the outside and to give me the strength to be myself. The support of the boning goes straight into my soul, strengthening me and showing to myself and others that wearing a mask is no longer necessary—I can be who I am, inside and out. My corset not only makes me look masculine; more importantly it makes me feel masculine. Defiantly using a garment that women use to enhance their femininity in order to show off my masculinity creates a rebellious pride in me that cannot be subdued. Without corsetry I would feel trapped; paradoxical for a garment that cages your torso with metal and string.

PART XV

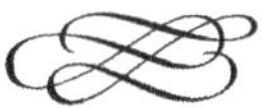

MENTAL HEALTH (ANXIETY & DEPRESSION)

REPROGRAMMING FOR LOVE

REV. KATIE NORRIS

I have been wearing corsets for three years now, and almost daily for the past two years. Contrary to what most people assume about corsets and corsetry, many of us who wear corsets and tightlace do not do it because we think we need to look different or want to attract a romantic relationship, and we don't wear corsets because we hate our bodies.

Most of us like corsets because 1) they are beautiful and carefully made garments; 2) they create a shape that appeals to us; 3) the back support they provide is a big benefit; and 4) in my experience, corsets feel good and have a calming effect.

I wear my corsets for all of these reasons, but especially because it calms me so well that I have not needed my anti-anxiety medication more than once in six months. I can also manage my bipolar disorder, especially manic episodes, by wearing a corset.

In 2013, I found myself on vacation in a situation that caused such panic I thought we would have to return home immediately. My husband, son, and I went to GenCon (a gaming convention), and while I had been to many conventions for all sorts of things before, this one was really crowded, and the convention center was so convoluted that I often found myself in areas that had no exit nearby. I panic when I do not know I can easily escape a room or situation. Thus, large buildings with few exits—like convention centers, indoor malls, movie theaters, and hospitals—scare me to death.

As soon as we walked into the convention center, I was a wreck. I got overheated and sweaty, I was hyperventilating, I was shaking, and I felt sick. I was having a terrible panic attack. No matter what I did—deep breathing, repeating to myself that I was safe, talking to my family to distract me—nothing helped, and I did not have my Ativan with me. Then I spotted a corsetiere's booth and knew I could stop my panic attack in two minutes.

At a previous convention I had bought a corset as a costume piece, and while wearing it I noticed I was calm and did not feel my usual constant anxiety. When wearing my corset, I had fewer panic attacks.

Remembering this, I headed over to the booth at GenCon and asked to try on one of their corsets. As soon as the corset was laced up, I calmed down. My husband and son were surprised at my almost instant turn-around. We were able to continue our vacation and I had no more panic that weekend, all because of the corset.

It is not surprising to me that a corset can calm panic, since deep touch pressure therapy has been used for many years with animals (such as the Thundershirt), and now for people with autism and attention deficit hyperactivity disorder (ADHD). Deep touch pressure became more widely studied and popular after Dr. Temple Grandin discovered that she was calmed by putting herself into a squeeze chute made for cows.

The corset is not that different than the weighted clothing they make for autistic children. The nice thing about it is that you can adjust the amount of pressure throughout the day. There are also different lengths of corsets, so you can get some that are shorter that cover mostly just your waist (short underbust or waist cincher), or some that cover your whole torso (overbust corset), depending on how much pressure over your body you need.

When I am really manic, sometimes I will put on my overbust corset. You can wear corsets under your clothes, but I find them more comfortable and easier to handle over my clothing, because I can easily adjust the pressure of the corset throughout the day. This is harder to do if your corset is under your clothes, especially under a dress.

For me, wearing a corset is a quick and safe fix for panic and mania. I can wear it all day, it's adjustable, and it does not cause addiction, as anti-anxiety medications such as Ativan do. I would need to use Ativan all day due to how much anxiety I have, but I don't because it is addictive. However, I can use the corset all the time.

Another benefit I've found, one that I really did not expect, was that wearing a corset has helped me accept my body as it is. For most of my life, whether I was a size 6 or 16—I had always hated my body. I had always been told I was fat, no matter how small I was. I bought into the thought that only skinny, tall women with thigh gaps were beautiful, rather than understanding that all bodies are beautiful.

I have had a binge eating disorder since I was in grade school. Eating a family-sized bag of Skittles on my own in one sitting was not unusual for me. Now I know that binging on food (especially sugar), was the only way I knew at that age to medicate my mental illnesses of panic and bipolar disorder. Sugar does a lot to the brain, especially by increasing serotonin, just as antidepressants do—except that sugar dosage is unregulated, and you need more and more of it to get the same effect.

Due to binge eating, I gained weight and then started dieting—mostly starvation diets and low-fat diets that made me feel horrible and wreaked havoc on my mental health. My anxiety and bipolar disorder went through the roof every time I dieted, but I didn't care because at least I was skinny and people treated me better. This is what everyone had encouraged me to do, even doctors.

With all of the dieting, I lost all awareness of my hunger cues. I ate processed foods with no nutritional value just because they were low in "points," and I rarely ate fruits (I was afraid of the calories) or vegetables (I couldn't find a way to make them taste good). Sandwich Thins and fat-free bologna made up every meal, while I binged on Skinny Cow ice cream bars in between. As long as I lost weight, the doctors were happy—and the weight loss company I was paying was really happy.

Then, two years later, I could not handle the dieting and I gained the weight all back. I swung to the other side, still eating processed foods, but not the low-fat ones anymore.

Whether I was dieting or not, I had constant stomach issues: rarely did food stay in my body for very long. I was sensitive to some of what I was eating and had terrible skin problems as well. Basically, I learned to destroy my body—to never listen to it and what it needed. I was told that my stomach issues were all Irritable Bowel Syndrome and that it was normal for me to be sick all the time. No doctor ever recommended that I should listen to what my body was telling me.

This cycle of binging and dieting slowly changed when I started wearing a corset daily. Wearing a corset requires you to know your body. You have to respect your body. When you get a new corset, it needs time to be seasoned and to mold to your body. You have to learn to listen to your body and to never wear a corset too tight or too long; and you need to listen if your body is telling you whether the corset is applying pressure anywhere that hurts.

I also find that I can't starve myself in a corset. Whenever I under-eat (such as with dieting), I get light-headed, tired, angry, and tend to have faster bipolar swings. In a corset, I become aware of my hunger cues faster, and I now eat small meals throughout the day, which is better for my brain. I think since the corset helps one learn to honor one's body and listen to it, corset wearers learn what pattern of eating is best for their bodies, which helps them function better.

Previously, I had been able to put up with the extreme stomach pain and other daily issues from eating things that did not work well with my body. I thought I could get away with ignoring my body and abusing it. Now, in a corset, when I eat something that bothers my stomach, I notice right away; the extreme cramps caused by allergenic foods are apparent while corseted. So I don't eat things my body does not like. The corset makes me very aware of everything my body feels and, for me, this change has resulted in awe at how my body works, respect for the way my body functions, as well as love for my natural body image.

You might think that wearing a garment designed to change my body shape slightly would make me unhappier with my body when I took the garment off. The opposite is true for me. The corset is a beautiful fashion piece that creates curving lines that I love, and so I love my body when I wear it—just like I love wearing bright red lipstick because it makes me happy. When the corset is not on, I realize that the body I loved while wearing the corset is still the same body. If I love my body when the corset is on, then I can't hate my body when the corset is off.

I truly think you can reprogram your brain into either positive or negative thinking. For example, our society programs us to see beauty in only one specific form, so if we look at ourselves and don't see ourselves mirroring that form, our brain automatically tells us we are ugly or not good enough. When I wear my corset, I feel comforted, safe, happy, and beautiful. These messages have been repeated over and over enough in my brain that I am starting to reprogram my negative thinking and beginning to see the positive reality.

I'm not saying reprogramming is easy, and I think the way it happens is different for different people. Corsets have improved my relationship with my natural body, but at the same time, my therapist uses the Emotional Freedom Technique (EFT) to help reprogram my brain to handle what previously were triggers for anxiety or trauma.

Wearing a corset has also allowed me to see the beauty in other people more than I used to. Different corset styles create different lines and shapes. As an artist, I see lines and shapes as beautiful and expressive. Consciously noticing the lines and shapes of bodies through corsetry has enabled me to look at other people and see them as a unique and beautiful combination of lines and shapes. No one can replicate who they are.

Learning to love one's body size and shape is a complex task when we live in a society that says that almost no one should love their body. The corset, combined with therapy, is slowly helping me overcome my eating disorder and resisting what society tells me about how I should eat and what I should look like.

My experience with corsets is not unique, but it is also not universal. I am sure some people continue to abuse their bodies while corseted. Different things work for different people. But there is so much negative stigma out there about people who wear corsets that it's important to shed light on the ways in which corsets help many of us. Society sees corsets as oppressive garments that women only wear for attention, but many of us who wear them have found them to be extremely helpful on our journey to radical self-love.

CORSET SOLUTIONS

ANDRÉA ~ CORSETPROBLEMS

It's hard to say exactly when my love affair with corsetry began. Maybe it was in early childhood and the fact that I was raised on Disney princesses and classical music, with images of beautiful women with perfect figures in period costumes. Or maybe it was when I went through my goth phase at 10 years old. Whatever the case, my adventures in corsetry began with cheap bustiers when I was in middle school—buying them at the mall and carefully hiding them from my conservative parents.

By the time I was 16, I gathered the courage to tell my parents that all I wanted for my birthday was a black satin, steel-boned corset I found online—with a price tag of nearly $350. After a few months of insisting that I had done my research and that it was safe, they agreed.

Around that same time, it came more clearly to my attention that I was not like other people. My mood swings were wider than most teens, sometimes entirely personality-changing. When very tired and stressed, I began to hallucinate, which caused panic attacks. I had been a self-harmer from the time I was 9 as well, just to cope with my constantly fluctuating state of mind. Although I knew there was something off through my teens, it would be another five years (at the age of 21) before I sought the help I needed and received a diagnosis.

Along with my mental issues, there were some physical injuries as well. During the first year and a half of my secondary education, I attended a school in a seven-storey building. Students were required to make the trek up and down those stairs unless they had an elevator pass. The stress from climbing caused a soft tissue injury (which my doctors couldn't detect on any tests) and I limped for nine months. Of course, that meant no physical activities—although I got the much-sought-after elevator pass.

When I left that school for an independent study school, I spent a lot of time at my desk. Being a kid, I would often rock onto the front wheels of my desk chair. One day, just as my knee was returning to normal, I was rocking in my chair as per usual—and in doing so, broke my toe. Alas, several more months of not being on my feet much.

These combined injuries boiled down to the fact that I gained nearly 50 pounds (23 kg) in a year. At 16 years old, I was 5′4″ (162 cm) and nearly 200 pounds (91 kg). I broke up with my significant other and spent most of my time in solitude, thinking about how few friends I had.

That corset my parents had bought for me had recently arrived and, surprisingly, wearing it helped. I wore it nearly every day, cinching my 33-inch (84 cm) waist down to 29 inches (74 cm). I remember spending a long time in front of the mirror (much longer than I'd like to admit), looking at my cinched waist. For the first time in my life, I could look at myself and think, "I guess I'm not so bad-looking." The more I wore the corset, the fewer panic attacks I had. My desire to self-harm finally completely disappeared. My mood swings were less temperamental.

All of this happened gradually, of course, and I had no idea that it was because of the corset. Then, in 2011, I saw the movie *Temple Grandin* by chance on a flight. Dr. Grandin is a professor of animal science who, among other things, discovered the positive effects of deep pressure therapy on people with autism. A little over a year later, Lucy of Lucy Corsetry posted a video on how corsets can mimic deep pressure therapy and its effects on conditions other than autism.

The changes that had occurred over the prior years finally started to make sense. In addition to the improvement in moods and anxiety, I gained confidence in my body image, which brought the energy and motivation to lose weight—reaping the benefits both physically and emotionally from my corset.

Corseting has also afforded me a different level of comfort while in costume, since I'm an opera singer. Most modern women never touch a corset, and the same is true of most young opera singers. I spent my first college opera (*Die Fledermaus*) laced comfortably at 26 inches (66 cm) in a genuine corset, while the other women in the cast were gasping for air in elastic-sided corsets—garments that did so little to cinch them that the bulk actually added to their waist measurement. My corset also gave me the correct posture and presence for the old Victorian baroness I played in the Belle Époque ballroom, contributing to the authenticity of my character.

Corsets have managed to pull me from some of the darkest places in my life. I've lost a total of forty pounds (18 kg), can look myself in the eye and say, "I love you" and mean it, and shed my fear of inconveniencing a doctor so I can get the help I need. I like to think that I've become a more confident, healthy person overall, in part due to my corseting. And, with the rest of my crazy life ahead of me, I'll need all of the health and confidence I can get!

A HEALTHIER APPROACH TO LIFE

ANJA W.

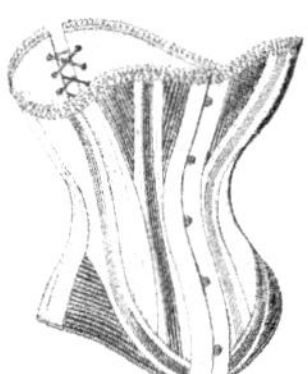

For as long as I can remember, I always wanted to own a corset. I don't know why, but for me they were a symbol of perfection and beauty. I am a big fan of illustrator Victoria Francés, and the women she features in most of her pictures are shown wearing corsets.

I didn't have a happy childhood. My parents used to fight all the time, even after their divorce. I was sexually abused as a child, and the trauma led me to self-harm by the time I was 12.

Whenever I felt overwhelmed by a situation or a problem, when I was sad, angry, or lonely, I used to cut myself. It created a rush of endorphins and it was the only thing that helped me to cope with the horrible things that happened to me.

I was 16 when I met my boyfriend. At that point I tried my best to stop my self-harm, because I didn't want to cause him concern. I suffered from panic attacks and depression though, and I didn't know of any other way to deal with these on a regular basis—harming was the only solution I knew that always helped. I was so full of self-hate that I couldn't look in the mirror without feeling disgust.

I spent most of my teenage years in therapy, and I spent one year as an in-patient in a mental hospital.

The first time I tried on a real corset was in a gothic shop. I was searching for a dress, but because of the medication, I was overweight and nothing fit me properly. I was so frustrated that I nearly cried, and the owner of the shop encouraged me to try one of their corsets. I was very skeptical, but also curious.

The shop owner helped me choose a black overbust corset for myself, and laced me in. The feeling was amazing. I could feel myself; I didn't feel numb anymore. For the first time in my life I looked in the mirror without disgust and hate.

This time, I nearly cried from happiness instead of frustration. What I saw was beauty and perfection, I transformed myself into one of the girls in Victoria Francés' illustrations. I purchased the corset that day.

Two years later, I started to wear corsets on a daily basis, and I began to see how they have helped me in different ways.

Suddenly I didn't feel the urge to cut anymore. I wasn't able to hurt myself.

They helped me to accept myself. I feel much more confident in a corset. The grounding pressure helped me to feel again. I also have terrible back pain and in a corset I feel so supported.

I feel more feminine in a corset. It is my protector, my shield.

The corset didn't solve all my problems, but it helped me to deal with them in a healthier way. I still have panic attacks from time to time, but the pressure that the corset applies to my body helps to calm me down. I am able to do things that I couldn't do before: speaking to other people, getting up in the morning and dressing myself, caring for myself. People are allowed to touch me now, which was something that made me freak out before.

The corset helped me to take those final steps into a healthier, happier life.

JUST WHAT THE DOCTOR ORDERED

CYNTHIA A.

I have struggled with depression for most of my life. First diagnosed in seventh grade, my biggest spectre is dysthymia (now called "Persistent Depressive Disorder"), occasionally coupled with bouts of Major Depressive Disorder. I am now 34 years old.

I'm a dreamer and have never felt that I belonged in the mainstream. I spent my formative years immersed in fantasy books and movies, wishing I could be a part of another world. The corseted aesthetic, from hourglass figures to corsetry itself, is very strong in the fantasy genre.

Even as a young girl I used to tell people that I would wear a corset every day if I could, just because I loved the look: powerful, intricate, and sensual. Much to my dismay, as I grew up I developed a very straight-waisted figure. Also to my dismay, growing up in a small town in the southern US limited my access to alternative clothing. I didn't do well as the odd girl out during my teenage years; I had a target on my back for bullies and mean girls. Depression isolated me.

Moulin Rouge (2001) came out when I was in college, and for the first time I saw corsets marketed to a mainstream audience. My time had arrived! I skipped straight over to Victoria's Secret and purchased a black lace, plastic-boned, Edwardian-style "corset." That single flimsy piece kicked off a style revolution for me—I went crazy! I started collecting everything corset-like that I could (affordably) get my hands on. When Express, Inc. got in on the trend, I picked up a black leather bustier to ostensibly wear over a collared shirt. I also snagged a couple of cinchers from local shops and a black leather, buckled waspie from a Renaissance Festival. Viva la Goth Revolución!

I wore them all proudly to my classes, usually coupled with a top hat or something equally ostentatious. Raised in a conservative household, my individuality was more comfortably expressed in the form of wearing funky clothes and dying my hair rather than getting piercings or tattoos. I finally felt like my external style matched my internal feeling of otherness. Those years saw a huge development of my previously nonexistent self-esteem.

It wasn't until I graduated from college that I discovered the possibility of waist training full time. I wish I could remember the maker's name; her website was, as most of them were in the early 2000s, extremely basic. I read and researched everything I could find, but, unfortunately, as a fresh graduate working for minimum wage, $300 for a custom corset at the time was financially out of reach. Disappointed, my plans turned to my wedding instead; my fiancé was very supportive and bought me a lovely cobalt blue and black velvet overbust corset as a wedding present. My wedding dress itself had a plastic-boned corset built into it.

Shortly after we married, we moved to the West Coast and I entered the jewelry industry—a conservative industry to be sure. I still picked up corsets for costuming purposes every now and then, but my dreams of waist training every day fell by the wayside.

As the years passed and I tried to blend in with SoCal culture, dysthymia crept back into my life. Everything came crashing down in 2014 when major depression struck; I became suicidal and gained weight from lethargy. For the first time in my life, I was hospitalized for my own safety. Upon my release, I was lucky enough to find a very good psychiatrist. He started me on a combo of medication and therapy, and encouraged me to not be afraid to match my appearance with my true personality.

A chance encounter with a friend introduced me to The Tightlacing Society on Facebook, and my fascination with corsetry flared. An entire, international community of people who shared my obsession! I hesitantly told my psychiatrist about it. To my surprise, he broke out in a huge smile!

"Yes, absolutely you should wear a corset! It would be perfect for you," he said. He went on to tell me that the corset would help with my anxiety, and it would bolster my damaged self-esteem to once again dress to reflect who I really am, and not merely who I was expected to be.

I proceeded to read every solid resource I could find on waist training and asked experienced waist trainers for their opinions on where to start. In short order, I had three off-the-rack waist cinchers and I started stealthing the corset under any outfit I could.

The effect was dramatic and immediate. Suddenly people were complimenting me on my appearance again. Suddenly, getting dressed in the morning was an adventure instead of a chore. Suddenly, I was sitting up straight! I felt confident! Lacing up in the morning was akin to putting on my armor for the day. My psychiatrist commented on it the very first time he saw me corseted, saying, "Everything about you is more confident! This is wonderful!" People started asking me for fashion advice—me, the girl who was bullied and picked on all through my childhood for being a weirdo! Friends saw my enthusiasm and results, and asked me for advice on how to get started. With my husband's support, I proceeded to order my first custom corset, in order to lace smaller with comfort.

A little over a year and three custom corsets later, waist training has helped me reclaim the missing parts of myself. Corsetry, combined with the right therapy and support, drove away my depression. I am stronger now than I have ever been! I haven't lost weight, but I have lost the need to feel ashamed of my body—and I am able to set new goals for myself through waist training. I'm only one inch away from my goal of an eight-inch reduction from my original natural waist.

Corsetry is synonymous with courage for me, a courage that helped me leave my job in jewelry and pursue a much more fulfilling Doctorate in Traditional Chinese Medicine. I still have that first cheapie Victoria's Secret "corset" from college. Although it's retired and falling apart, I'm just too sentimental to let it go.

When the whole world is falling apart, corsets hold me together. If I am feeling particularly anxious or insecure, I just lace a little tighter and find I can breathe again.

PULLING MYSELF TOGETHER

VALERIE LEE

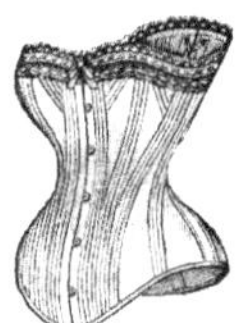

Corsets probably saved my life, frankly. You wouldn't know it if you looked at me: I'm a tall teenage black belt under the Singapore Tae Kwon Do Gymnasium; I attend one of the better local secondary schools; and I have a loud, deep voice for a girl.

I've also been dealing with chronic depression since I was 12, and anxiety since I was 15. I won't bore you with the details, but the short story is that the national exam that chose what secondary schools I could go to is taken at age 12, and I had gotten into my school by the skin of my teeth. First I was stressed by the exam, and then terrified that I'd be expelled for poor grades or poor conduct once I got in.

I've always had a fascination with history, especially historical clothing. They're so beautiful and different from what we usually see nowadays, and I ended up spending quite a bit of time researching them, which led to researching one garment in particular—corsets. I was lucky that by virtue of most of the TV shows I watched, my first encounter with corsets was through Wikipedia, and I didn't have that many preconceived ideas about them.

My research eventually expanded into corset videos, then reviews of corsets, websites about them, and so on. When I was 13, I presented my mum with a request to help me buy a corset—a cheap fashion one that would buckle the moment I put any real strain on it, so I couldn't reduce my waist even if I impulsively decided I wanted to—and a thesis on why I should be allowed to. I got what I wanted, each step closely supervised by my mum, until I had given her the money for the corset and the order was confirmed.

I knew I had depression, and I didn't like it. Depression, to me, seemed a sign of weakness in myself. I was exhausted. Exhaustion forced my shoulders down and my back to hunch as I tried to curl up and hide from everything. So the easiest way to combat exhaustion, and thus depression, was not allowing slouching to happen. And I knew that I couldn't slouch in a corset.

I used the corset as a form of exoskeleton. While I was wearing it, I could relax for a while and let the corset support me. It was like I was borrowing strength from the rigidity of it until I had rested enough to handle everything on my own again.

Pulling the laces closed also felt as though I was metaphorically pulling myself together, that I wasn't mentally fraying at the edges anymore. The feeling of it had a grounding effect, keeping my mind in the here and now. I didn't see how important this would be until I was a bit older.

The issue with depression is that, without someone knowledgeable keeping an eye on it, it tends to get worse. Case in point: my third year of secondary school.

Secondary 3 was a rough year for me. Everyone was moved around to different classes, leaving me in a class surrounded by students unknown to me, feeling isolated whilst also dealing with new subjects and increased pressure from the Cambridge O-Level examination I would take when I turned 16.

My depression took a turn for the worse that year: in three separate occurrences of depression-induced dissociative fugue, I attempted suicide; one attempt including hanging myself with my own black belt, until I finally snapped out of that state.

My corsets, now heavier, steel-boned affairs, served as a grounding tool again, though not so much as a means of physical support other than when I was working my Sunday morning retail job. The tightness and the feeling of a hug was a constant sensation, now keeping me from slipping into one of those fugue states where I couldn't think clearly and most of my logic and self-preservation instincts were muted, if not switched off outright.

In that kind of state, I can, and have in fact, often hurt myself simply because I was no longer attending to the fact that harming was no good and to be avoided. Every single time I had self-harmed or worse, I had been in such a mental state. I'm not sure how many such slips wearing a corset had prevented. Whatever it was, it was one less chance for me to hurt myself; and when it takes just one go to do something irreversible, my corset may well be—and probably is—the main reason I am still alive.

THE STAYS THAT SOOTHE

HAZEL T.

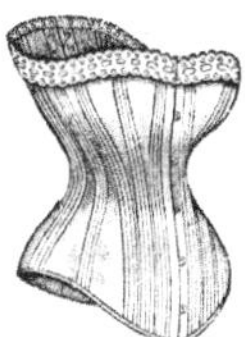

I have always been fascinated by corsets. When I finally decided to start researching corsetry looking to buy one, I came across the amazing, diverse corset community. I have learned so much. When I found Lucy's YouTube channel, I discovered her video outlining the physical benefits corsets provide. I have even been able to begin educating curious people around me by either pointing them to reliable resources within the corset community, or by relaying the valuable information I have learned so far.

For the past three or four years, my struggle with depression and Attention Deficit Disorder has gotten more severe. Only a few years ago I was officially diagnosed with both. Even though the diagnosis is recent, I had struggled with depression and ADD for at least 15 years. In retrospect, the signs were always there, but I never really received proper mental health care until I was diagnosed.

After I purchased and wore my very first corset, I noticed a significant rise in my self-confidence. It felt incredible wearing a garment that could alter the way I looked and the way I carried myself. In one of Lucy's videos, she mentions that wearing corsets forces her to stand up straight and address people head-on.

As a hairdresser, I have to be straightforward as I counsel my clients with honesty, tact, and creativity. Having to physically stand up straighter with a corset on has helped to change the way I consult with my clients. Even in daily life outside the salon, I have learned to carry myself in a more assertive way.

Being able to alter the way my body looks with a corset has also been a blessing. During my high school years and into my early twenties, I struggled with anorexia. Even now, dieting is a huge trigger for me. If I'm having a particularly bad day regarding my body image, a corset is just the thing to make me feel a little better about myself; not only for the figure shaping, but also because it is quite literally like wearing a hug.

The past three years have been an immense struggle with my depression and ADD. Even that is an understatement. When I am having an extremely low day, I don't want to be by myself; this is a huge indicator of a change in my wellbeing, as I normally value and enjoy my solitary time very much. During times when I've not been able to have a friend come over or wasn't able go out myself, and I was stuck at home alone, I put on my corset. The deep pressure provided by corsets has soothed and comforted me like a warm, intimate hug.

A corset is not just a beautiful garment. It is one of the life preservers thrown to me during one of the many dark times in my life. For me, corsets aren't just about the aesthetics. They are a tool I use to better my mental health and body image.

THE PEANUT AND THE KNIGHT

MIMI

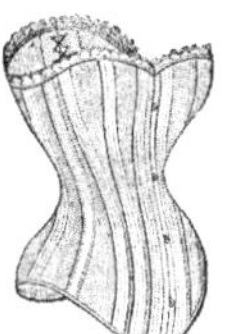

I've owned a corset for less than a year, but it has helped me in more ways than I thought it ever could have. It has helped me with my insecurities, which had led me down a road toward depression and occasional anxiety attacks. But at first all I wanted from it was to lose weight and feel beautiful.

I've had Lupus (a damaging auto-immune disease) since I was 9 years old. In the beginning it just looked like a rash across my face. Kids can be cruel, and I quickly realized that I could never fully do what the other kids did—I could never fit in with certain crowds because I was nothing more than hideous to them. I was a burnt peanut. A rotten tomato.

For years they never knew how much their words had affected me. There would be times I didn't want to get out of bed because I wanted to hide my face from the world, and couldn't get out of that bed because my aching joints just didn't allow me to. I cried because I didn't want to feel like a monster. My mother didn't want me to wear makeup, and she would always say "you are who you are," but I was very conscious of the way she would freak if a blemish or pimple appeared on her face. I developed a fear of looking in the mirror; I started to believe I really was a monster.

Time passed and I gained weight, became anti-social and housebound, until I told myself, "I am in my early 20s, I shouldn't have to hide anymore." More than anything I wanted to get into shape and do something good for my body, and I soon became a YouTube junkie. I looked into many videos about health, foods that could help with dieting, and much more, until I stumbled across the YouTube channel of a makeup artist who mentioned that she had lost a ton of weight by waist training.

I instantly became interested in corsets, and when I searched for waist training, part of me was scared for dear life. YouTube has a habit of showing a lot of negative images at times, which left me with a lot of doubt. One part of me said, "No, this isn't something I could consider," yet at the same time I didn't give up my search.

I stumbled across Lucy's Corsetry on YouTube and learned the logic behind wearing corsets; I finally decided to order one. After receiving my first corset and trying it on, I felt a small but noticeable gain in confidence—and something about it made me feel really special. My corset hugged my body tighter than any person ever could, and in a good way.

I started wearing my corset when I went outside, and even when I went out with no make-up covering my rash, the negative looks from other people slowly faded. I actually caught myself smiling in public. I didn't care so much about the temporary curvy look, but the corset made me feel at ease. I felt like my corset was my armor and I was a female knight ready to take on anything.

Even while I slept, the anxiety attacks happened less. I would wake up and smile because I knew I had nothing to fear and I had comfort on my side. Plus, corsets have helped me with my posture—losing weight is one thing, but carrying around a heavy bosom is another thing. My corset literally has taken a weight off my back—and chest!

All in all, I've learned to value corsets, not so much because of the shape they give, but because with each corset there is a new story of adventure and hope.

PART XVI

AUTISM SPECTRUM

UNEXPECTEDLY EMPOWERED

BECCA N.

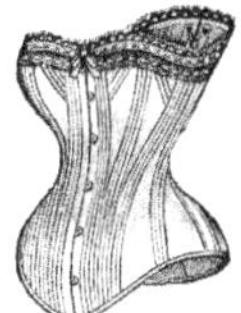

I've always been a person of eclectic interests, and those interests tend to be obsessive and short-lived. Most of the time when something strikes my fancy, I research it heavily for about three days, and that is enough to satisfy any curiosity.

Corsets were different. Corsets would not be a fleeting three-day passion; I knew that they were going to be one of those things that would preoccupy me until I had one of my own. They not only combined my love of vintage fashion and science, but most importantly they looked like the answer to my biggest concern at the time: my back.

A combination of lifelong poor posture, weak muscle tone, and a recently misaligned pelvis had progressed to the point where my sleep was suffering due to back pain. I had regular physiotherapy for some time, but it was quite expensive and not as helpful as I'd hoped. The idea that something could force me into proper posture was especially intriguing, because trying to maintain correct posture in class often took up so much energy that I couldn't pay attention to the material being taught.

So when I discussed the idea with my mother and she agreed, I made a big leap and bought two corsets off the rack, along with cotton tube tops as liners. My original intention was to wear them only on school days, and go from there. If they didn't help with my pain, then I wouldn't be able to personally justify the cost of buying more, but I loved them enough anyway that I would be okay with their not working out as intended.

Taking a few weeks to season the corsets helped me become comfortable wearing and removing them. I also became less self-conscious about whether people could see them under my clothes, and actually enjoyed the feeling of wearing them. Honestly, it felt a bit empowering. Not only that, but it was calming; and I later discovered that this effect was a common phenomenon.

Deep-pressure therapy is often used for people with autism spectrum disorders (which includes me!). The most amazing thing to me was putting on my backpack for the first time in my corset. The way it redistributed the weight made me realize just how much I inadvertently abused my back muscles. Since my college had no lockers, and I had no car, it was incredibly important that I carry my backpack properly.

Wearing a corset in speech class provided these benefits: calming my nerves, encouraging good pace of breath, and providing proper posture. Eventually I became so comfortable that I even did a presentation and demonstration on the science of corsets, misconceptions about them, and how they are properly worn—which I never would have been comfortable doing previously. It was one of the first presentations I was excited about, and definitely the first where I didn't blush as red as a lobster!

Eventually, I started to see enough improvement in my posture and my back such that my pain lessened, and so my quality of sleep improved. I was able to do core exercises and actually lost weight during this time.

Unfortunately, when I lost the fat around my ribcage, the corsets were a good 1-2 inches too large when completely closed. This provided far less support in my mid-to-upper back. So for a long time I stopped wearing my corsets, and my back still had some issues but never again to the point I had previously experienced.

A decent made-to-measure piece would be a large investment, and the continuing weight loss makes me nervous about purchasing too quickly.

Looking back, those corsets were worth so much to me. I've wholeheartedly endorsed them since, and really enjoy talking to people about my experiences and helping to educate friends who are interested in the subject. There are so many beautiful and varied pieces out there and you never know, they might change your life in some very unexpected ways.

MORTICIA'S SUPPORT

YVONNE R.

I was diagnosed with autism at the age of 9. It is one of the consequences I have from getting brain damage at birth, along with a form of ataxia (which makes me shaky 24/7) and balance problems.

Because of my autism I have a very scheduled life and when something doesn't go as planned, I get scared. New things, or situations I've never experienced before, can flip my entire life upside down. There has been some progress over the years but the problem is always there.

And when I get really scared, I tend to show other emotions. My parents used to think I got angry about things that seemed so small to them. But to me these things were huge! And they scared me—I was terrified. But all I could show was anger.

As a child, I tried many different therapies that were supposed to help me deal with these fears. I learned a lot about myself and about autism, but the fears never left. Living in fear is very exhausting, which sometimes makes me cranky. And for a time the only thing that could lower the anxiety was when my mom held me very tight. But in the moments that I was so overpowered by these fears, there's no way she could hold me. Also, there comes a certain age when your mother can't always be there for you.

I was 20 when my dad passed away and my entire life fell apart. I was so scared of everything and my mom was mourning the loss of her husband. There was no way that she could give me the comfort I needed, so I started looking for things that could. One of these things was corsets. It felt like someone was hugging me all the time. It made me stronger to deal with all the emotions I was going through. I was very depressed at the time, and the feeling of the corset was kinda soothing for me. I somehow knew everything was going to be okay.

My autism makes it difficult to have social contact with others. People who don't know me might consider me shy, and maybe it's partially true. But for me it's also hard to recognize facial expressions and intonation. I know what sarcasm is in theory but I do not know when someone is serious, sarcastic, or joking. These things make me very insecure. I'm always scared someone will get mad at me or that I might offend someone.

My corset helps me with these insecurities. It sort of feels like a shield to protect me from the outside world. Yes, people can still be offended by things I say. And no, I still can't hear sarcasm or see expressions. But I feel less vulnerable because, at the end of the day, I have my Morticia corset from What Katie Did to "protect" me.

At the moment I'm doing well. I live a structured life and although I have had some setbacks, I still manage to stand up for myself and live my life. I used to be ashamed of my autism. I wanted to be "normal." Now, thanks to the WKD Morticia corset, I accept my condition. It's a part of who I am, and I learned to be okay with it by wearing Morticia. I don't want to be like everybody else anymore.

I don't wear my corset on a daily basis: it's not always convenient in my everyday life. But it somehow makes me feel safer just knowing that my corset will always be in my closet when I do need it.

PART XVII

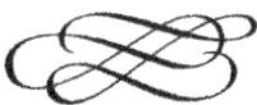

PTSD & COPING WITH ADVERSITY

HEALING LACES

LEAH B.

My journey began as a child, way before I even knew what a corset was. I grew up in a home which was always in some kind of turmoil—whether it was my parents fighting about money when there wasn't quite enough to pay the bills, or my half-siblings' family screaming at my parents in our front yard, once again threatening to take them to court for some unknown reason. My mother did her best to envelop me in love, to shield me from the ugliness around me. Despite her best efforts though, I never felt at ease as a child.

As can be expected in situations as poor as these, my family deteriorated. My half-sister left when I was 10 and disowned my family, never to speak to any of us again. My half-brother left home less than a year later after an altercation with my father. He tried to stay in contact with me for a while, but it wasn't long before that ended forever too. So, at the age of 10, my life, which had already been rough, was completely and utterly turned upside down. I didn't know how to function as an only child.

My mother fell into a deep depression. My father was there, but very distant. I was trying to figure out what I did wrong. My siblings had abandoned me and wanted nothing to do with me. I was lost. I remained that way for a long time.

I'm not sure when it happened, but I started thinking about swerving into traffic, whether it would hurt to hang myself, wondering how long it would take to die if I bled out.

My father's short temper snapped one day when I was crying over an overwhelming school assignment that I wasn't confident I could complete. He yelled at me to quit crying and when I couldn't stop, he grabbed me by my hair and threw me across the room. He had his fist raised to hit me when my mom came into the room. They divorced. I quit eating.

When I entered high school, I was 5′5″ (165 cm) and weighed 125 pounds (57 kg). My decision to quit eating had nothing to do with a desire to lose weight. I was abandoned, alone, scared, depressed, lost, and completely helpless. I wanted something I could control. When I quit eating, it hurt. I focused on the pain. It didn't leave any marks, so no one would notice, and it gave me something to feel grounded to. I didn't notice that it was changing my body; although my mom did. She took me to the doctor before my senior year.

I weighed 90 pounds (41 kg). I was completely shocked. The doctor didn't believe me when I said I wasn't happy that I weighed so little or when I said I wasn't drinking or on drugs. He told me that I should just quit lying. He diagnosed me with anorexia nervosa, and because of how he approached it, I was completely convinced he was wrong. I never wanted to lose that much weight; it scared me, so surely I wasn't anorexic—and if I wasn't anorexic, I didn't need help. I have no idea how much more weight I lost, but I kept getting smaller and smaller. I didn't want to weigh myself or even look in a mirror because then I'd have to face what I was doing to myself.

I was an emotional, self-loathing wreck. It was my boyfriend (now husband) who began to help me out of it. He slowly helped me through all of my baggage. (He has a degree in rehabilitation counseling now. He's very good at helping people.) It's taken years, and I'm still not 100% every single day, but I'm not a danger to myself anymore. I like myself, and I can admit that I'm a good person and deserve the life I have.

I started wearing corsets during this healing period after I saw some videos online. One person I saw described her corset as though it were hugging her, holding her in. Then I found articles online explaining that corsets didn't have to be dangerous. The wheels started to turn, and I talked with my husband about getting one. He didn't like the idea at first, but I relayed the information that I had learned, and he eventually agreed to let me splurge on buying one.

That first corset was amazing for me. When I wore it, it gave me that focus back: here was something I could control, something tactile to keep me grounded (I was still struggling with not wanting to eat at that point). The constant pressure around me was comforting. After wearing it for several weeks, my posture changed. I was standing taller, and somehow it helped me believe in myself a little more. Wearing a corset didn't completely fix all of my problems, but I honestly believe that it aided me tremendously. It gave me a little more strength, power, and clarity, which helped me to focus on healing myself.

I still struggle with my emotions when it comes to my siblings (despite the fact that it's been close to two decades since they left), and I still doubt myself from time to time, but I can say with confidence that I'm okay now. My husband continues to support me, I continue to receive a feeling of control from my corsets, and I keep striving to better myself. I wish I could go back in time to meet my younger self, and show that little girl how much better life will get.

My corset may just be fabric, thread, and metal—but, to me, it's a reminder that I can take back control of my life. I can seek out connections that will make my life richer. I can use my knowledge to help people so their world can be a bit brighter. Joy is all around me, and my corset was just a stepping-stone to me being able to see it.

MY LIFE JACKET

CECILIA V.

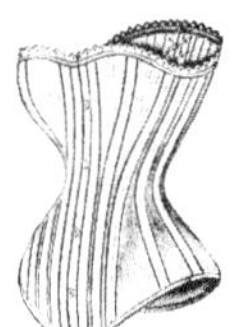

I first became interested in corsets when I came across a photo of a girl wearing a simple black underbust on some random website. Even though she wasn't what most people would call beautiful, her smile was. At that time I was depressed and was constantly being bullied; many things in life seemed to be going wrong for me.

I had just had my last growth spurt, which was a surprise because the doctor had told me I had finished growing—all of a sudden, none of my clothes fit me; everything I tried on was either too short, too wide, or too small. It got to the point that when I went shopping for school clothes, I would end up crying in the changing rooms until I finally gave up finding new clothes. Even though I was tall, I was still shaped like a child: no hips and no breasts. My only solution at the time was to wear my older brother's clothes, and clothing designed for adolescent boys in general. In my high school, if you're a girl wearing boys' clothing, you become an instant target for bullies. When changing in the locker rooms for gym class, the other girls would tease me and scream, "There's a boy in here! Get him out!"

Sophomore year came around and I caught a stomach virus. One of the effects of the virus was spontaneous allergic reactions, and these reactions could be to anything at all. Suddenly I couldn't eat any of the food offered at school, and I had to have blood tests and skin-prick allergy tests every week. One week I'd be allergic to rice, meat, and cod; the next week I would be allergic to oranges and milk. The medication they put me on caused my skin to break out and made my weight fluctuate daily. My hair became dry and brittle (even now, looking at the length of my hair, you can tell the period of time when I was ill). The stomach bloating was so bad it looked like I was pregnant. I started wearing baggy sweatpants and hoodies to school just to conceal my shape.

When I saw that photo of the girl in her plain black corset, I was of course impressed by the corset, but it was her expression that caught my eye. She looked totally happy; completely content with herself. I ended up spending hours in front of the computer, searching for photos of women wearing corsets—and they all looked so beautiful, confident, and happy. I wanted to know that kind of happiness.

I saved up my allowance, got a ride to a mall, and bought myself a corset. It wasn't an authentic corset (it was a plastic-boned and polyester lace-monster from Hot Topic), but it did what I wanted it to do. I wore it the next school day under my sweats (I was still very shy) and deliberately didn't change for gym, just so I wouldn't have to take it off. I felt so happy and confident in that corset that I think even my bullies noticed a change that day, and every day after that. Slowly, things started to get better. I started ignoring the bullies, and my body eventually adjusted to the medication (although at the time, I actually thought that my body's adjustment was due to the corset!). My body grew out of that awkward stage and the virus died.

After a while I bought myself a proper corset. When I grew out of it, I got another ... and then another. I have been wearing corsets for over five years now. My corsets are like my little private lifejacket. They make me feel safe, beautiful, and confident. Whenever life feels overwhelming and it seems that I'm drowning, it feels as though my corset is there to save me. I can't imagine not wearing one anymore.

As I type this, I'm crying from joy. I am now truly happy, and I never want to go back to how I was before—no one deserves to be made to feel so awkward and ugly and unwanted. Thinking now, I don't believe that my corset was the only factor in my life's improvement—I know that it was only a tool that made me feel better about myself at the time—but sometimes just one small change can lead to a big difference. The corset still means so much to me, and it's a continual reminder of how far I've come.

For senior prom in high school, I wore a corset over my dress. I wanted to show it off proudly, and let it be my armor instead of a life jacket for once. I wanted to show everyone that I feel beautiful and confident—I don't feel like I have to hide my corset or who I am anymore. I knew that the corset was not responsible for making me feel beautiful that night—my confidence became my truth, and no one could take that away from me. Even though I experienced hard times at the start of high school, I was determined to graduate with so much happiness that I would always be able to look back on my time there and remember it with pride.

Corsets are many things to many people: to some people a corset is a fashion choice, or a sexy object, or a form of body modification—but not to me. It was the one thing that kept me up during those difficult years. It is what stopped me from slouching to hide (figuratively and literally), and what encouraged me to stand tall. It was my comforter, giving me a tight hug when I was depressed. It was my support and morale-builder, telling me to keep going and not give up. It is now my armor against a life that probably would have crushed me if I had kept going down the track I was previously on. Even now, when I like to think I don't need a corset anymore, it still serves as a reminder to not let myself be pushed around or fall back into negative thoughts. It reminds me that I can do anything, and overcome any obstacle.

One day the time will come when I will be so totally happy with myself that I won't need to look at pictures or wear my corset to know this. I'm definitely already on that path, but I continue to wear my corset because I choose to and because the world is a hard place and I still have lots of fight left in me. Every warrior needs her armor, and sometimes it comes in the form of cloth and steel.

A REMINDER THAT I AM ENOUGH

AMANDA T.

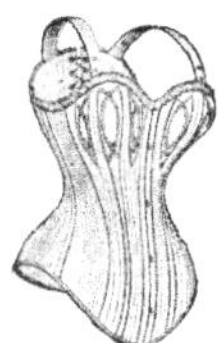

It all started on a day in November, many years ago. He seemed so sweet and thoughtful in the beginning. He made me feel like I belonged somewhere. I felt safe, happy, and madly in love.

A few months into our relationship, I moved into his place, excited to start my new life with him. Soon though, he started telling me that my family hated me, and that they were ashamed of me. Young and naïve as I was, I believed him.

He started to go out at night, and often returned home drunk. Those nights, he used his intoxication as an opportunity to berate me about all of the things I was doing wrong, and how stupid I was.

He would tell me that I was ugly, and that I was a slut for having sex with him as young as I did. I began to feel ashamed of my body, and believed there was something wrong with it.

He used confusion as a weapon, and fed me conflicting words to the point where I did not know what was true, so I just would believe him. I was stupid. I was ugly. I was a slut. I was an embarrassment to my family. I was hated.

Again, I believed only in him.

Then came a day where I was home alone, searching the internet and looking at antique garments and Victorian dresses. I spent hours looking at product reviews, finding pictures, and researching their history.

He soon came home, saw what I was researching, and laughed at me. He then took my phone and deleted all my messages and contacts.

There would be nobody in my life other than him.

He told me that only whores dressed like that, and that the ideas of others were infecting me, corrupting me. He wanted to help me get rid of my bad habits.

All I could think of were all those beautiful Victorian women, and how confident and strong they looked. Something about their strength drew me to them; something I wanted, and more importantly, needed.

I wanted to be beautiful, modest, confident, and strong.

And that would never be allowed.

August was approaching, and with it the urge to feel the sun on my skin and the summer breeze in my hair.

I put on a summer skirt and my favorite shirt—some of the few clothes that I was allowed to keep.

I then asked for permission to go outside.

I wasn't allowed.

Instead he shoved me in to the wall and laughed at me.

In that moment, I was again ugly, stupid, and a slut.

I couldn't take it anymore. I wanted to be independent and free.

I wanted to get out of the apartment that held me prisoner, but it didn't seem possible.

No job, no school, no family or friends.

All I had was the same four walls and the one person who brought doubt on myself and my world.

I then decided that if I could not make a decision for myself, no one could.

I swallowed an entire bottle of painkillers. Then I waited.

Fear suddenly came over me. I wanted to live, but not like this. I frantically thought of what to do, but my head was spinning, and I was quickly getting faint.

He wasn't worth this. I would not let him have this satisfaction of finally breaking me.

I called the emergency services.

I was in the hospital for eight days.

When I was released from the hospital, 11 days before my 17th birthday, it was the first time in forever that I felt truly free.

Several months later, I met another guy. This one treated me like a person who was worth something, and he even bought me my first corset—the garment I dreamed about for so long.

I was no longer ugly, stupid, or a slut.

I first wore a high-quality corset on my 18th birthday. That long-awaited moment finally came true. I felt beautiful, confident, feminine, strong, and independent. It was like a hug that would never lose its grip around me.

I suddenly felt safe in my own body.

When I got my first corset, I knew that this would be my constant reminder that I am good enough. Never again will I let another person tell me how to look or how to live. I have damn great taste, and I look and feel amazing in my corsets and Victorian dresses.

Now I have a fiancé and a daughter who both adore me.

Through one-hundred-year-old fashion, I discovered a new side of myself: a stronger, independent, self-respecting woman.

FINDING JOY

DANIELLE H.

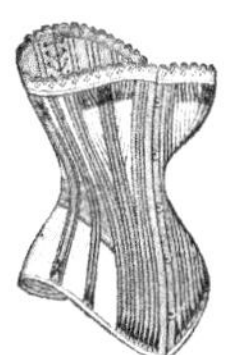

Corsetry has always fascinated me, and in the summer of 2009 I finally had the money to purchase a corset that was of good quality. It was a fully custom piece from Electra Designs, and I still love it. It remains the only fully custom corset I own; although I have other corsets I wear from time to time, that particular piece is still my favorite.

In early 2013, my life as I'd known it for six years was torn apart. I discovered that my (now ex) husband, who had fully relapsed into his painkiller addiction, was deep in an emotional affair that turned physical soon after I became aware of it. I was devastated.

Over the next three months I tried to put my marriage back together, for the sake of our young daughter, who was only two years old at the time. I quickly learned that a relationship won't survive if only one person is putting any effort into it. So the week of my 30th birthday, I asked him to leave—and I began the slow, painful task of putting myself back together.

Not long after he left, I went for my annual check-up with my doctor, and they discovered a mass in my neck. I was diagnosed with thyroid cancer, and I underwent a full thyroidectomy. Before I had the surgery, however, I had to endure a month of testing until my hormones were all at the correct levels.

In the midst of all that pain, turmoil, and uncertainty, I found myself seeking comfort and solace wherever and whenever I could. It was in my Electra Designs corset, the only one I owned at the time, that I found an easily accessible, readily available source. I could lace myself into it and immediately feel as though I was wrapped in a warm, steady, strong hug. It became something I wore frequently, nearly every day for a time, as I healed from both my emotional pain and my physical illness. My divorce and my surgery occurred within months of each other, but my corset remained there for me.

As of 2016, I have been cancer-free for over two years. I know I would still have recovered had I not had my corset. But I believe I recovered more quickly than I would have without it, and I will be forever thankful for that.

So now when I wear my corsets, and I get questions about it (as I'm sure most corset-wearers do), I always make sure to set the record straight if the other party has been misinformed or holds misconceptions. And I always try to share why my corsets mean what they do to me, and how they've made my life immeasurably better. I like to think I leave people a little better informed than they were about the joys and benefits of owning and wearing a corset.

A PRACTICE IN REMAINING PRESENT

SARAH C.

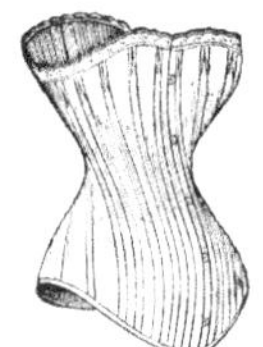

While I was attending university, I developed Generalized Anxiety Disorder (GAD), which was linked to a previous incidence of PTSD. It took about two years for me to be properly and officially diagnosed with GAD, and some time after that for me to begin Cognitive Behavioral Therapy as treatment.

Two of the tools for managing anxiety that were most helpful to me were deep breathing and mindfulness meditation. However, they didn't always prevent an anxiety attack or panic attack from occurring—and once an attack started, it was essentially a point of no return. It is a very helpless feeling, as though your mind is declaring mutiny.

I discovered corsets soon after I started therapy. In fact, my psychologist encouraged me to purchase a corset since I had always been fascinated with them and wanted to explore their possible benefits. I had no idea what those benefits would be for me, but I was intrigued and wanted to find out.

My first steel-boned corset was cheap and not very good quality, but I discovered that wearing a corset helped me focus my breathing and be more mindful and grounded. Without a corset, breathing feels subtle and even when I try to focus on it, it can slip away from my attention. My anxious mind is always busy and always ruminating. Wearing a corset brings me into the present. The weight of a corset and its "hug" keep me grounded; it's a feeling that is never outside my awareness. I become more conscious of my breathing and more conscious of any tension in my body.

I have never had an anxiety attack or panic attack while wearing a corset. It's a complementary tool I can use that works together with everything else I've learned to help manage my anxiety disorder. (Side note: I'm pleased to say I'm doing much better now; GAD is no longer debilitating for me and it's not holding me back from things I want to do in life.)

Since educating myself about corsets, I have purchased higher-quality corsets that have a better fit and shape for my body. I have used these as "armor" when I go out. I currently live alone in an urban area and I am a petite woman. Although I don't know if a corset would literally provide extra protection like real armor, I do feel safer if I wear a corset when I go out. Feeling safe encourages me to walk and hold myself in a way that is more confident. I act more assertive and self-assured. In other words, I think I look like less of a target for someone with malicious intent. I have no family or friends living in my city, so it's important for me to find ways to feel secure and safe here.

Beyond that, I have acquired a very Victorian taste since wearing corsets. This is one of my primary interests and hobbies now; I collect corsets and I collect Victorian and Neo-Victorian style garments. I love reading and learning about the Victorian era, and I just recently finished reading Sarah A. Chrisman's book, *Victorian Secrets*. I enjoyed it so much that I'm looking forward to reading her other books as well! Maybe one day I will be sewing my own clothing and corsets ... who knows! Looking back, I'm impressed that a single garment has affected my life so greatly and in such positive ways.

AN INSTANT METAMORPHOSIS

LANA H.

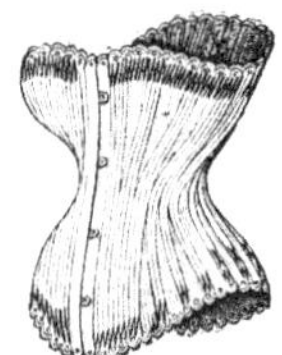

I struggled with body image and confidence during my teens. I was a very happy child, but that changed when my innocence was cruelly taken due to sexual abuse at the age of 10. Add to that an absentee father, and it was no wonder I felt worthless. With the love and support of my family and close friends I slowly began to regain my self-esteem ... but something was still missing.

I met my husband-to-be at the age of 16. Without him, I don't think I would have ever taken the plunge and bought my first corset. A university friend of his suggested I try one once she learned of my background. She used them for her own mental health issues and she firmly believed I could also be helped. I didn't think some material and steel could make much of a difference, but it was worth a try.

I admit I had always been curious about trying them, but I was always told how they were "bad" for you, and very uncomfortable. Seeing how easily the friend moved; how good she looked (confidence-wise as well as physically) began to change my opinion, but I was still not totally convinced.

Along with a small group of friends, I took a trip to one of the places we knew where we could buy off-the-peg corsets without breaking the bank. I chose one in my favorite colors (purple and black), and let the lady who owned the shop work her magic. That moment, when I wore a corset for the first time, still sticks in my mind today. It is strange how a piece of clothing changed my life. The change in my behavior was instant. My first corset acted like the suit of armor that I was struggling to build on my own. It showed me that I was beautiful, something that I had never believed before. It helped me to be the happy-go-lucky girl I had been before the abuse.

I was as surprised as my friends by my transformation from meek, mild-mannered geek who only wanted to fade into the background, to an assertive woman, unafraid to take center stage. I was hooked. I soon gathered a collection, and wore them at any opportunity, from going drinking with the girls (where I rarely got comments other than compliments), to somehow incorporating them into costumes, and sometimes wearing them just for the hell of it.

I am unable to wear my collection these days (children have seen to that), but despite the stretch marks and the body shape changes from my two wonderful pregnancies, corsets are still one of my favorite items of clothing. One day, once my baby-making days are done, I will be wearing them again.

CONFIDENCE IN MYSELF

ZARIAN V.

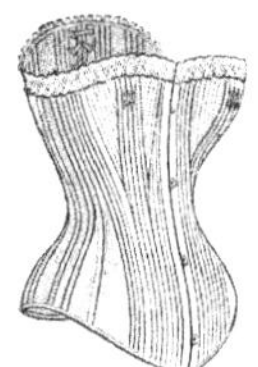

From a very young age, there was something different about me that I couldn't quite understand completely until I was a teenager. I am asexual, and from a very, very young age I couldn't understand why the world seemed obsessed with sex. Yes, I can appreciate outer beauty like everyone else, but the behavior of everyone relating to it just baffled me to no end—even when I was much too young to know what romantic kisses were. This confusion I felt didn't help my confidence as I grew older and began to understand the subtle rules of society—those non-verbal cues of sexual attraction that human beings display as signs of affection.

How was I supposed to fit into this "natural" puzzle if I didn't experience those cues? I grew up with low self-esteem, living in a very isolated area, and was bullied for my interests and my appearance: my fascination with books, the color of my skin, and the curls of my hair. I was a dork who would rather sit in the corner and draw than participate in the weird mating-dance practices of high school interactions.

But I was still human, and I needed something—anything—that would somehow help me find my place in my community; make me feel like a piece in the puzzle. I turned to the elegant women of the past. Period clothing always stood out to me; it enraptured me with its patterns and silhouettes, and as a young artist they seemed like the most beautiful works of art. I wanted to wear them all, but simply settled with drawing them and, eventually, trying to learn to craft my own.

I got my first corset when I was a teenager. It wasn't a real corset (with its plastic bones and all), but it brought my confidence out. Sure, I knew it wasn't quite as high quality as I wanted, but it was enough at the time to force my head high when I walked down a street or a corridor. Enough to feel my voice had some weight to it. Corsetry has served as a reassurance to me, like the kind you get from the hug of a close friend or relative. Wearing a corset gives me a soothing feeling of being in control.

There even came a time when I didn't wear my corset all that much because that confidence eventually became part of me and I had become more comfortable in my own skin.

When I left for college, I was still very confused about how I fit in the world. Even with the confidence I managed to keep, I still felt that part of me was broken. Everyone I talked to or consulted with seemed to confirm this. Everyone said it would be all right once I found "The One"—meaning I needed to find someone else to fix me.

Looking back on it, it wasn't the best advice, but ignorance can only teach ignorance, right? I began a relationship with the first person who seemed willing enough for something long term. Yes, I'm not kidding—I used to think that relationships simply happened, because I was never taught or had experienced otherwise. How was I to know that it is not how healthy relationships begin, if all through my young life I believed myself to be too ugly and broken to start one?

Anyways, I began the relationship. It had its ups and its downs. But still I took things as they came, believing that it was just simply how relationships went. I lost my virginity, I got engaged, and the bastard took the liberty of throwing away every single one of those plastic corsets I had, saying, "You won't need these trashy clothes anymore." Suffice it to say I was miserable, but I tolerated it because ... I just believed that is how it was supposed to go, at least if I wanted to be fixed.

Silly me.

After all of this, I made a decision for myself. I left that previous college and moved from the Caribbean to the US so I could study art instead of science. I LOVE both, but doing something interactive really pulls my passion strings. Through all of this, I was still engaged, but I was very vocal that I would not marry until I received my degree. After enduring four and a half years of abuse, cheating, and broken promises from my fiancé, I found myself more broken than I thought possible. And in all of this I still believed it was my fault. Can you believe that? Guilt is a silly, illogical thing, yet it consumed me nonetheless.

There was one moment in which I sat with a friend pondering, and I unexpectedly started sobbing. My poor bewildered friend didn't know what to do but just hold me. I made a decision that moment, a decision I should have made years earlier but hadn't.

After a short plane ride to the Caribbean and a drive up to my close friend's house, I told her everything. She hugged me; just gave me that long, comforting hug. She was delighted that I made a decision for my own well-being, but was angered over the abuse that I had silently endured for so long.

I drove the next day to my fiancé's house and picked him up; I decided to take him to one of the secluded spots we always used to go on our dates many years ago. In retrospect, that was a very stupid decision on my part. He could have killed or severely hurt me in one of his violent fits. But we were already there, and I wanted to talk to him in a private setting that was off of his property.

There was no consoling him—and yes, I had to be the one consoling him because he damned every last cell of my being. Even as I tried to settle things peacefully and gather my belongings from his place, he burned a good portion of them and almost crashed my car on the highway. Not a very happy ending.

Again I digress. After this whole snafu, I was incredibly torn. Yes, I was happy to be free, but my depression persisted and once again came the outside opinions that "someone else will come to fix you." I grew tired of that narrative, and instead of relying on those opinions, I went to the internet for my torch and shield whenever I became too depressed or too bogged down by my studies.

It was there where I learned what asexuality was, and thereupon after lots and lots of research I discovered that I am not in fact broken. I'm not broken at all, I'm perfectly fine, and I am beautiful. So I started dressing up again! On the worst days of my depression, I made the effort of looking my best because I wanted to show the world that I would not allow others to tell me that "someone else will come to fix you."

In this moment—the moment when I finally allowed myself to feel good about myself—I gathered the money I had saved and recalled the hours of research I had done over the years and finally got my first real corset. I still admired them from afar all those years, even after my ex threw away my clothes and discouraged me from wearing them, but it was a defining moment when I finally let myself enjoy one. I wore my corset proudly despite the questions and incredulous looks of those I knew—and you know what? I loved it! It gave me real confidence—and it alleviated my bad back problems.

I still remember the first time I found Lucy's corset blog and clicked over to her YouTube channel. I spent a week going through every single video. I'm now the proud owner of two real corsets and can only hope one day to have a vast and beautiful collection of couture corsetry. Corsets make me feel right with myself.

I am very prone to panic attacks and bad back pain from my days as an athlete, but whenever I have a corset on (whether under or over my clothing) it feels as though I have this one thing that no one can take away from me. It's like a security blanket. I feel empowered and I feel beautiful, graceful, and in control of my life.

My corset is something that not many people understand, somewhat like my asexuality. I find parallels between the same funny looks I get from people when I tell them about either my corset or my sexual identity. But now I'm relaxed and assertive enough to take a second to educate people properly on both topics, and to refer them to other resources.

I've realized that I am indeed beautiful enough to wear the beautiful garments I've always loved and admired. I now know that I don't need anyone there to reassure me about it. With my corset on, and now even on the days without my corset, I feel confident, and I feel that confidence is a solid part of my identity.

STRENGTH

VIOLET M.

I have anxiety and depression, which grew from a hurtful past, namely an abusive relationship. My ex-boyfriend was very controlling. He wouldn't let me hang out with my friends. He wouldn't even let me eat. I was so hungry and sad. He would force me to kiss him and touch him. It felt wrong and I felt degraded. It gave me a skewed perception of what was expected of me as a woman. I felt like I couldn't be attractive or happy the way I was because I was being forced to live my life differently.

I was able to break off the relationship before it could escalate further. I went back to eating a healthy diet, and started hanging out with my friends again. I realized that I am always there to help myself and I can stand up for myself. But I was afraid of sex or looking sexy.

I overcame that obstacle with my current boyfriend of five years, but I still needed help to overcome my depression and anxiety. For years I had resisted taking medication. I know prescription drugs have helped many people with anxiety or depression; however, I wanted to heal the root of my problem rather than masking it. At my first meeting with a psychiatrist, she heard my story and my emotional struggles, and she told me I had PTSD.

My nerves and emotions used to be very unstable and erratic. I would say things to friends and family that I regretted because I was too stressed out. It was embarrassing to start shaking and crying during an argument. Situations that would seem normal to other people would cause me to panic. I cried very easily, got excessively upset over trivial situations, became suddenly paranoid, and had panic attacks. It was very difficult for me to go through college with my uncontrollable anxiety. I started missing school due to sleepless nights, constantly vomiting from anxiety.

One of the most difficult periods of my life was my father's struggle with epilepsy. He was diagnosed a few days before his 50th birthday, shortly before I started college. A brain tumor had been found from the scans and the doctors estimated that removing the tumor would give a 96% chance of him being seizure-free.

Unfortunately, after the surgery, his seizures only became more frequent. He had seizures up to three times a day, and the doctors tried many medications in succession to stop them. It broke my heart to see my dad slowly losing brain function from the seizures and medications—he was helpless and housebound. It was hard for me to be away from my family while at college, knowing that my dad needed more help than my mom and brother could provide.

I never cried around my father during his illness. Even as his condition progressed and he started having memory lapses. Even if he forgot my name, I bottled up my emotions until I could go to my bedroom to be alone to cry. I didn't want my parents to argue. I didn't want to see my brother depressed like me. I wanted to help, and I helped as much as I could.

But while I was constantly helping my family and friends with their problems, I never stopped to consider helping myself. I worked myself to my breaking point and never repaired myself. I would put up a façade in public. I smiled at my father to give him hope and I told him that his problems would go away. I wished so hard that my words would come true.

I had few friends in college, so I was often alone with my thoughts and had few reminders to keep me strong. People thought I was quiet and weird. Most people didn't bother to get to know me since I didn't have the fun "party" college personality. My boyfriend attended a different college, and without him by my side, I found myself falling back into depression and being continually stressed by the long-distance relationship. I realized that I had become dependent on having a boyfriend to bring myself happiness. I became aware that I needed to love myself for who I was instead of depending upon receiving affection from others.

I had fainting episodes multiple times during college whenever I became overwhelmed, and I ended up moving into a dorm room by myself since my roommate was uncomfortable with my condition and was very rude to me. By then I was completely isolated.

I learned that there are people who don't understand that depression is a serious issue. Support and happy reminders keep depression at bay, and they are essential to keep us strong.

I went home during vacation and learned that my father had had a reaction to a combination of his medications. For one week, I stayed by his bedside while he had severe hallucinations, vomiting, and seizures. I slept only a few hours that week, and I felt myself going crazy from insomnia. That week was so disturbing I just wanted it to end. I screamed at my mother that I wanted him to die so he didn't have to suffer anymore. I started to cry. I felt guilty for wishing for him to die.

Then the doctor told my family that my father could have another surgery. The scar tissue from the original tumor removal surgery was causing the seizures, so the removal of that scar tissue would likely end his epilepsy. I was so excited and I told my father that he should do it. I had faith in him and the doctor, and I believed it would work.

The surgery was a success and he was seizure-free. I had tears of joy. But I was unable to visit him for several months because the hospital had strict visitation rules to avoid compromising his immune system. When he was transferred to a new hospital, I could finally visit him.

I saw him for the first time all summer and he was so happy to see me. It was the first time I saw my father so emotional. He told me he was scared that he was going to die when the hospital staff had to perform a barbaric test to locate exactly where the seizures started in his brain before they could operate. During the test, the hospital staff waited too long to pull him out of his seizure and they couldn't stop it. His seizure lasted six hours. I was horrified and enraged at that hospital. I hugged my father and told him that he was going to have a better life now.

The next morning, I got a call that my father had passed away due to a blood clot. The hospital had him sedentary too long and they did not take preventative actions to avoid clotting. My world turned upside-down, and it was the lowest point of my life. I didn't eat or sleep for several days. Everything felt so surreal.

I immediately went back to college after the summer because I was determined to finish and get a degree. But my grief made me feel so disconnected from reality. I became irritable and cold-hearted towards others. I felt ugly. I felt like I was in a dream and that nothing mattered.

My first visit to a psychiatrist helped me realize that I didn't take enough time to do things to make myself happy. I have forgotten to recognize how strong I have been these past few years, despite my past and current problems. I would hide my body under my coat and slouch. I needed a way to remind myself to be strong and remind myself that I am beautiful. I needed to embrace my body and be proud of myself. Corsets, in part, provided that embrace.

I believe that corsets boost my confidence and lessen my depression and anxiety. A corset is a lifeguard for me. It holds me up high and saves me from drowning in my thoughts and emotions. It is my shield against the sorrow and negativity. It is my hug when I have no one else to embrace. It is a reminder that I am beautiful.

Corsets have lifted my spirits many times, and make me feel glamorous and confident. I began connecting with the corset community, which is full of so many beautiful and kind-hearted people. I felt surrounded by positivity and excitement for corsetry.

My hobby was initially a distraction from reality. But over time, thanks to it, I have learned to accept what had happened in the past and to be proud of how far I've come in life. I've become happier and made new friends. Random people in public smiled at me or politely talk to me when they saw me wearing one of my corsets. Then I began to notice that people would talk to me even if I wasn't wearing a corset. I became more confident whether I was wearing a corset or not. I became more adventurous, started new hobbies, and met new people.

For the first time in my life, I feel genuinely happy with myself. I have found happiness in my friends, family, and in myself. I am thankful for corsets helping me love myself and my life. I finally feel like I am true to myself and others. I have grown to be a strong, beautiful person.

PART XVIII

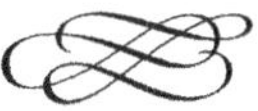

MATURE CORSETING

THE ART OF AGING

ROSE GUILDENSTERN

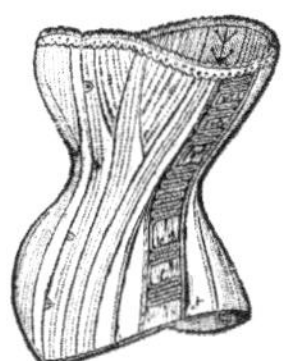

Being an aging woman in this modern world can be either tragic—or *magic*.

We watch the body of our youth go through such "socially unacceptable" changes: jiggles, furrows, dimples, puckers, and scars. So many of us feel trapped in a body that is now judged "over the hill" instead of over the top, "seasoned" instead of sexy, or the dreaded "matronly" instead of magnetic. We watch our diets and work out harder than we ever did when young in the attempt to lose those love handles, stop those spreads, or at least slow those sags, but the years and gravity are against us: We are aging, and we live in a society that still worships youthful beauty above all else in half of its population.

Nothing ages a woman's body quite so quickly as having children. After the birth of my youngest child, I felt old for the first time. It's much harder to bounce back from childbirth at 40 than at 26 (my age when I had my first) and I felt frumpy, uncomfortable in my softer stretch-marked body, and tired. Monumentally tired.

As every mother of a small child knows, you tend to lose your own identity in the all-consuming task of raising little human beings. Totally and completely worth it, but there comes the day when every mother eventually confronts herself in the mirror and says some version of, "What happened? Where did I go?" It might be returning to the workforce, or the first day of preschool, or the first day of college, but eventually we all have to redefine ourselves within the context of being "mother."

I began to make excuses to myself, of course: I looked so wan and tired because I hadn't slept, in, well, YEARS, and I was waiting for when I had time to put on makeup, or to go to the store to find the right moisturizer for those dark circles under my eyes. My clothes looked atrocious because I was waiting for when my kids would be old enough to stop staining them, so why go shopping and buy more nice clothes that would either get messed up or I'd never wear? Although I'd always preferred myself in short mod hair, long hair pulled back in a ponytail was more sensible for a mom, because who has time to style and get it cut regularly? And what's the use when my body has changed so much? No one will think that this irrevocably altered mommy's body is beautiful. I'd wait until...

Oh my god.

I was living in a perpetual state of waiting. I was fast becoming that sweet old lady who is only noticed as a placeholder in line, as a person who is in your way.

Prior to motherhood, I had been an artist by trade. My first career was a high school theater arts program director, I ran the vocal arts program at my church, I was a published author, and even when home with my youngest I crafted meticulously handmade art dolls. Some might say that my children are the greatest artistic creation of my life, and while there is definitely truth to that statement, I had lost myself as an artist while I invested myself into my children's becoming.

As I gazed into my mirror at 45 years old, I felt that with regards to my physical self, I had failed. I'd continuously failed to achieve the beauty standards that society set for me—I'd never been model thin, I'd never had a hard body, I'd always looked awful in the popular shapeless fashions that were so svelte on my friends. And now I was getting grey hairs and showing laugh lines, the final proverbial nails in the coffin of my dream of having a socially approved feminine body.

But here comes the magical wisdom of aging: I just didn't care anymore.

As I stood facing the naked truth of my body in that mirror, I decided to also shed the false dictates of what I had been tutored to believe was beautiful by fashion magazines, advertisers, and the media. I decided to befriend my body, rather than try to change it into something it wasn't. It was time to embrace my aging, flaunt my natural assets, and stop waiting for that distant "someday" that was NEVER going to come.

Rather than systematically cutting away parts of me, living in a state of perpetual diet deprivation, or just plain giving up and "aging gracefully," it was time to reclaim my inner artist, discard the physical ideals of my youth, and transform my 40-something body into my own unique work of art.

I refused to go gentle into that good night.

I'd often flirted with corsetry throughout my lifetime—from my first Renaissance Faire to the corselets of Frederick's of Hollywood, and even retro fashions when they made a resurgence—but now, after myriad hours spent researching, I decided to use the corset to artistically sculpt my body into an *objet d'art*. I purchased a bespoke corset, custom-made for my own unique curves, and began the process of waist training: wearing a corset for long hours daily with the purpose of retraining my natural waist to be smaller.

The corset as used in the modern corset movement is not, as many of its critics accuse, "sexist" (although it is supremely sexy in an in-your-face sort of way that can make those who are insecure in their own body and sexuality uncomfortable). It is not conformance to an imposed norm, but rather the height of individual expression.

My corset may bind my waist, but it frees *me*. I do not wear my corset to please a man, or because fashion dictates it, or because my peers judge it acceptable. My corsets are the height of my personal physical aesthetic. Unlike the fashion trends that I followed (often unsuccessfully) in my youth, my corset expresses what is unique about my particular body type: I am round, curvaceous, zaftig, with huge hips, a smallish waist, and an even bigger bust.

Corsets worn under the clothes are a guilty pleasure—a secret indulgence that is mine and mine alone. Corsets worn over the clothes (a thoroughly contemporary manifestation of personal fashionista expression) are, contrary to criticisms, physically and psychologically liberating. I wear my corset on top of my clothes to openly display my assets, to celebrate the extreme expression of my uniquely feminine form, to glory in my hills and valleys *with* you.

Just as a girl with lovely legs wears a mini skirt, a woman with a glorious bosom wears a push up bra, or a lady with lovely eyes wears dramatic eye makeup, my corset enhances what is most appealing about my figure: the difference in size between my bust, waist, and butt.

In addition to wearing corsets, I began to pamper my body: I dressed it only in lush fabrics that hugged my curves, I invested in portraits taken by professional photographers, I delved into sumptuous skin care and makeup, and I began luxuriously stretching and moving my body through daily yoga.

After nearly two years of regular corset wear, I have sculpted my body into a striking corseted hourglass shape. Initially I could only cinch down to 31.5″ (80 cm), but now I regularly cinch down to 26″ (66 cm), measured over my corset. When wearing one of my corsets my dimensions are 45-25-45 inches (114-64-114 cm). But my corset has brought more *dimension* into my life in other ways I could never have predicted: weight loss, better health, easier menopause, more happiness, and more sensitivity to my body's cues.

Everyone in our society wants to lose weight it seems, and I was no different for most of my life. Yet the statistics of weight loss failure are astounding: 95% of us will fail at our diets (or, as I now believe, 95% of our diets fail *us*), with many regaining even more weight than their body's original set point at the start of their diet. With the decision to corset, I threw away my diet books and the desire to be thin. Nevertheless, my natural waist was 33″ (84 cm) when I began waist training—now it is 30″ (76 cm).

Rather than making weight loss my marker of health, I worked to love my curves, eat mindfully, and move my body joyfully every day. I did lose some weight during the process, but this was a by-product rather than a goal. As I corseted my waistline, however, my blood pressure and other blood work resolved to not just normal, but more akin to that of an athlete (who knew corseting could be a competitive sport?). My blood sugar and hormones stabilized. I am perhaps having the most relaxed perimenopause that I've ever heard of. My daily mood and energy are what can only be termed *effervescent*.

Wearing corsets makes me intimately more aware of my body—that gentle hug of pressure throughout my torso keeps me attentive to what my body is experiencing moment by moment. As a result, I make better choices for my body's wellbeing much more often.

Is corseting responsible for all my health improvements? Of course not. But choosing to corset was the catalyst that propelled me to alter a succession of poor health fixations and choices. Wearing my corsets helped me give permission to myself to create my own physical reality, rather than hopelessly chasing the rules prescribed by the "experts" and the "well-intentioned." Choosing to corset—to revel in my own body and all its marvelous complexity and wonder—propelled me to view aging as a ripening rather than ruin.

My corset has transfigured my life and my experience of aging. With my corset, the most magical years of my life are yet to come.

And I can't wait.

Rose Guildenstern is an author who pens weird fiction that appeals to all ages, writing the edge between eerie and enlightening. She also creates cartomancy decks and books about tarot under the pen name Juno Lucina.

Find out more about Rose/Juno at— roseguildenstern.com

CORSETING FOR THE NOT SO YOUNG

CARYN G.L.

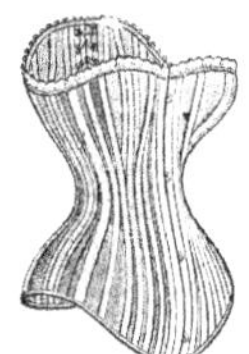

I came to corseting the same way I have about many things: by accident. I love to learn, and for me one thing always leads to another. So while learning about European royal houses, I became interested in what women wore over the years—and this led to learning about corsets. I was startled to find that corsetry still exists in this day and age, but I was also too fascinated by the beauty of corsets, their unparalleled femininity, and what they can do to change the body to ignore them. I wanted in!

I ordered one from Isabella Corsetry with no thought of anything but a possible improvement to my 59-year-old body. I have borne two children and have a serious medical condition (namely stage IV breast cancer) that has altered said body. Between the reconstructed breasts and the medication that keeps me going, my body has suffered a bit. My oncologist is a wonderful woman and I asked her about corseting. She was, like me, surprised that corsets still existed, but felt there was nothing health-wise to stop me from giving them a try.

I loved my corset from the moment I put it on. Yes, it made my waist look amazing—but I also loved the way the pressure on my torso slowed my breathing and calmed me. This was a surprise. I had known about weighted vests that help calm children with certain conditions like autism (I am an elementary school teacher), but I didn't realize that a corset could function in a similar way.

Corseting has been a rather private affair for me. I live alone and view corseting as part of my private time, though I have stealthily worn my corset under my clothes on occasion while out of the house. What the world sees, however, is a somewhat sleeker body, a bounce in my step that had gone missing since my breast cancer diagnosis, and a less tense approach to the daily trials of modern life.

So, what has corsetry done for me? It has helped restore my body image and the confidence that goes with it, served as a healthy way to calm and de-stress, and given me an insight into why pressure on the torso works for some of my students. I suppose I could say that wearing a corset has made me a better teacher. And, could anyone deny the utter beauty and femininity of a well-made corset?

OUTDOING THE SPRING CHICKENS

SHELLY P., LVN

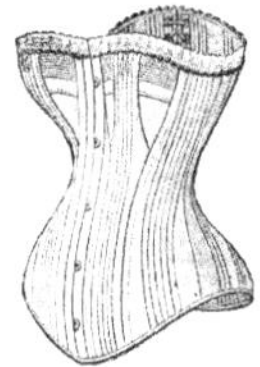

I am a 67-year-old hospice nurse. My skeletal frame is very small—my wrist's circumference is 5.75 inches (14.6 cm). In addition to my "bird-bone" skeletal structure, I have osteoporosis (which is being treated).

I am responsible for turning patients that weigh more than I do. Some of my patients suffer from dementia or mental illness and can become combative. Sometimes, especially when the shift is unusually long, my back hurts. There is also my ongoing concern that if a patient hits or pushes me, or twists when I support or move them, or if I fall, I could break one of my small and fragile bones.

I took up wearing corsets strictly for ornamental reasons. However, I quickly learned that if I wear a steel-boned corset under my scrubs, my back is fully reinforced. I also find that I can work a longer day. In addition, my corset protects me against aggressors: if I am struck or punched in the torso by an agitated patient, they get badly bruised hands, and I am able to hold my ground. If I get pushed or fall, the corset provides some protection from hip fractures, and from vertebral micro fractures that may otherwise lead to kyphosis.

Many hospice facilities offer a sort of "back brace" to staff, for use while working. A well-constructed, steel-boned corset is *ten times better* in my opinion! I feel safe and comfortable, with no fear of injuring my back, or breaking a hip. The comfort of a good corset enables me not only to work more hours, but also to be happy and cheerful while doing it. Because I am not fighting pain, fatigue, or injury, I can out-produce nurses who are decades younger than I am!

On a more personal matter: a good corset feels like an "all day hug." It somehow adds a feeling of security, and brings me increased confidence.

I have developed an elegant and graceful carriage due to the corset, which has given me a more youthful appearance and led to my receiving many compliments from those around me. The benefit to my shape and my posture often cause people to mistake my age, to my advantage! (I am tired of people telling me that corsets will hurt my childbearing capabilities—at 67 years of age!)

My corset has helped me to control my portion sizes, as it acts like a mini lap band, thereby helping me maintain my weight. I weigh the same as I did in college, and have also preserved my natural hourglass figure into my senior years—I'm even getting invitations from guys 20 years younger than I am! And the longer I wear my corset, the more benefits keep surfacing.

In summary, the personal gain that I have enjoyed is extremely satisfying. The physiological benefits are irreplaceable, and, to me, spending $300 for a well-made, custom fit corset is a small investment for all those benefits!

PART XIX

CORSETS & METAPHYSICS

CORSETRY & REIKI

REBECCA CAPLE ~ ICRT CERTIFIED REIKI PRACTITIONER

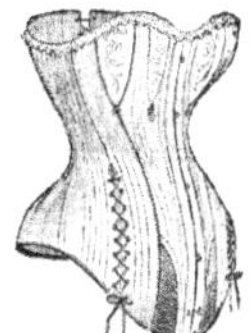

Corsetry is not just art or just history; corsetry can be a wonderful catalyst for helping one address various conditions: back pain relief, lessened anxiety, and improved posture, to name a few. I feel the qualities go further than alignment and deep pressure therapy. About 10 years ago I was involved in a car accident, leaving me with chronic back pain and anxiety. This accident manifested itself in an ongoing battle with panic attacks and stress. Since this event I have been searching for a way to manage my ailments without prescriptions.

After years of trial and error I found my first breakthrough. It was with Reiki. Reiki is a Japanese technique for stress reduction and relaxation that also promotes healing. This is achieved through visualization, meditation, and touch. Some would refer to this practice as "massage for the soul." Reiki can be described as manipulation of the energy that flows through our bodies.

This flow of energy has natural pooling areas. In Eastern belief, the body has seven energy centers, running from the base of the spine to the crown of the head. These are known as chakras. Each of these energy pools governs a set of functions.

In Hindu and many new age belief systems, pain and emotional distress are a physical manifestation of imbalance in the body. Typically, this is associated with an imbalanced or blocked chakra, and the symptoms will tell you the source of the ailment. I use Reiki energy to remove these blockages to help soothe pain and manage anxiety. This is done by visualizing the chakra, or by touching the corresponding region.

To practice Reiki you must be trained by a certified master. However, Reiki is not the only way to balance these energy centers. Acupressure, acupuncture, massage therapy, and deep pressure therapy are other external ways of stimulating the flow of energy throughout the body.

My second breakthrough with pain and anxiety management was from corset wear. As an adolescent I had a fascination with Victorian-era clothing and historical art. It didn't cross my mind until recently that corsetry had uses other than fashion. Subsequently I began researching corsetry as a supplemental means of pain relief.

These garments, after all, were intended for support. I noticed upon wearing my first corset a sense of well-being, calm, minimized pain, and hyper awareness. The constant pressure from a corset, specifically one with steel boning, provides support to the lumbar region.

There are also many who claim it helps them manage anxiety due to its functional deep-pressure therapy. I agree with these observations, since I have experienced this first-hand. My posture has improved, and in combination with core strength exercise, the hyperlordosis in my spine has been minimized.

It wasn't until I decided to wear my corset during my daily meditation that I had discovered one more interesting side effect: after having worn a corset while giving myself Reiki, I noticed the steel boning serving as a conductor and magnifier of the vibrations from the Reiki traveling down the boning along my spine. It felt as though I had just received an hour-long massage at my favorite spa. Typically, when I meditate I will spend the first 5–10 minutes letting go of whatever floods my mind. In this particular instance, I felt immediate calm and comfort. Only then did I remember that metal is a conductor.

Upon further research into the metaphysical properties of steel, I learned that it is defined as a great projector, conducting your intention effectively. This can be useful when trying to balance a chakra through meditation. Simply relax and focus on balancing the intended chakra. If you are familiar with meditation, I recommend trying this for yourself and comparing it with and without a corset. You may find that it is easier to relax and focus, and that you find balance in a shorter period of time.

I also found that steel has protective qualities, sort of like spiritual armor. Steel has been said to protect from others' negativity and attack. You may hear many in the tightlacing community make the claim of feeling safe, perhaps even invincible, while being laced.

This is just another interesting parallel.

As a certified Reiki practitioner with a strong belief in the power of energetic healing, I feel the relief that is brought on by corset wear is more than just a physical aid; that it's due to a way of life that helps heal the soul.

ACTIVATION OF THE MANIPURA CHAKRA THROUGH THE PLEASURE OF CORSETING

DAISY RAE

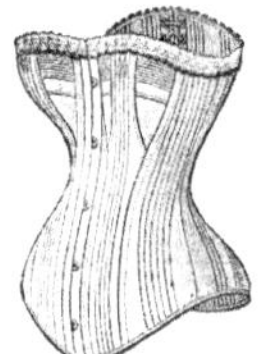

In the modern mindset, corsets are often thought of as an instrument of torture. A typical reaction is, "Why do women torture themselves just to be fashionable and to have a smaller waist?"

On the other hand, if you read the statements of long-term waist trainers and tightlacers, they almost all refer to how comfortable their corsets are. They love their corsets and use words like "pleasurable," "enjoyable," "cozy," and many can hardly imagine not wearing their corsets. They are ecstatic about the experience. In fact, you'd have to admit that anyone who would wear a corset from 8–23 hours every day must actually *enjoy* wearing their corset.

Let's rule out a couple of negative reasons one might think of for enjoying corsets.

First, the corseting experience is clearly not usually a masochistic one. All responsible waist trainers try to avoid pain and discomfort. They advise that if you start to feel uncomfortable, loosen the corset or take the corset off. Rather, they view the restrictiveness and tightness of the corset as a positive experience.

Second, serious waist trainers are well aware that in the long run, if they stop wearing their corset, their waist size will return to normal. They are not fooling themselves that they are permanently altering their waist measurements.

Third, although waist trainers may initially launch their programs with a goal of looking more fashionable, many long-term trainers who achieve dramatic results in waist reduction may eventually try to *hide* their new figures under loose clothing, an action called "stealthing." Thus, in the long term, even one's outer appearance is not the most important criterion for many waist trainers.

So just how do waist trainers describe the pleasure they gain from corseting? At the first tightening of the laces, I feel a strong and unique pleasure that does not seem to be related to life's other pleasures. What a wonderful feeling! It is almost as though that tightening pushes a magic button or flips a switch of contentment. This reaction is reported by other corset users, as you have by now read in earlier chapters.

This relaxing or calming effect while wearing a corset can be related to "Deep Pressure Therapy." This is the calming feeling some people have when being hugged or swaddled. In fact, Deep Pressure Therapy is used in treatment for several syndromes.

In this regard, Dr. Temple Grandin's work on her "squeeze machine" is instructive.

Grandin reports that the machine also works with many neurotypical people, in addition to autistic children. Deep pressure applied to a wide area of the body, administered by the squeeze machine, has a relaxing effect on everyday adults. In the present study, college students were found to feel relaxed after use of the squeeze machine.[1] However, the result is not the same for everyone: for 40% of subjects, the machine appeared to have no relaxing effect.

Grandin concluded that the feel-good experience can be achieved despite societal opprobrium; that is, it makes or incites positive emotions even if other people are telling you you're crazy.

Lucy's Corsetry compares corsets to the squeeze machine: the corset simulates the pressure of a hug and makes the wearer feel more secure. However, a hug around the shoulders should have the same deep pressure effect as around the waist, as shown by the squeeze machine. Why, then, do we not see devices sold that create tightness around the shoulders? What is so unique about the waist area? I will return to this point soon.

Most waist trainers report "feeling good about themselves." Indeed, Lucy has already written about this at length. Several questions arise about this "feel-good" phenomenon. How is one to explain of some corset wearers who "stealth" under their clothing? Do some of them feel shame from societal opprobrium and, if so, how do they still "feel good about themselves" in the corset? Do they feel good about the accomplishment of reducing their waist size? Or do they feel good about successfully keeping their secret from the public?

Another experience worth illuminating is that of Heidi of Strait-Laced Dame, who describes her "Waist Training Journey" as a life-changing experience and not just a fashion statement:

> This was the first time I had felt an embrace by anyone or anything in months, and I felt just a little bit more alive right then than I had the day before ... If I could have mastered sleeping in a corset so soon, I would have lived in it right from the start. It felt safe. It was my armor. Wearing a corset had, in a short period of time, progressed far beyond a way to change my body into some nonexistent ideal.
>
> An entire change in my attitude toward life was inspired by this simple steel-boned garment, as inconceivable as it may seem. What's more, in corsetry I found myself inexplicably passionate—it was something I never thought I would experience regarding any subject.

Lucy's theory about her own experience is that the confidence mechanism was related to her improved posture and powerful body language when corseted. Still, many corset wearers have naturally good posture. So in their cases, the confidence phenomenon is probably related to something else.

The following passage by Ava Strange describes a whole range of reasons for feeling good: pride, deep pressure therapy, anxiety-comforting, and the "journey":

> I'm very proud of the shape I've been able to achieve over the years, but unless I'm going to a special event where I feel it will be appreciated, I tend to somewhat hide it. Corsets are capable of performing a version of deep pressure therapy, and can be extremely comforting, especially to those with anxiety issues. You're wrapped in a firm hug for as long as you want to be, and you feel protected. It's comforting and calming...
>
> Also something to be proud of is not just the shape itself, but the time that it took to achieve it. It's the fact that I've been disciplined enough to make it this far, that I've really earned this. It's about the journey.
>
> You need to really be comfortable with yourself and your decisions to go against the social grain like that, because there's nothing quite like hearing a stranger tell you that you're killing yourself and you look disgusting.

Thus, you can be comfortable with yourself for corseting, even when society is sending the opposite message.

All the above is simply a compilation of various articles and theories. But now I come to some thoughts that are uniquely mine. I have not seen anything remotely similar to them anywhere.

I kept thinking about the effect achieved by the squeeze machine, similar to the feeling of putting on a corset. But why does deep pressure work so well around the waist? What is there about the waist region that is so special? I thought of the mysticism surrounding the solar plexus, or how Yogis "contemplate their navel."

I haven't read any accounts relating waist training to mysticism. The closest I have come is Ava Strange's account, comparing it to "zen":

> It's in this way that corsets really get you acquainted with your body in a way that virtually nothing else can, and really help you to connect with it. You'll become hyper-aware of your body inside the corset. Most of all wearing a tight corset on a regular basis teaches you how very unique we all are, and that this is beautiful in itself. There's something very earthy and zen about all this ... But "zen" only begins to cover it.

Although I don't consider myself a New Ager or a mystic, I thought about New Age mysticism, and the fact that the chakras are supposed to be mysterious energy centers located in various parts of the body. So I looked up the solar plexus chakra, called the Manipura chakra, and found some quite surprising coincidences:

The solar plexus chakra (Manipura chakra) is referred to as the home of self-esteem, asserting ourselves, finding our place in the world, and our inter-personal relationships with those people outside our lovers and family units. This chakra represents self-confidence, understanding of oneself and others, and ultimately personal power.

If the Manipura chakra becomes blocked, the affected person may experience low self-esteem and assertion, may become hypersensitive to criticism, may fear rejection, and may not consider themselves equal to others.

The solar plexus chakra is activated when one asserts one's willpower and stands up for oneself, especially when one stands tall and speaks with a clear voice.

To clear a blocked Manipura chakra, one must build self-confidence. One source, ChakraHealing.com, advises one to "set goals that challenge you a little and excite you a lot, and take small, consistent steps to achievement. You'll gain confidence as you see progress!"

You couldn't find a better description of corset pleasure. Unblocking your Manipura chakra sounds exactly like the pleasures of corseting. Notice the references to posture and "standing tall." Also note the concept of setting goals and taking small, consistent steps to achievement (cf. waist training).

Thus, it seems plausible to suggest that the tightening of the corset places gentle pressure on the solar plexus and activates the Manipura chakra, which then causes one to feel more self-confident and good about oneself.

In my own case, this explanation makes even more sense. I am 67 years old and had never worn a corset in my life until recently. I have always been successful professionally and otherwise, and have had a pretty positive self-image. I have always been physically fit as a distance runner, bicyclist, and swimmer, but it has only been recently that a heart problem has kept me from strenuous exercise. I have gained weight and developed a potbelly, which makes me feel bad about my self-image.

Moreover, I have recently experienced a total failure of a business venture, and this, too, has damaged my self-esteem. It was only at this point, in my 68th year, that I decided to purchase a corset. Somehow, I knew what I wanted and needed, although I told myself at the outset that I might decide this was a totally stupid idea and give it up immediately. However, I found that lacing and wearing the corset did have the magic self-esteem effect, even the first time I put it on. I have trouble ascribing this good feeling to anything other than the Manipura chakra effect.

Finally, let me reveal that I am a male waist trainer—I didn't want to cloud the discussion with that fact by saying so earlier. My whole point is that for long-term waist trainers, the allure of the corset applies to both males and females. The main difference is one of degree—the difficulty males have to overcome societal opprobrium as compared to the increasing acceptance of corset wear by modern women.

However, once this societal resistance has been overcome, I believe that the waist training pleasures apply to all sexes equally. The twin benefits of increasing one's self-esteem and gradually controlling the shape of one's body (through exercise and/or waist training) are pleasures that are available to anyone, and are not necessarily gender-specific. But aside from those psychologically describable joys, I can't dismiss that magical, irrational feeling that might just be ascribed to the activation of the solar plexus chakra.

---

1. Grandin, Temple. "Calming Effects of Deep Touch Pressure in Patients with Autistic Disorder, College Students, and Animals." *Journal of Child and Adolescent Psychopharmacology* 2, no. 1 (1992): 63–72. https://doi.org/10.1089/cap.1992.2.63.

PART XX

NOTEWORTHY NEWSPAPER CLIPPINGS
(PUBLIC DOMAIN)

PLUNGES A BUTCHER-KNIFE INTO HER SISTER'S BOSOM

Cincinnati Enquirer, 24 October 1859

Yesterday morning two abandoned women, Emma Raynor and Judith Miller, living in a bagnio on Sycamore street, between Third and Fourth, quarreled about a lover, of whose attention they were both desirous, and began scratching and biting each other like tigresses. At last one of them (Emma) grew so infuriated that she ran into the kitchen, and, seizing a butcher knife, rushed back into the room where the trouble occurred, and plunged the weapon, with a murderous intent, at her sister's breast. The blade struck the board of her corset—a circumstance which saved her life—and, glancing off, entered her breast half an inch to the left of her heart. The sanguinary Emma would have completed the fearful deed she had undertaken had she not been prevented by two or three inmates of the house, who were compelled to employ violent means to disarm her. The woman seemed demonized with rage, and would have killed those who had prevented her from committing murder had she been able to do so.

HER CORSETS SAVED HER

Los Angeles Herald, 4 January 1891

FRANK H. MANDEVILLE ATTEMPTS MURDER AND SUICIDES

A Tragedy Last Night in a Main-Street Lodging House—The Horrible Sight Witnessed by a Ten-Year-Old Child.

"I will blow your brains out if you open the door!" shouted Frank H. Mandeville about 10 o'clock last night. Mandeville was locked in room 26 in the third story of the Roberts building, at the corner of Seventh and Main street, and Officer Farmer was attempting to get into the room.

"I command you to open the door. I am an officer, and will burst open the door," shouted back the officer.

The officer had no sooner spoken than he put his shoulder against the door and burst it wide open.

"Stand back, or I'll shoot" hissed Mandeville, as he leveled a revolver at the officer, who had stepped to the side and warned Mandeville that he was an officer and that he had better not shoot.

"Stand back a minute and I will come," said the man with the gun. These were the last words spoken by Mandeville, for he held the pistol close to his face and put a bullet in his head.

A HERALD reporter arrived a few minutes after the tragedy. Mandeville lay on the floor of a room occupied by Mrs. Millie Shaw. In his right hand was an ordinary revolver, in his left hand was a razor, and after the coroner's arrival a bottle of poison was found in his pocket. The deceased was dressed in black, and on his vest was displayed a grand army badge. As he lay on the floor he appeared to be a man of about thirty-five, but it was afterwards learned that he was almost fifty years old.

Before Mandeville took his life, he labored under the impression that he had shot and killed Mrs. Millie Shaw. Three times he fired at the woman, and it is only a miracle that she escaped with her life. It appears that early in the evening, Mandeville must have sneaked up stairs and secreted himself. Mrs. Shaw suspected that she heard somebody and stayed in Mr. and Mrs. Humphrey's room until they came home. This room is opposite the hallway and in close proximity to the two rooms occupied by Mrs. Shaw. At about 10 o'clock, Mrs. Shaw, lamp in hand, started to go into her room. She was about to enter when Mandeville rushed out and, without speaking, fired three times at her in rapid succession. Mrs. Shaw ran screaming down the hall, the lamp falling to the floor. In a minute, all was confusion—men and women rushed all over the building.

Mandeville, however, entered Mrs. Shaw's room and locked the door. The arrival of Officer Farmer and the succeeding event of Mandeville's death, has already been told.

At first it was thought that Mrs. Shaw had been killed or seriously wounded. An examination showed that she escaped without injury, except a powder wound on her right wrist. Two of the balls struck her corset and glided off harmlessly. Nothing but the corset saved her life.

Johnny, the ten-year-old son of Mrs. Shaw, occupied a cot in the room all the while the shooting was going on, and from under the bedclothes saw Mandeville send a bullet crashing through his brains. It must have been a terrible experience for the little fellow.

Mandeville is well known all over California. He is a manufacturers' agent. Recently he was the agent for an elastic tug spring and a patent mop. He was apparently infatuated with Mrs. Shaw, who is a dressmaker. His visits were objectionable, however, but he continued to force himself upon her until she asked Mr. Pearson, the landlord, not to allow him to enter the building. One of the roomers at the Roberts block told the HERALD reporter that Mandeville had threatened Mrs. Shaw several times.

Mrs. Shaw was interviewed by the reporter. She did not throw much light on the mysterious affair, being in a very excited and nervous state.

It was ascertained that Mandeville and Mrs. Shaw were school mates in New York. Mandeville had been seen prowling around the neighborhood of the Roberts building since early yesterday morning. He evidently watched his opportunity to get up stairs, as Pearson had previously threatened to throw him out if he ever crossed the threshold of the building.

The coroner found a letter on Mandeville's clothes. On one side was written:

My Last Request
F. H. M.
Over.

On the reverse side was:

Please deliver letter to W. H. Shinn, Esq., First and Broadway, before coroner's jury report.

Three other addressed letters were afterwards found on the mantel piece. They were turned over to Under Sheriff Moran. The body was removed to the undertaking parlors of Orr & Sutch, where an inquest will be held today. The letters left by Mandeville will doubtless throw some light on the subject.

STARTLING OCCURRENCE IN A TEA-ROOM

Evening Post, 28 October 1898

Two Women and a Revolver
Three Shots Fired.
One Advantage of Wearing Corsets.

An incident having all the elements of sensational tragedy, without its reality, took place in the tea-rooms on the first floor of Messrs. Kirkcaldie & Stains's new premises late yesterday afternoon.

At about 4.30 o'clock Mrs. McWilliam, who was a not infrequent visitor to the shop and the tea-rooms, ordered afternoon tea for herself, her daughter (about 17 years of age), Mrs. Coleman (a friend), and a child. The party took a table overlooking the stairway, and close to the counter where the refreshments are dispensed. Just as the party had partaken of the tea, Mrs. Dick, who has been in charge of the tea-room since its opening, came across to the counter. Mrs. McWilliam immediately rose from the table, and withdrawing her hand from under her cloak levelled a large six-chambered revolver deliberately at Mrs. Dick and fired.

Mrs. Dick was passing sideways through the opening of the counter at the time, and was not more than half-a-dozen paces away. The bullet struck her on the left side just under the ribs, glanced off, and tore a hole in the side of the wall. Mrs. Dick ran through into the kitchen, the door of which she had just passed when two more shots were fired, the bullets passing through the panel within an inch of each other, and on into the wall of the kitchen. Miss Holmes was making scones at the time, and the bullets passed within a few inches of her back.

At the time of the firing of the first shot every table in the tea-room was occupied by ladies. After the shot was fired about the only ladies left in the room were those of Mrs. McWilliam's own party, Mrs. Coleman having fallen into a hysterical swoon. The Sheriff of the Supreme Court and a male friend were witnesses of the whole incident.

When Mrs. McWilliam levelled the revolver Miss Roach, an assistant, was standing at the counter between Mrs. Dick and her assailant, arranging some cakes upon a tray, her back being towards Mrs. McWilliam. On the weapon being fired Miss Roach jumped round, saw the revolver being levelled again, saw Mrs. Dick stagger, and caught Mrs. McWilliam's wrist with the cry, "You brute! You've killed her!" Mrs. McWilliam replied to the effect that she was glad that she had, and accused Mrs. Dick of having robbed her of some "thousands," Miss Roach not being certain whether it was the word "five" or "ten."

"As Mrs. Dick was opening the kitchen door," said Miss Roach to the POST representative, "Mrs. McWilliam gave me such a fierce look that I was afraid she was going to fire at me, and I let go of her hand. She immediately raised the revolver, and fired two more shots rapidly." Miss Roach's interruption probably saved Mrs. Dick's life.

Another assistant, Miss McFarlane, was behind the counter at the time of the firing, and narrowly escaped the two bullets, as she was just coming out to see what was the matter when she saw Mrs. Dick running into the kitchen.

After firing the third shot, Mrs. McWilliam quietly walked out of the tea-room and was half-way down the first flight of stairs when Mr. Teasdale, the shopwalker—who had heard the shots and at first thought a gas explosion had occurred—on running upstairs saw the woman with the revolver. He immediately seized her, and in pinioning her arms his hand came in contact with the hot barrel of the revolver. Close behind Mr. Teasdale came Mr. S. Kirkcaldie, who disarmed Mrs. McWilliam. "Here's the revolver," said the woman as he took the weapon from her, whilst to her captor she remarked, "It's all right; leave go, I won't run away." Mr. Kirkcaldie rang up the police, and a constable took Mrs. McWilliam to the Central Police Station.

Some long-standing feud has existed between the two women, and whenever Mrs. McWilliam came into the tea-room Mrs. Dick has been accustomed to keep out of sight as much as possible, remarking that the woman had threatened her with mischief, and she was afraid some day the threat would be carried out. Yesterday morning, we were informed by the assistants, Mrs. Dick came to business in a very depressed state, and on being rallied by the girls she said, "I feel as if something was going to happen to me to-day." Mrs. McWilliam when she came into the room was wearing a pair of coloured glasses, which was not her usual habit. Miss Roach remarked to Mrs. Dick, "There's your friend," to which she replied, "I'm afraid her disguise means mischief to me." It was whilst endeavouring to get out of the room quietly that Mrs. Dick was shot at.

Mrs. Dick behaved very coolly during the incident. Mr. Kirkcaldie found her sitting in the kitchen, and when she complained of a pain in her side she sent for Dr. Henry, who arrived within a few minutes. On making a casual examination—the three bullets having been found in other places than their intended billets—the doctor found a contusion just under the ribs on the left side.

"Your corset saved you, Mrs. Dick," said he. "Had that bullet struck a man where it struck Mrs. Dick," said Dr. Henry afterwards to the pressman, "it would have killed him." Later in the evening Drs. Henry and Cahill made another careful examination of Mrs. Dick, and found that no serious injury had been inflicted. After a few days' rest Mrs. Dick will be enabled to resume her duties.

The injured woman was for many years a resident of Reefton. While living there she took over a hotel in the town belonging to the woman who shot at her yesterday. Some trouble in reference to the purchase-money occurred, and Mrs. McWilliam has brooded over it ever since. After leaving Reefton Mrs. Dick kept a boardinghouse at

Belnheim, where she alleges she was also shot at by Mrs. McWilliam. Three years ago Mrs. Dick took up her residence in Wellington, and until 18 months back she kept a boardinghouse in Boulcott-street. Ever since Mrs. McWilliam came to Wellington Mrs. Dick has been afraid of her—so much that she states that in view of Mrs. McWilliam's frequent visits she has several times been on the point of asking Mr. Kirkcaldie as a personal favour to exclude her from the establishment.

H/T: Katie Fordyce, National Library of New Zealand

LIFE SAVED BY CORSET

St. John Daily Sun, 26 September 1903

WOMAN HUNG FROM BRIDGE HALF AN HOUR BEFORE SHE WAS LASSOED.

SALISBURY, N.C., SEPT 23.— The corset of a neatly dressed woman saved her from death here today.

She had come in from South Carolina and was walking along a steep embankment on the line of the Southern railway, when she fell a distance of several feet and her body struck the end of a cross-tie in the bridge connecting the two sections of the city.

There she was suspended in an upright position for half an hour, supported by her strong corset, which had been caught by a projection from the tie, while several trains passed under her.

Finally some railway men succeeded in looping a rope around her waist and dragging her to safety. She was then locked up for intoxication.

CORSET STEEL SAVED LIFE

Los Angeles Herald, 8 January 1906

Knife Aimed at Heart Was Deflected.
Husband Made Savage Attempt at Murder.

PHILADELPHIA. Jan. 7.— The steel in her corset probably saved the life of Margaret Bruce, whose husband, Walter, made a savage attempt to murder her at their home on Ashland heights, West Manayunk. Crazed by drink and provoked over a remark the woman made regarding his condition, the man jumped from his seat at the supper table, seized a sharp carving knife and plunged it into the left side of his wife.

As she dropped to the floor Bruce grabbed his hat and overcoat, rushed from the house and succeeded in escaping arrest, though he almost ran into Mounted Policeman Broadhead, who had heard the Bruce children screaming for help. The policeman had a short tussle with the man, who succeeded, however, in breaking away. Then he ran into a nearby woods and was lost sight of.

Broadhead was not aware of the crime that had been committed, but on going to the house found Mrs. Bruce on the floor and bleeding profusely. He rode with breakneck speed to Manayunk for the patrol, and had the supposed dying woman taken to St. Timothy's hospital. The wound in Mrs. Bruce's breast is one and a half inches in length and two inches in depth, but the knife had been deflected by the corset steel and the physicians have some hope that she may recover, although her condition is serious.

CORSET STAYS SAVED HER LIFE

Spokane Daily Chronicle, 25 January 1908

The unrequited affection of a man for pretty Geraldine Ballou of Seattle led to an assault on the girl in that city a few nights ago. Only the approach of the girl's parents saved her from being murdered, or worse. As it was the girl was badly choked and her dress cut in shreds by the assailant's knife. Who the man is, the girl is unable to tell, but she was given a fair description and the police and detectives are searching for him.

The beginning of the affairs dates back to more than a year ago, when the girl was first approached by the man who she says attacked her on this occasion.

She never learned his name, but accepted his attentions to a certain extent. One evening, however, she awoke to what was in his mind and stabbed him deep with a hatpin. He vowed vengeance and disappeared.

Miss Ballou left her home the other evening to mail a letter. A few feet from her doorstep she encountered her erstwhile admirer with a companion. The admirer seized her by the throat and with an oath tried to strangle her. Failing in this, and observing the approach of her father and mother, who had been summoned by her cries, the man drew a stiletto and slashed at the girl. Happily for her, he only succeeded in ruining her dress waist, her corset steels preventing the blade from going deeper.

Both men then fled, and, accompanied by her parents, the girl went to police headquarters, where she told her story.

BULLET HITS CORSET STEEL

Chicago Tribune, 22 December 1909

ATTEMPT IS MADE TO ASSASSINATE MISS ETHEL EITELHUBER.
ADMIRER UNDER SUSPICION
SHOT IS FIRED THROUGH WINDOW OF THE WOMAN'S BEDROOM.

A corset steel probably saved the life of Miss Ethel Eitelhuber, 36 years old, 350 Wendell street, when a shot was fired through a bedroom window in her home last evening in an attempt to kill her.

John Schreckel, 40 years old, 29 West Chestnut street, said to be a special policeman employed by the George W. Jackson company, is being hunted by the police as the would-be assassin.

The shades were drawn, but as Miss Eitelhuber was standing near the window her shadow on the curtain gave the would-be murderer his mark. When the bullet struck her she ran out into kitchen, where other members of the family were seated, crying: "I am shot; I am shot."

SEES MAN RUNNING AWAY.

Michael Griffin, her brother-in-law, went in search for a doctor. When he reached Orleans street, he said, he saw Schreckel run east in Elm street. The belief he did the shooting is strengthened by the report to the police that on several occasions he threatened to kill Miss Eitelhuber. Schreckel is said to be married and to have a son 13 years old.

Two months ago, when Miss Eitelhuber learned that Schreckel was married and told him she did not care to see him again, she dreamed that he shot through the window and fatally wounded her. She said last night the dream was borne out in every detail of the attempt on her life. Miss Eitelhuber said she had been afraid of him ever since she dismissed him, and whenever she went out she had an escort with her.

Says She Was Threatened.

Schreckel, she said, has threatened to kill her on several occasions, and only on Sunday, when she saw him last, he repeated the threat. Several times he has been seen lurking around the house and Miss Eitelhuber usually extinguished the light in her room for fear he would carry out his threats. He is said to have told her at one time that if shooting failed he would blind her with acid.

The bullet struck Miss Eitelhuber over the abdomen. It went through her dress, but when it struck the corset it glanced off.

CORSET SAVES HER LIFE

The Spokesman-Review, 22 June 1912

Woman Is Thrown From Buggy on Barbed Wire.

MOSCOW, Idaho, Jun 21.— Mrs. W. G. Barge was thrown from a buggy to a barbed wire fence yesterday and her life was probably saved by reason of her corset, which was torn into pieces. Mrs. Barge was rushed to a hospital here. Returning home she met a runaway horse dragging a post. The post struck the buggy and frightened the horse.

PART XXI

POTPOURRI

WISDOM AND AUTONOMY

TARA MOSS

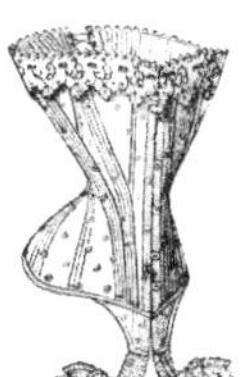

There is a reason the eye is drawn to the silhouette of a corseted form. First there are the proportions, the curved lines. Then the shining busk pins, the pattern of laces, the often sensuous, shining fabric, the contrast of soft curve and rigid boning. There is more to a corset than aesthetics, however, and this is where my real corset story begins.

I first came to view corsets as more than attractive additions to my wardrobe last year. You see, headaches and back pain have been regular companions to my career as a novelist and writer for the past twenty years, in part because of scoliosis (curvature of the spine). After two full decades of wearing corsets for pleasure and fashion, and collecting no less than 12 of them, I experienced yet another of my "writing aches" and laced myself into an old underbust one afternoon. Perhaps I had medical corsets in mind that day (they are often structurally similar) and I unconsciously craved the stiff posture support.

Whatever the reason, by the end of that day, I discovered something curious—my neck and upper back felt "lighter." Despite long hours at the keyboard, I was without a discernible headache or neck tension. The next day I tried it again, to the same result. And so finally the penny dropped: the corsets I had loved the look of for as long as I can remember could do far more for me than I'd given them credit for.

Why had it taken me so long to make this obvious connection? I soon began reading everything I could on the topic, from blogs and news articles to W.B. Lord's *The Corset and The Crinoline,* Ann Grogan's *Corset Magic,* the work of Dr. Valerie Steele, and Lucy's many informative web posts. Reading the bulk of the literature on corsetry, it was easy to see that the terms "corset" and "medical benefit" were rarely found in the same sentence—not since some questionable Edwardian advertisements for the S-curve, anyway.

Search for "corset" and "pain" and the dominant story becomes quite clear, with the mainstream narrative being one of corsets causing, never relieving pain. Though I had not taken as fact the more outrageous claims about corsets causing frequent broken ribs (I would guess they have caused somewhat fewer broken bones than the far more accepted fashionable women's heels), etc., it was good to read many of these hyperbolic claims forensically debunked step by step in the work of Steele, Grogan, and on the website of the author of this book, among others.

Yes, it is possible to wear an ill-fitting corset and hurt yourself by making it bruisingly tight, just as you could with another piece of rigid clothing—again, shoes spring to mind—but the question is, why would you?

Legitimate issues of social pressure and body dysmorphia aside, the root of the hysteria about women and corsetry seems to be the idea that women, as an entire sex, cannot be trusted to know their own minds and bodies. There could apparently be no comfortable or moderate corset wear for women, only masochism and dangerous vanity. For this reason, perhaps, it was puzzling to many dedicated dress reformers that all women didn't simply toss out their corsets as soon as it became acceptable to do so. Didn't they all hate the things? Well, apparently not.

As Steele writes in *The Corset: A Cultural History,* "Behind the dress reformers' belief that menswear was intrinsically superior to women's clothing was the assumption that men themselves were more rational than women."[1]

Wasn't it possible, at least for some percentage of women, that a life with corsets was superior to a life without, and that they were reliable witnesses to their own feelings and experiences on the matter? Could this be one of the reasons foundation garments, from corsets to girdles to shapewear, have never quite disappeared, even if they have gone underground, as it were, becoming hidden elements of dress?

Tellingly, men's corsetry is almost entirely left out of the "corset debate," despite their historically documented use for the military, in fine men's dressing, on the stage (more than a few male performers wouldn't be caught dead under stage lights without one), and of course, for personal expression and pleasure. This speaks, no doubt, to anxieties about male identity, perhaps once the focus on the corset as a feminine article became so entrenched in the collective consciousness.

No, the focus of the "debate" remains fixed on familiar anxieties about women, namely notions of female frailty and women's dangerous sexuality. Both ideas have passed down from century to century, from the preposterous "wandering womb" theory originating in the work of Plato and taught right up to the modern era of medicine, to the antiquated but oft-taught idea that women need masters, do not have the capacity for rational thought, and should not speak up in public spaces or exert public authority, lest we all be led astray: Eve and the apple; Pandora and her box.

What we find again and again is the idea of the corset itself—or the woman who wears one—as a corruptor. A woman with a corset is a threat or a victim. The femme fatale, the dominatrix, the masochistic maiden, but never, it seems, the sensible (if finely dressed) writer. With this history in mind, it's little wonder it took so long for me to see the obvious benefits a corset could provide, beyond what was aesthetically clear.

I have now, like many women before me, discovered the benefits of moderate and regular corset use. It is something I do for myself—

for my pleasure, yes, but also to avoid chronic pain. My doctor is aware of this, and I am aware of both the benefits and limitations of these lovely additions to my wardrobe. I exercise to pick up what back strength I can, with the scoliosis I have, and I wear my corsets as an aid to those parts of me bent by nature, not as a substitute to my real back muscles.

In this way I can hike for hours without a corset, and write for hours with one, both comfortably. Whether "stealthing" or proudly showing off a corset, I feel good, and if I don't, I know something is wrong. I know my own body.

And when my leggy 5-year-old daughter runs into my arms, and I pick her up without hesitation, and I keep holding her thanks in part to my stays, I am grateful for the special moments these steel-boned creations afford me. A contemporary mainstream acceptance and understanding of it is of little matter. The sensation of holding my child without fear of hurting my back is just one pleasure among the many that I will not soon care to give up.

---

1. Steele, Valerie, *The Corset: A Cultural History*, page 61.

Tara Moss in a corset by What Katie Did. Photograph by Berndt Sellheim.

Tara Moss is the author of 11 books of fiction and non-fiction, a journalist, TV presenter, human rights activist, model, and corset collector. Visit her at taramoss.com

PUBLIC FIGURE

QUINN B.

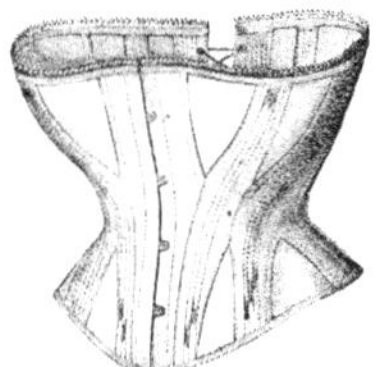

Corsets can make you feel like a rock star. It's not the reason I got into them, but it did come as a nice added surprise.

No, the reason I got into corsetry was my love for all things Victorian. This love started so early in my life, and so naturally, that I scarcely recall when exactly it was that I first decided that I needed to have a corset. I definitely know that the desire was there by the time I was 16, and because I couldn't afford one yet, I spent all the time I could learning about them. Teenagers have a tendency to be broke, so this period of study before experience lasted for years. And with every new thing I learned, I fell more in love. It's hard to come across something that combines beauty, history, psychology, biology, art, engineering, sex—and probably more that I'm forgetting—as corsets do. I could talk about them for hours.

Of course, no amount of studying is going to teach you everything; certain things you only learn from experience. I feel much more acquainted with my body now, as well as with other people's minds. Corsets tend to elicit very strong opinions.

Some of those opinions are negative, but negativity has been only a very negligible part of my now ten-years' experience. When something feels this much like a part of you, unfavorable opinions don't have much power to bring you down. Besides, positive ones are much more common. Which brings me to how corsets can make you feel like a rock star…

I must have been about 20 years old. This was very early on—long before my first corset had been literally worn to pieces, but after I had managed to train my waist down to 20 inches. The corset was my pride and joy, and I wore it everywhere, especially for a night of clubbing. When the bar closed, the Subway shop across the street would be filled with people eating and winding down until past 4 A.M. I only needed to use their restroom, and as I walked past the crowd, every head turned. I didn't really know what to do about this, so I did nothing. I did my business and then I left.

Except one person didn't want me to leave. I was being chased down. I had barely even begun to brace myself before seeing that there was nothing threatening at all about this woman. She only had a favor to ask, as she tried to catch her breath. Now I paraphrase, because this was many years ago:

"You're going to laugh … when you were in the bathroom my friend wanted to knock on the door to talk to you. I thought it would be rude so I wouldn't let him. It would be so great if you could just go back in there and say hi to him."

Of course I would! So we went the short distance back to the Subway, and at first her friend was nowhere to be found. It turned out that now *he* was in the bathroom. So of course I knocked on the door. When he opened it he laughed, "I can't believe this!"

It was a great moment that I'll always remember. They had a lot of questions for me about corsets that, thanks to my years glued to a computer screen, I was easily able to answer. Finally the woman asked where I had bought mine, and as I wrote it down for her it felt almost as though I was signing an autograph.

Maybe one day I'll be signing real autographs. Corsets have been with me throughout my career, from office jobs, to a ton of blog articles, to modeling, and now to the exciting world of burlesque. They've enhanced every single one of these things, whether it was because they stopped me from ruining my back in a bad office chair, because they kept me feeling safe and secure, or because they make me look amazing.

And I'll keep wearing them for as long as I can, because you're never too old for fabulous. Corsets have been around for centuries, and they'll be around for centuries to come.

FINDING MY VOICE

ALEXA H.

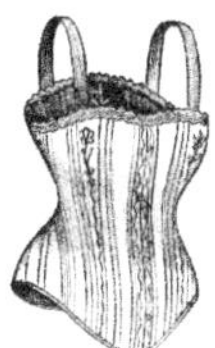

I don't remember exactly why I put on my first corset; it was sometime in college, before discovering much information about it, but I remember how oddly confident and safe it made me feel. That was enough to get me hooked: I bought a cheap underbust corset with my spending money for the month the next day. (I was attempting to pay tuition/living expenses with a fast food job and loans, so a better corset was not a possibility at the time.) That corset became my lifeline through my undergrad years.

You see, I am painfully shy—like serious-anxiety-problems shy: one of my first memories of the fourth grade was passing out during a book report presentation. Since then, I had gotten through any necessary public-speaking (or even participating in large discussion groups) more or less by just blanching and stammering my way through, and then running away to go freak out elsewhere afterward, but it was not a comfortable arrangement.

My little purple corset changed that. I, of course, was scared to death of someone noticing it, so I always wore a baggy t-shirt over it. For four years I wore it to most classes because it did something to make me feel safe enough to speak and participate in class—even when I wasn't required to. Although I'll never enjoy giving presentations, my corset stopped the shaking and other, more extreme stress response symptoms. Maybe the theory about dominant posture and cortisol reduction is really on to something.

My original purple corset was very straight and caused hip bruising, which I didn't want to repeat, so I retired it and purchased two other "public speaking corsets"—which recently I also retired due to my weight loss.

I kept them for as long as I could, repairing them and sewing darts into them so they would continue to fit me as I lost weight. As little time as I had to continually repair and alter them, they taught me how to "make do and mend" and brought me a greater understanding and appreciation of the intricate construction of corsets.

I was recently accepted to graduate school and I'm really excited about it. I have been working in the lab, and my Principal Investigator has said that while my work is fantastic, he would like to see me work on communicating my research to others (via posters, presentations, etc.) more often and more confidently. Knowing that I will likely have to take on a more active public speaking role in pursuit of my PhD (not to mention a future thesis defense) is, frankly, terrifying, but it comes with the territory of the work and learning I love, so I will do my best to adapt. With this adaptation, of course, comes more corsetry.

Now I am proud to refer to myself as a no-longer-quite-so-shy fledgling neuroscientist, and corset addict!

LIFE WITH INTRACRANIAL HYPERTENSION

GRACE A.

I'm Grace, and this is the story of how corsets changed my life. I first started wearing corsets years ago to help improve my posture, back pain, and mild scoliosis. My doctor said that to improve my back pain, I needed to improve my posture. He suggested that I wear an elastic posture belt, but it felt horrible, so then I decided to look into corsets as an alternative. Thankfully my doctor has approved me wearing my corset for back support; he said he thinks it's a great tool to help with my posture.

In September 2012, my world changed—and so did my need for corsets. I was diagnosed with a brain disease called Idiopathic Intracranial Hypertension (IIH). Normally a person's brain and spinal cord is bathed with cerebrospinal fluid, and fluid pressure is balanced. Intracranial Hypertension is too much fluid on the brain and it results in daily chronic migraines and visual disturbances; in some patients it can lead to blindness. It's a rare condition, the odds of having Intracranial Hypertension are 1:100,000.

How I got Intracranial Hypertension is not common either: it was a result of taking an acne medication!

The two most common treatments for Intracranial Hypertension are lumbar punctures and medications. During a lumbar puncture, a needle is inserted into my spine and the fluid is partly drained to reduce the pressure. For a week or two after getting a lumbar puncture, it's very painful to move and bend my spine.

I spoke to both my doctor and my neurologist about using my corset to help, and they think it's fine. Neither doctor seemed too interested or worried that I use them. The only time I've been told not to wear my corset is immediately after I get my lumbar punctures, so for that first day or two I go without the corset. After those few days, I wear my corset very loosely and it supports my sore back muscles and helps immobilize my torso so I don't twist and hurt myself. Within a week I'm usually back to normal; I've found that I feel loads better with my corset than without it.

Wearing a corset also helps me with my daily eating patterns and nausea. My migraines always come with nausea, and I am rarely able to keep down a normal-size meal. My neurologist was one of the first to advise me to try smaller portions through the day, to control my nausea. The corset makes it much easier to cut down the amount I eat in one sitting, and to eat more frequently. It does help with the nausea, which I'm thrilled about because that's one less medication I have to take to treat the symptoms of this disease.

The final way corsets have helped me is they've improved my confidence in my body shape again. When I started putting on considerable weight as a side effect of the medications, I remember being so upset: I missed the body I used to have. Even with a healthy diet and healthy portions, my body kept gaining weight as a result of the medication. Discontinuing this medication is not an option, but wearing a corset has helped me to accept my new body and become confident in the way I look. Due to the pain, I rarely get the chance to get dressed up and go out to enjoy myself, but when I do, the corset is there with me.

DENT REPAIR

MARY W.

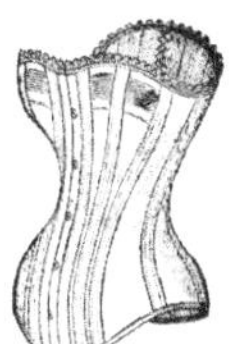

I went through a bad depression in my teens. For years, almost every day I'd wear the same pair of low-rise jeans (that quickly grew too small for me), and this one bra that I never knew or cared if it fit properly. They'd both pinch and chafe so much that they'd cause bruises and rashes, but I just ignored it and hid behind baggy jackets. The jeans caused my body to form an extreme indentation just below my hips. Some people call it a "hip dip" and a lot of people have it naturally, but mine was so very deep that I was certain it had something to do with these jeans—my hips more resembled the shape of a mushroom at the sides. Same problem with my bra; as it became too small, the straps would dig into my shoulders and leave strap-sized grooves. The back of the bra band left a nasty ridge across my back and under my arms, which remained there even by the next morning after wearing loose pajamas all night. My mental health was in bad shape, and the last thing I needed was to be self-conscious as well.

In my early 20s and in a much healthier place, I got to thinking: women who were raised to wear corsets from a very young age grew into adults with cinched waists since their bodies had grown into the corset's shape—so surely the same thing would happen to modern-day women with tight, low-rise jeans or ill-fitting underwear; it seems that the same process is at play. It may also be a contributing factor to how the modern day woman's waist is apparently much larger than decades ago—not just from changing diet, but from underwear and changing fashions as well.

Now in my 20s and having begun wearing comfortable clothes in my size, I decided to experiment: hopefully I was *just* young enough to reverse some of the damage I'd done in my teens, and the use of alternative fashions would grant me the opportunity to be more satisfied with my silhouette. I bought a few different corsets that varied in shape and length. The corsets sat directly on top of some dents and ridges, and issued an evenly distributed pressure on and around them. My theory was that the corset could push away the flesh from my waist and this fullness would eventually settle smoothly into these depressions—if not with bone or muscle, then at least with fat under the skin.

After a year of wearing corsets regularly, I realized that all the dents on my shoulders, back, and underarms had filled in entirely. Now there's only the slightest dip below my hips that is only noticeable without a corset—while wearing a corset, that dip fills in and disappears entirely.

The whole experience opened my eyes to how modern-day girls and young women are raised to know the standard hipster panties, low-rise jeans, and mono-breast bra as wardrobe staples, and are made to believe that anything else is inadequate and old-fashioned. Corsets were a huge gateway to alternative modern-day fashion for me.

A good overbust corset eliminates the need for a bra altogether, and some underbust corsets can improve a bra's support, helping to take the weight of the bust (if a person wants to wear a bra in the first place). Wearing a mini cincher or waspie means I'm still able to wear a bra and low-cut pants if I like. With an arsenal of different styles of corsets, I can mold my body and silhouette the way I want it to look.

This wasn't about having a conventionally beautiful body—to me, being able to remove all these grooves I'd inadvertently formed on my body was like erasing an awful reminder of the mistreatment of myself in the past, and giving me back the body I was meant to have—lovable mini hip-dip and all.

SHATTERING THE STIGMA

JENICE M.

I had been interested in, and researching, corsetry for a few years before "taking the plunge" and buying my first one from Orchard Corset in early 2014. Lucy and Orchard Corset's YouTube videos helped break down the basics for me. I bought one for the same reason that many others do: because I'd always liked how corsets looked and I wondered what I would look like in one.

At the time, I was suffering from strained lower back muscles from incorrectly lifting a heavy object at work, and various pain medications weren't working. After trying the corset, I discovered that it was the only thing that relieved my pain due to the support that it provided. Needless to say, I was in love from the beginning. You could say I became addicted. In less than a year, I purchased at least ten different corsets as I tried to figure out what styles and shapes fit me best. The benefits I discovered heavily outweigh the costs.

With the permission of my chiropractor, physical therapist, physician assistant, and doctor, I began wearing my favorite corset to relieve my back pain and to help my mental health, with which I struggle greatly.

It eases my anxiety symptoms (when I can muster the energy to put a corset on) by helping me feel calm and protected. There is the odd occasion when my anxiety makes me claustrophobic and I feel inexplicably "trapped" and have to remove the corset, but this is rare.

My corset can keep my depression at bay by embracing me in a hug, and by generally elevating my mood.

It inspires me to lose weight, which I need to do for my health. It helps me picture what I could look like if I lost an extra 50–70 pounds (23–32 kg). I know my corset could aid in weight loss too, by compressing my abdomen and not allowing me to overeat—a bad habit of mine.

When I wear it as outerwear for others to see, I'm complimented more often, and I tend to feel more confident in myself. Even when I wear it under my clothing, the corset provides that illusion due to the posture correction.

I'm also grateful for the new friends I've made from corset-based internet groups, some of whom I have met, or plan to meet, in person. That wouldn't have happened if not for our shared love of corsets.

I've become so enthralled with the world of corsets and the positivity they have added to my life that I have begun to hold local Corset 101 classes for the genuinely curious, as well as becoming a moderator in several online groups to help others around the world. It's important to me, and I think to any corset wearer, that people are properly educated on the safe use of corsets. We truly have to work at shattering the stigma.

LONG-TERM RELATIONSHIP

JEN H.

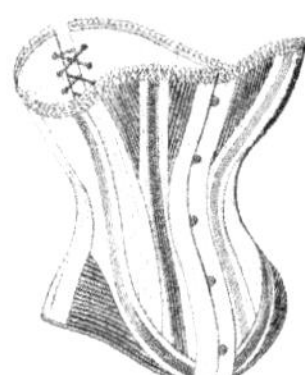

I don't feel I had one single, definitive, life-changing moment with corsets. It's more like a relationship that's grown over time.

I got my first corset after losing 25 pounds (11 kg). That loss was a huge milestone for me then, and I decided to get one to celebrate. I was working at a Victoria's Secret store at the time, and we had just gotten them in. I fell in love with a look that Express Clothing had on display: a leather corset with a white blouse and jacket, and I was determined to recreate it.

I was so excited to have access to these corsets at work, and my first piece was a black and red satin number. I looked fantastic in it ... Okay, maybe it wasn't the curviest corset ever, but it triggered a new interest in me. I felt so beautiful in it. It was so versatile! Sexy for going out, edgy professional with a blouse under my suit at work, fun for costumes—what couldn't a corset do?

Fast-forward a few years. It was Halloween, and my husband looked at my then well-worn Victoria's Secret corset and suggested I look for a new one. He didn't have to ask twice! But the more I looked around for a good corset, the more I realized that they weren't inexpensive.

By that time I was no longer working for VS, and my tastes had evolved anyway. If I couldn't afford to buy a new corset, the next best thing would be to make one, right? After all, if it didn't work out, what did I have to lose? So, Simplicity pattern in hand, I borrowed my mom's Singer Genie and collected the necessary supplies: some fabric, steel boning, grommets, and a real front busk. Then, I went for it.

This sparked the next level of obsession: soon I was swooning over the couture work of Sparklewren and Electra Designs, gathering pictures from every corner of the internet, reading old LiveJournal corset tutorial archives, joining a corset making group on Facebook, correcting construction mistakes with my first few corsets, learning to draft my own patterns, upgrading my materials, enlarging my tool collection, and talking with amazing people from all over the world.

In the five-year process of making my own custom designs and wearing them, I learned several things about my body. Corsets provide abdominal compression that eases my menstrual cramps. My compulsive eating is curbed when I wear them. The tight hug makes me feel more confident and less susceptible to anxiety. It helps support my back when I'm at work, standing for hours on a concrete floor. I've become more in touch with my body, and I'm more familiar with its idiosyncrasies, like my slight asymmetry due to scoliosis. My hips might be too glorious for a string bikini, but a corset shows off my natural hourglass shape like nothing else. Even at 100 pounds (45 kg) overweight, I am stunningly, incredibly beautiful.

I think the biggest change of all, though, is in the people I've met. Not only have I joined a few online groups that have increased my knowledge of making and wearing corsets, but I've made some closer friends as well. We can be silly and excited over frippery of all varieties, but these are also people I can message in the middle of the night with a problem for a sympathetic ear. We've celebrated new tattoos, new pets, new babies, and we've mourned together. So many times we sign off with the term "corset hugs," but it really means that no matter where I go in the world, there's someone waiting for me with a real hug.

BIKER 'CHIC'

APRIL BROOKS CLEMMER ~ THE POWDER ROOM

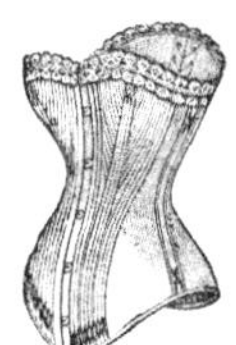

Today is my first motorcycle ride with my boyfriend. I've never ridden at all, and though I trust my boyfriend with my life, I am a bit nervous as I mount the bike. No seat belts, no doors to close, no airbags … how is this legal? I can get a ticket for not wearing a seat belt in my car fully equipped with modern safety features. But sitting on the back of a bike completely unprotected feels like it should be forbidden. I basically feel naked.

The first part of the ride I close my eyes and concentrate on staying as still as possible so as to not throw our balance off. My boyfriend even checks to make sure I'm still back there, and reminds me I don't need to be a complete statue! We eventually find our comfortable place, me leaning slightly forward and resting my hands on him so I can anticipate and go with his movements. It's fun.

But I find myself thinking also of my corset, left at home. I'm slouching uncomfortably, then oddly arching my back at intervals to counter the ache the slouching causes. My corset would fix that … in fact, my corset would fix a lot of things. I miss the way it sits snugly around me, protecting and supporting me. It slowly dawns on me that the corset is exactly what I need right now.

The second day that my boyfriend invites me out for a ride, I show up for it laced down in my custom-made corset by Romantasy Exquisite Corsetry. It's made especially for the unique contours of my body, but its steel bones gently demand that my posture remain erect and poised with an air of confidence. I feel the corset's protective covering over my organs and the strong back support it provides. It keeps me warm against the wind during the ride, and the laces remain tight and secure. My corset has taken care of my nerves and my discomfort. Today, my only concern is capturing the exhilarating feeling of freedom as we race through the countryside. Today, I'm able to relax and look around, catching as much of the amazing scenery as possible.

I also feel like a total hottie whenever we stop and I take off my jacket, realizing I'm rocking a corset with my riding boots and totally pulling it off!

Exactly one year from the day of this ride, my boyfriend became my husband.

April and her now husband on their motorcycle

April is a writer and researcher, focused on classic Hollywood and all things vintage. She works with various groups for historic Hollywood preservation. Visit her at The Powder Room.

ACKNOWLEDGMENTS

First and foremost, deepest thanks to my family for loving my weirdness, for nurturing my creative madness, and for supporting me unconditionally as I navigate this unconventional career path. Mom and Dad—I'm sure this is not at all what you had in mind when a multi-passionate, six-year-old Lucy said she wanted to be an author, film-maker, scientist, musician, *and* fashion designer when she grew up, but thank you for allowing me to forge my own path. To my husband—you are my best friend, and you bring out the most in me. You are the greatest person I know.

Heartfelt thanks to Jody Hewitt and Christine Wickham, two wonderful friends who continue to inspire me even after their passing. I miss you both; you are never far from my mind. I hope this book would have made you proud.

Sidney Eileen and Rosalind Guder for their beautiful cover art; thank you for bringing my vision to life.

Cora Harrington for paving the way for intersectionality through fashion and wearable art, and for emboldening me to use my own platform to amplify the voices of others.

Michael With All the Cats for his sage advice and for funding so many previous giveaways, supporting corsetières and corseters alike.

Diana West for her indispensable wisdom regarding the traditional publishing industry.

Marion McNealy and Cathy Hay for providing resources on self-publishing as well as taking oneself seriously as an entrepreneur in an ultra-niche artistic industry.

Janelle Aleff for her tireless footwork—after years of my false starts, thank you for lighting a fire under me to finally make this paperback a reality.

Roger K. and Ann Grogan for their editing and proofreading, but more broadly, for being among the first to accept and welcome a young and shy (but eager) Lucy into the corset community more than a decade ago. In an industry that can be incredibly competitive and exclusionary, the potential you saw in me and the kindness you showed from the beginning is a huge reason why I'm still here today.

My sweet pup Tibby, who has now passed on—for loyally curling yourself around my feet through countless late work nights, and incentivizing me to be as good of a human as you believed me to be. You are forever in my heart.

My friends, near and far, for being my constant cheerleaders and believing in me when I couldn't believe in myself. I consider you my global family.

My patrons for making this project financially possible and for helping me over the hurdles when I endured decision paralysis. You've made this paperback something we can all be truly proud of.

Last but not least, I must give credit to the over 100 contributors who have generously opened up their lives and shared a piece of themselves to make this book possible, who made themselves vulnerable so we could feel a fraction of what they experienced, and invited us to laugh or cry with them.

This book is truly a group effort *by* the corset community, and is therefore dedicated *to* the community—the contributors, editors, and supporters who believed in this project and helped bring it to fruition.

Thank you.

BE PART OF THE SOLACED PROJECT

If you are a corsetière who makes therapeutic braces, orthoses, and medical corsets for others, or if you are a wearer who has noticed a measurable improvement to your quality of life through the use of a corset, you are invited to share your true story for possible inclusion in future volumes.

If your story is eligible for inclusion, you will be asked to sign a legal form (publisher release agreement and oath to ensure the verity of your narrative). Apologies, fictional stories will not be accepted. However, names can be omitted or modified in the final published work to maintain your anonymity. Eligible entries will be rewarded/compensated.

If interested, please email a synopsis of your experience to corset.benefit@gmail.com.

Made in the USA
Las Vegas, NV
01 May 2022

48273244R00246